Bookmarks
London, Chicago and Melbourne

Fascism, Stalinism and the United Front

Leon Trotsky

with commentary by Chris Harman
and an introduction by Steve Wright

Fascism, Stalinism and the United Front / *Leon Trotsky*
First published in German in various editions 1930-33.
This edition published by Bookmarks May 1989
Bookmarks, 265 Seven Sisters Road, London N4 2DE, England
Bookmarks, PO Box 16085, Chicago, IL 60616, USA
Bookmarks, GPO Box 1473N, Melbourne 3001, Australia
Introduction copyright © Bookmarks and Steve Wright

ISBN 0 906224 48 9

Printed by Cox and Wyman Limited, Reading, England
Cover design by Roger Huddle

Bookmarks is linked to an international grouping of socialist
organisations:
Australia: *International Socialists*, GPO Box 1473N, Melbourne 3001
Belgium: *Socialisme International*, 9 rue Marexhe, 4400 Herstal, Liege
Britain: *Socialist Workers Party*, PO Box 82, London E3
Canada: *International Socialists*, PO Box 339, Station E, Toronto,
           Ontario M6H 4E3
Denmark: *Internationale Socialister*, Morten Borupsgade 18, kld, 8000
           Arhus C
France: *Socialisme International*, BP 189, 75926 Paris Cedex 19
Greece: *Organosi Sosialistiki Epanastasi*, Menandrou 50, Omonia, Athens.
Holland: *International Socialists*, PO Box 9720, 3506 GR Utrecht.
Ireland: *Socialist Workers Movement*, PO Box 1648, Dublin 8
Norway: *Internasjonale Sosialister*, Postboks 5370, Majorstua, 0304 Oslo3
United States: *International Socialist Organization*, PO Box 16085,
           Chicago, IL 60622
West Germany: *Sozialistische Arbeiter Gruppe*, Wolfgangstrasse 81, 6000
           Frankfurt 1

Contents

Bookmarks would like to dedicate this edition
to *Harry Wicks*, lifelong revolutionary socialist
and founder-member of the Balham Group,
the first British Trotskyist organisation,
who died on 25 March 1989
while this book was in preparation.

This book is published with the aid of the **Bookmarks Publishing Co-operative**. Many socialists have some savings put aside, probably in a bank or savings bank. While it is there, this money is being loaned out by the bank to some business or other to further the capitalist search for profit. We believe it is better loaned to a socialist venture to further the struggle for socialism. That's how the co-operative works: in return for a loan, repayable at a month's notice, members receive free copies of books published by Boookmarks. At the time this book was published, the co-operative had more than 300 members, from as far apart as London and Malaysia, Canada and Norway.

Like to know more?

Write to the **Bookmarks Publishing Co-operative**, 265 Seven Sisters Road, Finsbury Park, London N4 2DE, England.

Steve Wright

Introduction

IN 1928 the organisations of the German working class were the strongest in the world. Five million workers belonged to Free Trade Unions affiliated to the main union federation, the ADGB.[1] The Social Democratic Party (SPD), with 1,021,000 members, reached deeply into the lives of these trade unionists through mass-circulation newspapers and 9,000 local organisations.[2] The Communist Party (KPD) also commanded substantial forces, but only a small proportion of its 130,000 membership was among unionised workers: here the SPD retained overwhelming dominance.[3]

Social Democracy stood for peaceful and legal reform; on the surface its prospects seemed good. German capitalism had apparently restabilised itself after the upheavals of 1919-23,[4] and in spite of the continued burden of heavy war reparation payments the economy seemed healthy and dynamic. After a sharp recession in 1925-26, industrial production had surged forward on an apparently inexhaustible tide of American finance. To most workers, the reforms which could be won in these circumstances seemed to vindicate the strategy of Social Democracy. To the German capitalists, such concessions certainly represented a price to be paid for continued (relative) social harmony, but a cheap one. Desperate remedies no longer appeared necessary. Adolf Hitler commanded few forces outside Bavaria and was widely regarded as a grotesque joke. And if the working class, in its majority, did not as yet understand the need for revolution, it nevertheless appeared impregnable in its defensive positions.

By the mid-point of 1933 this entire edifice was in ruins. Hitler was Reich Chancellor, and most of the workers' leaders, reformist and revolutionary, bureaucrats and shop stewards, were in concentration camps. No coordinated resistance had inconvenienced the Nazis in their work.

The most fundamental cause of the rise of Nazism was the international economic crisis triggered by the stock market crash in the USA.[5] In Germany the process was especially violent and anarchic, as its industrial and financial conglomerates strove to renegotiate with labour's leaders the terms of bargains struck in 1924-28. In those years of restabilisation it had become the established practice of trade union leaders to look to the state to arbitrate between their members and the employers. In 1923 arbitration boards, composed of equal numbers of employers' and trade union representatives, were set up to sort out 'industrial relations' disputes. Either party could reject the board's decision, but such cases would then be passed to a state official whose ruling was compulsory and binding. In 1927 special labour courts were created, also on a collaborative pattern; employment exchanges were regulated by similar methods. Consequently, the machinery of the state intermeshed with that of union officialdom, which was also involved in an impressive array of other enterprises. All in all, as Franz Neumann explained:

> The trade union bureaucracy was much more powerful than the corresponding party [SPD] bureaucracy. Not only were there many jobs within the unions but there were jobs with the Labour Bank, the building corporations, the real estate corporations, the trade union printing and publishing houses, the trade union insurance organisations... And there were innumerable state jobs: in the labour courts, in the social insurance bodies, in the coal and potash organisation, in the railway system. Some union officials held five, six and even ten positions at the same time, often combining political and trade union posts.[6]

Neumann saw that the union leaders' mental world, their 'psychological attitude of dependence that discourages strikes,' grew from material roots in this ramifying bureaucracy. The very close relationship between the trade union bureaucracy and that of the SPD did not guarantee an identical reaction to particular events, but they shared a deeply held core faith in the possibilities of peaceful advance within the legal and constitutional framework in which their apparatus functioned. In 1928, they could point to improvements in housing, education and social legislation as evidence for the practicality of this strategy. But the internationalisation of the crisis in the years which followed demonstrated its bankruptcy.

At the end of 1929, the Wall Street crash led to the abrupt withdrawal of much of the foreign capital upon which the German economy was especially reliant, and also resulted in a sharp contraction of world trade, with disastrous consequences for industrial exports. Bankruptcies, sackings and plummeting tax receipts followed. Now the possibility of making gains by playing to the constitutional rules of capitalism vanished, but the devotion of the SPD leaders was to the constitution itself, not to the gains which it had once permitted—and this commitment remained unbroken.

The government crisis of March 1930, in which union pressure prevented the Müller cabinet (a coalition in which the SPD was the senior partner) from loading increases in unemployment contributions onto their members, was a direct consequence of the economic crisis. Müller's resignation was merely a minor tremor compared to the earthquake to follow, but it illustrated that social democracy was no longer useful as a party of government: the sheer scale of ruling-class demands far outstripped its ability to implement them. Even the bourgeois centre parties were unwilling to take responsibility for the austerity measures required by German capitalism. Müller's successor, Brüning, could find no stable majority in the Reichstag, and ruled increasingly by emergency decree.

The impotence of the Reichstag both reflected the social *impasse* and illustrated the inability of parliaments to decide great social issues; its continued veneration by Social Democracy was an expression of the party's own impotence. In opposition, the SPD could escape direct responsibility for the ruthless wage cuts and tax increases initiated by Brüning's dictat. But it did nothing to prevent them, continuing to 'tolerate' his government as the 'lesser evil' in comparison with Hitler.

In mid-1931 the failure of the Kreditanstalt Bank in Vienna threatened to plunge the German Deutsche Bank into liquidation. The finances of the government itself deteriorated. Tax receipts declined, just as spending on unemployment benefits, and subsidies to farmers and industrialists, were increasing. Spiralling government debts in turn threatened its ability to prevent the entire financial system from collapsing.[7] Further austerity measures followed as the crisis gripped every sector of the national economy. Unemployment, 1.3 million in 1929, advanced to three million the following year, 4.3 million in 1931 and 5.1 million in 1932 (all September figures), rising to over six million at the start of 1933. Afraid of the capitalists, and afraid of mobilising the workers in defensive action, the SPD and the unions shrank into a legalistic shell. Too enervated to advance, and too strongly entrenched to retreat, the organisations of labour were paralysed.

Neither the SPD nor any of the other traditional parties of the Weimar Republic seemed able to deal with the crisis. In an atmosphere of mounting chaos, it was the Nazi Party which was able to present itself to the swelling ranks of the desperate and disoriented as the movement which had what others lacked: the energy and courage to impose drastic solutions. In the presidential elections of March-April 1932, Hitler polled 37 per cent of the vote. He refused subsequent offers of a share in the government, however, and resisted pressure from within his own party to make a *putsch*, swearing that his programme would be carried through legally, in accordance with the constitution. However, in September, the Nazis suffered a reverse in the Reichstag elections. Commenting on the significance of this, Rudolf Hilferding, former Marxist, and Reich finance minister till 1930, wrote of the 'downfall of fascism':

> Legality is his [Hitler's] own undoing. In the second elections to the Reichstag, Hitler lost two million votes; the aura of invincibility was broken; his decline had begun...[8]

> The National Socialists are now confined within the bounds of legality...[9]

One year earlier, Leon Trotsky had commented upon the fantasies of Hilferding and his like, warning that Hitler's apparent attachment to constitionalism served an important purpose:

> Under the cover of the constitutional perspective which lulls his adversaries, Hitler aims to reserve for himself the possibility of striking the blow at a convenient moment. This military cunning, no matter how simple in itself, secretes a tremendous force, for it leans upon not only the psychology of the intermediate parties, which would like to settle the question peacefully and legally, but, what is more dangerous, upon the gullibility of the national masses.[10]

Hitler became Chancellor at the end of the very month in which Hilferding had written him off. He was able to achieve this only on the basis of the passivity of the working-class organisations, of which the Social Democracy was politically dominant. But how was it that millions of worker-supporters of the SPD could continue to believe in their disastrously feeble leaders even up to the end? For there existed a strong Communist alternative: the KPD, German section of the Communist International set up in 1919. This counted in its ranks the most advanced and militant workers and claimed to stand in the Bolshevik tradition. That tradition comprised not only the basic principles of revolutionary internationalism, but a rich store of tactical and strategic lessons learned not only by the Bolsheviks themselves but by all the sections of the International in its early years.

In 1922, Benito Mussolini had taken control in Rome. The recently formed Italian Communist Party (PCI) was led by Amadeo Bordiga, an intransigent and dogmatic ultra-leftist. It rejected all cooperation with the Socialist Party on principle. This important mistake, however, ultimately reflected its inexperience in the face of the explosive and bewildering growth of fascism, which was at that time a uniquely Italian phenomenon.[11] No such difficulties confronted the German Communist Party in 1929. With more than a decade of activity in the most varied of circumstances behind it, and with the events in Italy to learn from, it could also call to mind its own earlier experience of fascism. For years before the final victory of Mussolini, it had became necessary in Germany too to confront the problem. Klara

Zetkin, a leading German Communist, had argued in 1923:

> Fascism does not enquire whether the factory worker owes his allegiance to the white and blue of Bavaria, to the black, red and gold of the bourgeois Republic, or to the red flag with the hammmer and sickle... It is enough that fascism sees a class-conscious proletarian in front of it; it strikes him down regardless. The workers must therefore make common cause in the struggle, without distinction of party or trade union. The self-defence of the proletariat against fascism is one of the strongest factors making for the organisation and consolidation of the proletarian united front.[12]

Fascism was not, at that time, the main enemy in Germany. But Zetkin's remarks did indicate (and still do) the only appropriate response whenever it develops into a major threat to the labour movement. From 1924 onwards, in extremely unfavourable circumstances, the Italian Communist Party, now led by Antonio Gramsci, began to apply such tactics, which were based upon the recognition that fascism is a specific form of reaction involving the smashing of *all* the workers' organisations, including those of social democracy. In 1926, Mussolini was able to complete this process. And two years later, Togliatti, a leading figure in the PCI, could still remember what fascism meant:

> ...fascism...rejects every compromise with Social Democracy; it has persecuted it mercilessly; it has deprived it of all possibility of legal activity; it forces it to emigrate.

But by February 1930, the experience of that terrible defeat had vanished entirely from his memory:

> The Italian Social Democracy turns fascist with the greatest readiness.[13]

For now, according to the new position held by the Communist International, fascism and social democracy were indistinguishable. In Stalin's understanding, 'Social Democracy is effectively the moderate wing of fascism'. Survival as a Communist leader was made dependent upon repeating and implementing this 'analysis'. It was echoed throughout the

Comintern, most importantly in Germany.

'*Social fascism*' involved forgetting all the experience of defending, alongside reformists, existing workers' organisations and the gains which they had won, when these were threatened by reactionary forces. It meant forgetting the joint defence of the Russian *soviets* against General Kornilov in August 1917, which had enabled Lenin's party to place workers' power on the agenda for the first time; forgetting the proposals for joint action against the bosses' offensive in 1922-23 in Germany and elsewhere; forgetting the words of Zetkin and many others; forgetting the consequences of establishing too late the united front in Italy, for which all the organisations of the working class had paid so dearly. 'Social fascism' involved more than amnesia; for Marxism, as a theory of the emancipation of the working class, seeks to understand both social democracy and fascism, by analysing their very different social and political content in class terms. 'Social fascism', therefore, was no mere tactical mistake: it represented a decisive break with the experience, and the basic method, of the International.

In resisting the 'theory' of social fascism, it was Trotsky, and not the 'official' Marxists, who stood in the tradition of the Communist International. And it was from this storehouse of experience, rather than the incontestable brilliance of his own mind, that Trotsky was able to assemble the fundamentals of his analysis of fascism and his powerful demonstration of the political necessity of a united front against it.

There is no doubt that the new line of the Comintern originated in Russia. Its origins were in two linked features of the interests of the group around Stalin. Firstly, the defeat of the British General Strike of 1926 and of the Chinese revolution of 1927 revealed the treachery of two sets of 'progressive' allies and brought to an end the period in which they could usefully be cultivated. These defeats also led both British and French imperialism to adopt a more aggressive posture. Secondly, growing economic difficulties inside Russia encouraged the Stalin group to gravitate, haltingly at first, towards a policy of confrontation with the peasants and to abandon attempts to secure economic assistance from abroad.[14]

The new line was not a turn to the left. Stalin did not

abandon 'socialism in one country' for an internationalist policy, as Trotsky and his supporters in the Left Opposition had urged; the failure of diplomatic friendships with the leaders of British trade unions and Chinese nationalism, so cogently criticised by Trotsky, was diplomatically covered up. The Left Opposition had argued for industrialisation in order to strengthen the capacity of the working class to influence policy. In the mid-1920s this was already severely restricted. In 1928-29 it was obliterated.

The Russian Party Congress of December 1927 *both* confirmed the expulsion of Trotsky from its ranks, *and* revealed for the first time a lurch towards the new line. Here Stalin proclaimed the end of the 'Second Period', of capitalist restabilisation, and the start of what came to be known as the Third Period, 'a new revolutionary upsurge'.[15] There was absolutely no evidence for this.[16]

The meaning of the new 'perspective', however, became clear as the drive towards the collectivisation of agriculture and forced industrialisation gathered momementum: 'class against class' was in no sense a strategy for international revolution, but reflected the standpoint of the Stalinist bureaucracy, as it drove towards violent and autarchic national development. For this involved a full-scale attack on the masses of Russian society, in defiance of all forces which might seek to resist the offensive or even to moderate its tempo.

The single force remaining within the leading circles of the Russian Communist Party which might impede Stalin's plans was led by Bukharin, whose supporters were for continuing to conciliate the better-off peasants and for retaining the mediatory role of the trade unions. From the Ninth Plenum of the Comintern executive committee (February 1928) onwards, a violent clamour was stirred up to purge such restraining influences, both within Russia and internationally.[17] The discovery of 'ascending revolutionary struggles', and the revelation that social democrats were in fact 'fascists', were the main weapons of this hue and cry. Those who opposed it were denounced as 'soft' on the social democrats, and therefore as their 'objective' allies; any realistic appraisal of the actual balance of class forces was cowardice or renegacy. The result was catastrophic:

Extreme verbal radicalism went hand in hand with practical passivity. The Communist parties isolated themselves, then shouted furiously from the sidelines.

This suited Stalin well. He still needed these parties, but mainly as propaganda agencies for the USSR. An active policy, for example an approach to the Social Democrats for an aggressive united front against Hitler, carried the risk of creating political upheavals. This was the last thing that Stalin wanted. His policy was conservative: avoid foreign entanglements and so avoid the risk of foreign intervention. The ultra-leftism of the Third Period fitted very well with this aim.[18]

In Germany, the new line was enforced ruthlessly by the Comintern's favoured leader, Thälmann. At the Sixth World Congress (May 1928), where Bukharin and his supporters still exerted a restraining influence, he distinguished himself by demanding that the resolution, which already urged 'an orientation totally antagonistic to the Social Democrats', should be 'sharpened' and focussed more on exposing the role of *Left* Social Democracy.[19] Between December 1928 and March 1929 the group around Brandler and Thalheimer, which was sympathetic to Bukharin, was routed and completely purged from the KPD.[20] By the Party Congress in June it was impossible to disagree: the only delegate to do so was barracked off the platform, and Thälmann's insights—he denounced the SPD government as 'an especially dangerous form of fascist development, the form of Social Fascism'—were greeted with thunderous applause.[21]

The SPD government was certainly capable of anti-working class actions. Notoriously its Prussian police chief, Zorgiebel, had defended his force when it attacked a Communist May Day demonstration in 1929, killing 25 people. But the KPD notion of how to win Social Democratic workers whose loyalty was tested by this behaviour was to abuse them as 'little Zorgiebels':

> We must ruthlessly purge the ranks of the proletariat in factory and trade union of all rotten elements. He who belongs to the SPD is rotten and has to go.[22]

KPD squads involved themselves in street brawls with Social

Democrats; KPD trade unionists initiated ill-prepared struggles which led to their isolation and frequently to expulsion from Social Democrat-led trade unions. KPD members were encouraged to regard these as secondary: the leaders were in alliance with the bourgeois state. From spring 1929, under pressure from Lozovsky, head of the Comintern's trade union work, the unorganised and those of the expelled who had formed 'Red' unions were seen as the main catchment area from which the swelling tide of radicalised workers were supposed to flood into the Revolutionary Trade Union Opposition (RGO). The effect of all this was certainly to purge the organised working class: to purge it of revolutionaries, who, sacked by the employers and expelled by the union leaders, nevertheless stood condemned in the eyes of the majority as thugs and splitters.

But was it not the case that the trade union bureaucracy *did* play the role of dampening down and betraying strikes, and were they not increasingly enmeshed in the state machine? Did not the Social Democratic leaders initiate repressive actions when in government, and were they not passive in the face of the rapid growth both of unemployment and of the Nazis? The Comintern was right, surely, in its assessment of their role as paving the way for Nazism. On the reactionary role of the trade union bureaucrats, Trotsky himself was in no doubt:

> In the capitalist states, the most monstrous forms of bureaucratism are to be observed precisely in the trade unions. It is enough to look at America, England and Germany.

And he goes on to remark on the absurdity of counterposing

> the trade union organisation and the state organisation. In England, more than anywhere else the state rests upon the back of the working class... The mechanism is such that the bureaucracy is based directly upon the workers, and the state indirectly, through the mechanism of the trade union bureaucracy.[23]

But even in situations where the reformists had themselves initiated a breakaway such that the majority of the organised workers were under revolutionary leadership, 'the Communist Party strives in action to reduce to a minimum those obstacles which are placed before the labour movement by an organisational split.'[24]

Neither did Trotsky have illusions about the role of the SDP leaders in 'paving the way' for the Nazis. Indeed he went further:

> There is no doubt that, at the crucial moment the leaders of the Social Democracy will prefer the victory of fascism to the dictatorship of the proletariat.[25]

Why, then, urge a united front with such traitors? Why not simply denounce them as social-fascists? Because, whatever their subjective intentions or beliefs, the Social Democratic leaders stood at the head of a political party organically linked to the strongest sections of German workers; their influence depended upon the continued existence of this base, which the *Nazis* aimed to destroy. Perhaps those leaders would cynically make their peace with the Nazis; perhaps, they might reassure their supporters that the police and army would uphold the constitution, that mass action was unnecessary, and thereby commit political, and possibly literal suicide. But this was not decided in advance: it depended on the Social Democratic millions, for whom individual solutions were impossible. For though they were not revolutionaries, the interests of these masses, in their attachment to their union organisations, and to the newspapers, meeting halls and clubs of the Social Democratic world, were placed in violent contradiction to those leaders who could and would abandon them.

But would the Social Democratic masses realise this and act in time? For they did not trust revolutionary leadership, and would not march under its banner. Could they be mobilised, and if so, how? *Yes* was Trotsky's answer, but by one method only: if the Communist Party, the only organisation with sufficient forces to influence events, were to propose a United Front, propose practical measures for the joint defence of workers' organisations.

In 1922 the executive committee of the International had written to its French section criticising its failure to launch a united front and explaining how and why it worked. The French party, which held the allegiance of a strong minority of workers, should have used this influence to mobilise wider layers against the political repression of a strike in Le Havre. It should have:

> ...made a direct and public proposal to them, the Dissidents,
> [socialists] for a conference. There is not and there cannot
> be a rational, serious argument against such a proposal.
> And if, under the influence of the situation and under our
> pressure, the Dissidents had taken a half-step forward in the
> interests of the strike, they would have rendered the
> workers a real service, and the majority of the working
> masses, including those who follow the Dissidents, would
> have understood that it was our pressure that made them
> take this political step.[26]

This followed from the basic principles contained in the theses
drafted for the Comintern Executive by Trotsky himself:

> The reformists dread the revolutionary potential of the mass
> movement; their beloved arena is the parliamentary tribune,
> the trade union bureaux, the ministerial ante-chambers.
> On the contrary, we are, apart from all other considerations,
> interested in dragging the reformists from their asylums and
> placing them alongside ourselves before the eyes of the
> struggling masses.[27]

To achieve this, the Comintern was clear in 1922 that the
slogan of the united front 'only from below', was 'sheer scholas-
ticism'. It was impossible 'to summon the organised masses to a
united struggle without entering into negotiations with those
whom a particular section of the mass has made its plenipoten-
tiaries. What comes clearly to the fore in this intransigence is
political passivity...'[28]

But in 1929-33 'political passivity' was rampant: Thälmann
denounced Trotsky for urging Communists to 'stand shoulder to
shoulder with the murderers of Karl Liebknecht and Rosa Luxemburg and with Zorgiebel.'[29]

The specific conditions of Germany in 1930-33 were, of
course, different from those of 1922 in France. But the *main*
difference was that the scale and seriousness of the reactionary
threat, which had posed the need for a united front then, was far
greater now: both Communist and Social Democratic organisations were threatened with obliteration. It was necessary firstly

for the Communists to *explain* to the Social Democratic supporters *the seriousness of the threat,* which many of them already sensed, but which was pooh-poohed by their leaders, and second to propose *practical* cooperation between the two parties for the defence of working-class trade union and political organisations.

This was not a bloc in which the Communists ought to sacrifice their independence by diplomatic silence about the role of Social Democracy: on the contrary, Trotsky conceived it precisely as the International had once done, as a powerful method of criticism. To the extent that SPD leaders refused joint defensive action, they would stand in the eyes of their supporters not just as non-revolutionaries, but as traitors, even to the Social Democracy itself. To the extent that they agreed, their illusions in the neutrality of the state machine (and therefore in the willingness of the police to defend the constitution against fascism), would reveal itself in inconsistency and half-heartedness in the struggle. Thus, *provided* the Communists maintained complete political independence, criticising all the hesitations and half-measures of their temporary allies, the united front could help to build a powerful defensive movement, which, discrediting and superceding reformist methods as it swept along, could lay the basis for a working-class offensive in the future, in which the influence of reformism was substantially weakened.

The united front, therefore, was a method of struggle for influence in the working class. But it was not a manoeuvre: common defensive action was in the vital interests of all working-class organisations. Proposals designed to initiate it had to be made genuinely and repeatedly, not brandished—as ultimatums, accompanied by violent tirades—and then withdrawn equally abruptly, which was the KPD's actual practice on the rare occasions that it made such proposals. This approach only served the Social Democrats as an excuse for their inactivity, as proof that the Communists were motivated by sectarianism, not by a serious desire to organise common action. The KPD's 'bureaucratic ultimatism' grew from the theory of social fascism, in which all its policy was framed in the period 1929-33.

This is not to say that KPD policy was completely consistent. In March 1930 the party journal carried an article by Remmele condemning 'loud-mouthed swaggering over the smallest advances and successes'. This unaccustomed modesty was in response to a Comintern Executive resolution of the previous month which warned against left 'revolutionary phrases'. As E H Carr explains:

> It can hardly have been mere coincidence that the resolution was drafted at almost exactly the same moment as Stalin's famous letter to the party, 'Dizziness through Success', in which he called a halt to the headlong process of collectivisation, and censured 'people who think themselves "leftists"...'[30]

Remmele's article also rejected the lumping of fascists and 'social fascists' into one reactionary mass (an understandable deviation given the terminology)—which might have represented an advance. But the implied concern to combat the real Nazis was translated into frantic KPD attempts to outbid them in nationalist demagogy. It scorned Nazi claims 'that they fight for the liberation of the German people', and condemned them as 'agents for French and Polish imperialism'.[31] Such antics only strengthened chauvinism, but again they fitted the purposes of Stalin, for whom the main danger was foreign intervention, and the main source of the danger was Britain and France:

> Thus **Pravda** rejoiced after the elections in Germany in 1930 that the Nazi successes created 'not a few difficulties for French imperialism'. The desperate hope that an extreme right- wing government in Germany would be principally anti-French dominated their thinking.[32]

Trotsky, in the the first of the articles reprinted in this book, presented the lurch into 'national Bolshevism' as a new turn, as a departure from the Third Period. In retrospect it appears as a continuation of the same disastrous politics, with the insertion of a further obstacle to gaining an audience amongst Social Democratic workers. Attacks upon 'social fascism' continued throughout the interlude. This theory isolated the KPD from Social Democratic workers, systematically obscured what real fascism was, and thus disarmed resistance to it.

Trotsky recognised fascism as a political movement arising within monopoly capitalism during a phase of crisis so acute that the normal methods of parliamentary rule cannot resolve it, in which even the most restricted capacity of workers to organise cannot be tolerated by the big capitalists. This does not mean, as is suggested by most would-be critics of Marxism— who think the word means 'Stalinism'—that Hitler's rise can be attributed to a capitalist conspiracy. Trotsky understood that fascism is to be distinguished from many other forms of reaction by its growth as a mass movement rooted primarily in the middle strata of society, the urban and rural petty bourgeoisie, and in large sections of the growing army of unemployed. Unlike large capital or trade unionists, these have little or no organised strength to ward off the catastrophic effects of the crisis.

All the evidence shows that these were indeed the social roots of Hitler's movement. Nazism grew disproportionally in rural areas and small towns where the social weight of the organised working class was smallest, and it grew as a desperate response to the calamitous effects of the economic crisis. From 1928, the scale of bankruptcies in the countryside rose sharply, (from an average 31 in 1925-27 to 64 in 1928, 85 in 1929, 94 in 1930, 135 in 1931 and 190 in 1932). Broszat comments upon these figures:

> This was the soil for the massive agitation of the Nazi party [NSDAP] which began in 1929-30... From the summer of 1930 onwards the NSDAP became the leading agrarian movement... Thus the Nazi share [of the vote in 1930] in the rural constituencies of Schleswig Holstein rose from 5.4 per cent to 35.1 per cent.[33]

> ...in the provinces and the small towns...the Nazi vote had risen above the average. This was particularly true of those regions where a traditionally established Protestant and 'nationally minded' middle class had come into conflict politically and socially with equally strong battalions of the Social Democrat or Communist working class. It was in these areas that the radically anti-Marxist slogans of the NSDAP fell on particularly fertile soil. Bourgeois animosities and fears of being swamped by objectionable cultural and social forces were widespread in these circles.[34]

In Berlin, by contrast, the Nazis managed only 15 per cent of the votes, gaining 'the largest percentage in the well-to-do bourgeois suburbs of the city,'[35] but also growing alarmingly in urban districts worst hit by unemployment—such as Friedrichshain in Berlin, where the Nazi SA battled with the Communist Party for control of the streets. In a district of Saxony for which there are figures, 61 per cent of the Nazi membership was aged between 18 and 30, compared with only 19 per cent of the SPD. It is likely that a high proportion of these were unemployed. In the urban areas, the backbone of the Nazi organisation was among the young unemployed, shop-keepers, students and unorganised white-collar workers.

The 'anti- capitalism' of many amongst these layers was real, and was articulated in the Nazi 'left' around Gregor Strasser, which made threatening noises about what it intended to do to finance capital. Their adherence to the Nazis was not inevitable, argued Trotsky, but depended first and foremost upon whether the working class could offer a prospect of ending the misery which stemmed from the crisis.[36] The failure of the workers' organisations to offer such a way out was at the root of the Nazi dominance, which was able to focus middle-class discontent on to the Jews and the working class itself.

Thus, to the small trader, large capital was only the enemy in so far as it was Jewish, and he went along with the Nazi brownshirts to smash the windows of the Jewish department stores; to the desperate unemployed or unorganised worker, trade union strength, which protected only others, appeared as the source of his suffering, and he assembled in gangs to break up Social Democratic meetings; to the student, the defeat to be avenged was of the German nation at Versailles, and not of the revolutionary internationalists in 1923; Communism appeared as a sterile and alien creed, and a beating seemed too good for its adherents. Thus the working-class movement paid for its mistakes, as broader and broader sections of its potential allies turned upon it.

The dynamic growth of the Nazis was a source of magnetic attraction for the uncertain amongst the discontented. In January 1931 SA membership reached 100,000. By the start of the following year it was 300,000, and by July 1932 400,000.[37]

These did not sit in their barracks. Eighty-six people were killed in 'political riots' in July 1932 alone.[38] These battles were for control of the streets and meeting places. Generally, in the areas of large- scale industry, wherever there were factories, mines or docks, Nazi dominance was achieved only after 1933, by dint of massive intimidation by the forces of the 'regular' state machine, in tandem with the brownshirt squads now organised as its auxiliaries. The working-class parties held 13 million votes until 1933; it was the electoral base of the middle-class liberals and moderate nationalists which collapsed into the arms of the Nazis. Less than 1 per cent of works council members were Nazis in 1931—710 out of 138,418.[39]

Fascism, then, was distinguished by its mobilisation of the masses in a campaign of violence against the organisations of the working class. It was not a capitalist conspiracy, but at many key points Hitler was helped both by big capital and by the state. Jailed for five years in April 1924 for his part in the 'Beerhouse *putsch*' in Munich, he was released less than eight months later. Other leading Nazis too were treated leniently by the German courts, which allowed themselves to be used as a platform for the Nazis: 'Wonderful propaganda for us,' commented Goebbels in 1930 upon being fined the sum of 800 marks.[40] Despite being 'controlled' by the Social Democrats, the police often failed to act against the Nazis, and increasingly displayed evidence of pro-Nazi sympathies. By mid-1932 'the attitude of Army officers was summed up in the phrase "What a pity it would be to have to fire on those splendid youths in the SA".'[41]

With the eclipse of the Reichstag, and the growing instability of civil government, the role of the army assumed pivotal importance. Amongst the senior officers, General Schleicher was the most influential figure politically. Schleicher's desire to take the Nazis into a coalition government was thwarted when Hitler refused the terms offered, but the general was able to bring together a ministerial combination of 'aristocratic gentlemen of conservative-nationalist complexion'. These 'were determined to do away with the last remnants of Social Democratic and unionist influence which Brüning had still taken account of.'[42] They acted to dissolve the Prussian government, not out of an abstract commitment to law and order, indeed, in contempt of it, but because of the Prussians' reluctance to grant the Nazi SA complete freedom of the streets and their 'failure' to use the police enough against the KPD. 'Wilhelm von Gayl, the new Reich Minister of the Interior, ...on 11 July bluntly declared that Prussian measures against the Communists were insufficient, adding that the surveillance of the Nazis was wrong and undesirable.'[43] Nothing could dent the constitutional cretinism of the SPD leadership. It abjectly surrendered control of the Prussian police force which it had always urged its supporters to count on. Yet:

> In all German cities formations of the Reichsbanner and the Iron Front were standing by, polishing their rifles and waiting for a call to action. If ever there had been a moment to defend the Republic it had come on 20 July 1932, when Herr von Papen entrusted the executive power in Prussia to General von Runstedt.[44]

The Social Democrats did not mobilise these forces; neither did they even make an attempt (doomed in advance) to mobilise the police. The ousted government appealed instead to the Prussian Supreme Court at Leipzig, which, of course, also did nothing. As a result, almost everywhere in Prussia Social Democrat or left liberal police presidents or regional administrators were replaced by conservative civil servants. Martin Broszat concludes from this that: 'The bulwark of the Republic was razed to the ground well before the Nazis took over in February 1933.'[45] It was true that, as Trotsky remarked, 'little now remains of the proud Weimar constitution save the bones and the skin.'[46] But the existence or not of leftish policemen and civil servants did not define what was worth defending in the Republic. It was necessary to assess the problem as Trotsky had urged, 'from the standpoint of *workers'* democracy'. The passivity of Social Democracy weakened and demoralised workers' democratic organisations and strengthened those forces—both the state machine and the Nazis—which could and would be mobilised against them. But the *destruction* of workers' democracy still lay in the future.

In the final stages of Hitler's rise to power, business finance was indispensible, particularly after the electoral reverses of late

1932 had drained his party treasury. The support of the central sections of big business, of the large landowners, and of the army, was assured when the last and most unstable government combination, under Schleicher himself, had attempted to withdraw subsidies to the landowners. Schleicher had an independent base in the army, but little outside it; like Brüning and Papen, he tried to play off one social force against another. But the decision between them could not long be postponed.

As the Nazi movement grew, the KPD evaluation of it collapsed into complete confusion. On 16 September 1930 *Rote Fahne* had responded to the increase in the Nazi vote from 800,000 to 6.4 million by describing it as 'the highpoint of the National Socialist movement'.[47] But seven weeks later the paper explained that it had meant the precise opposite: 'Fascist dictatorship is no longer a threat, it is already here.'[48] And if it wasn't, then, said *Rote Fahne* in March 1931, 'no one has any illusion that Fascism can be smashed in alliance with social fascism'.[49] If fascism was already in power, if, notwithstanding, the KPD was not strong enough on its own to prevent it from coming to power, if it could not outbid the Nazis in rabid nationalism, and could not beat them in alliance with the Social Democracy, only one possibility remained: Hitler's victory was inevitable, and the job of the KPD was to project the inevitable as a victory of the revolution:

> ...once they [the nazis] are in power [note that it is no longer even 'if '], the united front of the proletariat will arise and make a clean sweep of everything... We are not afraid of the fascist gentlemen. They will shoot their bolt quicker than any other government.'[50]

This was empty bluster; confused and politically paralysed, the KPD leaders *were* afraid of the fascist gentlemen (and with reason): in June 1932 Thälmann appealed on behalf of the KPD to 'the unknown SA soldier' to join 'the revolutionary army of freedom against the Young Plan and German capitalists'. As Carr comments: 'In a desperate and baffling situation every rallying cry must be tried.'[51] The massive Nazi vote of the following month (13.7 million) was discounted: 'the KPD was the only victor of July 31st,' proclaimed Thälmann.[52] This was a repetition of **Rote Fahne**'s appraisal in September 1930, and the Nazi vote had more than doubled since then. It seems unlikely that his judgement convinced even Thälmann himself.

It will be recalled that after the next batch of elections, in which the Nazi vote was reduced by two million, Hilferding of the SPD had proclaimed 'the downfall of fascism'. The KPD for its part celebrated 'the disintegration of the Fascist mass movement'.[53] The cowardice of the leaders of both parties in their refusal to look at reality honestly, or to do anything meaningful about it, was completely symetrical. On 30 January 1933, Hitler assumed the Chancellorship.

Even now, Social Democratic eyes remained firmly closed: neither they nor the trade union leaders were prepared to mobilise, and neither should anyone else: 'undisciplined procedure by individual organisations or groups on their own initiative would do the greatest harm to the entire working class'.[54] Meanwhile, according to the later testimony at Nuremburg of the leading Social Democrat, Severing, the party top brass was anxiously seeking assurances from the army that it would defend the constitution. None were forthcoming.

> During the last open air meeting which the socialists were allowed to hold in the Berlin *lustgarten* Otto Wels, chairman of the party, gave his estimate of the situation by quoting the comforting proverb *Gestrenge Herren reieren nicht lange* ['strict masters don't rule for long'].[55]

In 1931, Fritz Tarnow, Social Democratic head of the Woodworkers Union, had clinched his place in the footnotes of history by asking of his party:

> Do we stand...at the sick-bed of capitalism...as the doctor who seeks to cure? Or as joyous heirs, who can hardly wait for the end and would even like to help it along with poison?[56]

Perhaps some of Tarnow's audience looked forward to the patient's early death, but their leadership aspired to the status of physician, having long ago shrunk from the role of executioner; for this post the KPD central committee saw itself as the only candidate. In the early 1930s both stood in attendance at the bedside of a capitalist system mortally ill. But the doctor knew no medicine but incantation—the economic situation will improve, said Kautsky. And the executioner had no weapon but empty threats: 'We are not afraid of the Fascist gentlemen,' blustered Remmele.

Meanwhile, the Nazis were assembling the instruments of surgery. In the weeks that followed Hitler's appointment as Chancellor, they set about tearing to shreds the venerated text of the constitution of Weimar. On 22 February an auxiliary police force of 50,000 was created which included 25,000 members of the SA and 15,000 of the SS.[57] Five days later, on the pretext of the Reichstag fire, mass arrests of Communists began. The March 1933 election was designed to bolster Nazi authority—by any means necessary. 'Social Democratic rallies were broken up, printing plants and campaign headquarters wrecked, in order to intimidate the SPD and the voters.'[58] Fifty-one opponents of the Nazis were killed. Even with all the resources of the state at their disposal, the Nazis were able to win only 43 per cent of the votes, but, as Goebbels exclaimed, 'What do figures matter now? We're the masters in the Reich and in Prussia.'[59] Communist deputies were prevented from taking their seats, and were seized wherever they were discovered.

On 21 March, the SPD voted against Hitler's Enabling Act, the only party thus to defend its beloved constitution. In April, Kautsky offered his own sage appraisal of the situation: support for Hitler was 'a passing fancy', particularly among 'politically and economically uneducated youth', and anyway, 'Avoiding a decisive battle under unfavourable circumstances is by no means a surrender'.[60] Hitler had little respect for Kautsky's acute tactical sense, and gathered his forces for a decisive battle which the SPD *could* choose to resist or to be dumbly massacred, but *could not* choose to avoid. In a final, criminal act of betrayal, the trade union leaders hastened to flatter their executioner:

> ...the victory of National Socialism, though won in the struggle against a party which we used to consider as the embodiment of the idea of socialism, is our victory as well; because, today, the socialist task is put to the whole nation.[61]

The occasion of this disgusting statement—by Walter Pahl in the federation's official publication—was Hitler's grisly parody of a May Day parade; it is not known what the marching trade unionists, mobilised by leaders such as Pahl, expected from it. But the next day, all trade union buildings were occupied and the most prominent leaders arrested; on 12 May trade union property was confiscated, and the following month the SPD was suppressed. The KPD's response?

> ...the complete elimination of the Social Fascists from the State apparatus and the brutal suppression of its press do not alter the fact that they represent now as before the main social buttress of the dictatorship of capital.[62]

In November the Nazis held a plebiscitary election with themselves as the only contenders, and claimed 92.2 per cent of the total electorate. The result, said the KPD, the result represented 'a great victory of Thälmann's Party' and 'confirms the correctness of the statement, made already by the Central Committee of the German Communist Party, that a new revolutionary upsurge has begun in Germany.'[63] Within six weeks of this utterance 130,000 German Communists were in concentration camps.

By now Hitler had at his disposal a formidable apparatus of supervision: block wardens and street monitors, supplemented by the workplace activities of the Nazi cells and the Nazified police, repeatedly wrecked the now clandestine Socialist and Communist organisations. The organisers themselves were forced to live under assumed names, continually changing their sleeping places, at the mercy of hunger and 'spy-psychosis', in constant fear of arrest.[64] A survivor recounts how during interrogation by the Gestapo he was dog-whipped until blood flowed from every part of his body, and how the wounds themselves were whipped till he did not know whether he was dead; how a comrade threw himself through the sixth-floor window of the Gestapo headquarters in Berlin because death was preferable to further torture and the inevitable betrayal of others.[65]

The German trade unions were formally dissolved on 7 December 1933, and replaced with the German Labour Front. This was primarily an instrument of indoctrination; workers

were made to suffer compulsory repatriation, compulsory training and deportation—total mobility of labour was the objective.[66] Works councils were suppressed and replaced with
'councils of confidence', whose members were elected through a
slate nominated by the employer and the chairman of the Nazi
cell: no other slate was permitted. Every independent workers'
organisation had been flattened without organised resistance in
the space of a few months.

The catastrophe was not confined to Germany, for it shifted
the balance of class forces internationally: in February 1934, the
extreme right in France was able to force the resignation of
Daladier and his replacement by the reactionary Doumergue;
that same month in Vienna, workers' apartment blocks, proudest
achievement of municipal socialism, were bombarded by the
artillery of Dolfuss' clerical-fascist coalition. In Spain, CEDA, the
political vanguard of Francoism, entered the government, and
the general strike mounted in protest was first confined to the
Asturias region and then crushed. Everywhere, energy and confidence bolstered the spirits of the most reactionary; for if the
legendary German workers' movement could be defeated without even giving battle, how much easier the task now appeared
elsewhere.

Leon Trotsky failed in his effort to prevent this tragic
outcome, which altered the course of world history along a path
which he had predicted with almost clairvoyant accuracy. But
his work remains significant today, and not only as historical
analysis which has rarely been excelled. For as capitalism moves
again towards a crisis which is part of its inner nature, it recreates
conditions in which fascism may grow. Nowhere is fascism the
main danger to the labour movement, though in France the rise
of the Fronte Nationale has illustrated that such movements are
no historical curiosity, or the product of 'the Germanic spirit'.[67]
Their re-emergence in the future would demand urgent action,
based in large part upon an understanding of past experience;
that experience is nowhere more forcefully and clearly analysed
than in the pages which follow.

Part One | **1930**

Chris Harman

Background

IN 1929 GERMAN SOCIETY entered a profound crisis for the third time in less than twelve years.

The first period of crisis had followed defeat in 1918. Mutinies in the navy, strikes in the factories and massive demonstrations led by revolutionary socialists forced right-wing Social Democrat leaders—who themselves believed in a constitutional monarchy—to proclaim a republic. For a time effective power lay in the hands of workers' and soldiers' councils. Only their ability to command a majority in these permitted the Social Democrats to rule, and to dissolve the councils in favour of a bourgeois parliament. Even so, until well into 1920 a stable unified structure hardly existed. The Social Democratic government was only able to restore 'normalcy' by relying on the army and the right-wing semi-official *freikorps*. These troops murdered thousands in putting down the Spartacist uprising in Berlin, in suppressing the Bavarian Soviet Republic and in occupying Bremen and Hamburg.

By 1921 this initial period of acute political instability had passed. An attempt by the Communist Party to stage a national uprising in March of that year (the 'March Action') was a disastrous failure. In 1923, however, a very large question mark was once again placed over the continued existence of capitalism in Germany. In their greed for the spoils of war the victorious powers had forced the German government to agree to reparations under the Treaty of Versailles that far exceeded the German economy's capacity to pay. The result was continual inflation of the mark. After the failure in 1922 to deliver the required quantities of reparation coal to France, the French army occupied the Ruhr in January 1923.

Immediately the whole of German society was thrown into crisis. The economy became chaotic. Inflation proceeded at an unprecedented pace. In January there were about 10,000 marks to the dollar, by June 47,000, and by September 200 million. German currency became valueless. Whole sections of the middle classes suddenly found their savings to be worthless. In the Ruhr spontaneous mass strikes broke out, not just against the French, but also for the nationalisation of the mines. In August there was a general strike throughout Berlin and other major industrial areas. Everywhere bitterness against the French occupation was combined with bitterness against the government for being unable to deal with it. There was complete disillusion with the *status quo*. On the political right people poured into the radical nationalist and fascist parties; on the left the Communist Party was for the first time commanding something like majority support among the workers. (Even a year later its vote was 60 per cent of the SPD's). And even many of those supporting the right-wing parties were prepared to accept any sort of change, even a revolutionary left change, which might solve the crisis.

Yet the bourgeois republic survived. The Communist Party at first ignored the implications of the crisis, then called for an uprising without adequately preparing its followers, and finally called this off at the last minute (in Hamburg a break in communications led a few hundred Communists to attempt to take power in isolation from anything happening elsewhere in Germany). The result was a rapid disillusioning of the millions who had momentarily turned to the revolutionary left. The only compensation was that in Munich a fascist coup—the 'beer hall *putsch*'—failed equally miserably.

By the sping of 1924, the government had begun to solve the crisis. The 'Dawes Plan' eased the burden of reparations; the currency was revalued and stabilised; a flow of American loans and investments gave a boost to the economy. The revolutionary left and the fascist right quickly lost the support they had gained. For the next five years it seemed that German society had at last stabilised. In 1928, although the Communists received three million votes, that was little compared with the nine million for the SPD. The Social Democrats seemed to be recovering all the strength and influence they had lost. One of their leaders, Müller, formed a coalition government. They also ruled in Prussia and many provincial cities. They had 900,000 individual members, 10,000 local parties, five million in the free trade unions.

At the same time, the Nazis seemed confined to the lunatic fringe. They received a mere two and a half per cent of the popular vote.

The Wall Street Crash and the slump that followed shortly afterwards transformed all this completely. The foreign loans upon which the German economy depended for its stability were no longer forthcoming. Thousands of factories closed down. The number of unemployed rose to three million by mid-1930, while the number on short time was similar. Whole sections of the middle class were poverty-stricken as large and small businesses went bankrupt. Agricultural prices fell and the peasants faced ruin. Everything that had seemed beneficial in the preceding period now seemed harmful. What had been marginal irritants—the effects of Versailles and reparations—now seemed major evils.

The Müller government was completely incapable of dealing with this new crisis. In March 1930 it fell, after disputes between the various parties in the coalition. The president, Hindenburg, then asked the leader of the Catholic Centre Party, Brüning, to form a right-wing government. This was unable to obtain a parliamentary majority, and elections were held in September.

The new feelings of anger and despair were recorded dramatically in these elections. The Communist vote grew by 40 per cent. But this was completely overshadowed by an 800 per cent increase in the Nazi vote. The fascists were suddenly a far greater and more menacing force than they had ever been in 1923.

The Comintern and the KPD

In the years 1925-28 the Comintern, under Stalin and Bukharin, followed a policy that laid stress upon alliances with non-revolutionaries as a way of obtaining mass support. This was known as the strategy of the 'second period', of capitalist consolidation (as opposed to the 'first period', of capitalist instability, in 1917-24). Trotsky criticised this policy (as he later did the 'popular front'), not because it involved united action with non-revolutionary bodies, but because in order to achieve this unity the Comintern leaders sacrificed the Communist Parties' independence and freedom to criticise.

In 1928 Stalin turned sharply against his previous ally Bukharin, and the previous policies. At the sixth congress of the Communist International in summer 1928 capitalism was proclaimed to have passed its second period of temporary stabilisation, and to be entering a 'third period' of 'rapid development of the contradictions in the world economy' and of 'maximum sharpening in the general crisis of capitalism' which would 'inevitably' lead to wars and revolution. From this the need for a complete change in tactics was deduced. Not only was the completely unsuccessful policy of uncritical dependence on 'left' Social Democrats abandoned, but now any sort of cooperation with them was ruled out.

At the same time all those in the different national Communist parties who had previously supported the rightist policies of Bukharin and who showed any degree of independence from Stalin were expelled (together with the remnants of the left opposition): in Italy Tasca, in India Roy, in the US Lovestone, in Czechoslovakia Hais and Jilek, in Sweden Kilboom, in Spain Nin, Maurin and Andrade.

It was announced that a 'radicalisation' of the masses was taking place; there was 'a loss of faith of the masses in Social Democracy'. The role of Social Democratic parties was seen to be a purely reactionary one in preventing the forward movement to the revolution. As such, it was argued that they were barely indistinguishable from the fascists. Stalin had written that 'social democracy and fascism are twins'. This slogan was taken up and elaborated by a host of functionaries. 'In countries where there are strong Social Democratic parties, fascism takes the particular form of social fascism...'[1] The term 'social fascist' was applied not merely to the hardened right wing of the Social Democrats, but especially to the left wing: 'As a matter of act it (the "left" wing of social democracy) wholeheartedly supports the policy of social fascism.'[2]

This designation was accompanied by a continuous failure to understand the extent of the real fascist menace. As early as

February 1930, the German Communist Party leader Thälmann was calling Müller's Social Democratic government a 'social-fascist gang' and announcing that 'the rule of fascism has already been established in Germany.'[3] If fascism already existed, why the need to fight against the Nazis, who only stood for a 'different form of fascism'?

Faced with the massive Nazi gains of the 1930 elections, and the rather smaller KPD gains, the Communist daily paper *Rote Fahne* could call this 'a victory for the Communists', and write that 'Last night was Herr Hitler's greatest day, but the so-called election victory of the Nazis is the beginning of the end'[4] and 'September 14th was the high point of the National Socialist movement in Germany. What comes after this can only be decline and fall.'[5]

The Turn in the Communist International and the German Situation was written immediately after the election of September 1930. It is one of Trotsky's earliest attempts to assess the new array of forces revealed, and to show the incapacity of the recently Stalinised Comintern to come to terms with these. It was translated by Morris Lewitt and published by the Communist League of America in 1931. To avoid later repetition, it is reprinted here slightly abridged.

Leon Trotsky

The Turn In the Communist International and the German Situation

1: The Sources of the Latest Turn

TACTICAL TURNS, even wide ones, are absolutely unavoidable in our epoch. They are necessitated by the abrupt turns of the objective situation (the lack of stable international relations; sharp and irregular fluctuations of conjuncture; sharp reflections of the economic fluctuations in politics; the impulsiveness of the masses under the influence of the feeling of helplessness, etc). Attentive watchfulness over the changes in the objective situation is now far more important and at the same time an immeasurably more difficult task than prior to the war, in the epoch of the 'organic' development of capitalism. The leadership of the party now finds itself in the position of a chauffeur who drives his automobile on a mountain, over the sharp zig-zags of the road. An untimely turn, incorrectly applied speed, threaten the passengers and the car with the greatest danger, if not with destruction.

The leadership of the Communist International has given us examples in recent years of very abrupt turns. The latest of them we observe these last months. What has called forth the turns of the Communist International since the death of Lenin? The changes in the objective situation? No. It can be said with confidence: beginning with 1923, there was not a single tactical turn made in time by the Comintern under the influence of correctly estimated changes in the objective conditions. On the contrary: every turn was the result of the unbearable sharpening of the contradictions between the line of the Comintern and the objective situation. We are witnessing the very same thing this time, too.

The Ninth Plenum of the Executive Committee of the Communist International, the Sixth Congress, and particularly the Tenth Plenum,[1] adopted a course towards an abrupt and direct revolutionary rise (the 'third period'), which was absolutely excluded at the time by the objective situation existing after the greatest defeats in England and China, the weakening of the Communist Parties throughout the world, and particularly under the condition of a commercial and industrial ascent which embraced a series of the most important capitalist countries. The tactical turn in the Communist International beginning with February 1928 was therefore directly contrary to the actual turn of the historic road. From these contradictions arose the tendencies of adventurism, the further isolation of the parties from the masses, the weakening of the organisations, etc. Only after all these phenomena had clearly assumed a menacing character did the leadership of the Comintern make a new turn in February 1930, backward from, and to the right of, the tactics of the 'third period'.

It is the irony of fate, unmerciful to all *chvostism*,[2] that the new tactical turn in the Comintern coincided chronologically with the new turn in the objective conditions. An international crisis of unprecedented acuteness undoubtedly opens perspectives for the radicalisation of the masses and social convulsions. Precisely under such circumstances, a turn to the left could and should have been made, that is, to adopt a bold speed on the path of revolutionary rise. This would have been absolutely correct and necessary if, in the last three years, the leadership of the Comintern had utilised, as it should have, the period of economic revival and the revolutionary ebb to strengthen the positions of the party in the mass organisations, above all in the trade unions. Under such circumstances, the chauffeur could and should have shifted his gears in 1930 from second into third speed, or at least prepared for such a change in the nearest future.

In reality the directly opposite process took place. So as not to go over the cliff, the chauffeur had to change from the prematurely adopted speed down to second, and to slow down the pace. When? Under circumstances which, with the correct strategical line, would have made necessary its acceleration.

Such is the crying contradiction between the tactical necessity and strategical perspective, a contradiction in which, by the logic of the mistakes of their leadership, the Communist Parties find themselves in a number of countries.

We see this contradiction most strikingly and dangerously now in Germany, where the last elections revealed an exceptionally peculiar relation of forces, resulting not only from the two periods of Germany's post-war stabilisation, but also from the three periods of the Comintern's mistakes.

2: The Parliamentary Victory of the Communist Party in the light of the Revolutionary Tasks

The official press of the Comintern is now depicting the results of the German elections as a prodigious victory of Communism, which places on the order of the day the slogan of a Soviet Germany. The bureaucratic optimists do not want to reflect upon the meaning of the relation of forces which is disclosed by the election statistics. They examine the figure of the Communist votes gained, independently of the revolutionary tasks created by the situation and the obstacles it sets up.

The Communist Party received around 4,600,000 votes as against 3,300,000 in 1928. From the viewpoint of 'normal' parliamentary mechanics, the gain of 1,300,000 votes is considerable even if we take into consideration the rise in the total number of voters. But the gain of the party pales completely beside the leap of fascism from 800,000 to 6,400,000 votes. Of no less important significance for evaluating the elections is the fact that the Social Democracy, in spite of substantial losses, retained its basic cadres and still received a considerably greater number of workers' votes than the Communist Party.

Meanwhile, if we should ask ourselves what combination of international and domestic circumstances could be capable of turning the working class towards Communism with greater velocity, we could not find an example of more favourable circumstances for such a turn than the situation in present-day Germany: Young's noose,[3] the economic crisis, the disintegration of the rulers, the crisis of parliamentarism, the terrific self-exposure of the Social Democracy in power. From the viewpoint of these concrete historical circumstances, the specific gravity of the German Communist Party in the social life of the country, in spite of the gain of 1,300,000 votes, remains proportionately small.

The weakness of the positions of Communism, inextricably bound up with the policy and regime of the Comintern, is revealed more clearly if we compare the present social weight of the Communist Party with those concrete and unpostponable tasks which the present historical circumstances put before it.

It is true that the Communist Party itself did not expect such a gain. But this proves that under the blows of mistakes and defeats, the leadership of the Communist Parties has become disaccustomed from big aims and perspectives. If yesterday it underestimated its own possibilities, then today it once more underestimates the difficulties. In this way, one danger is multiplied by another.

In the meantime, the first characteristic of a real revolutionary party—is to be able to look reality in the face.

3: The Vacillations of the Big Bourgeoisie

With every turn of the historic road, with every social crisis, we must over and over again examine the question of the mutual relations of the three classes in modern society: the big bourgeoisie, led by finance capital; the petty bourgeoisie, vacillating between the basic camps; and finally, the proletariat.

The big bourgeoisie, making up a negligible part of the nation, cannot hold power without the support of the petty bourgeoisie of the city and the village, that is, of the remnants of the old, and the masses of the new, middle classes. In the present epoch, this support acquires two basic forms, politically antagonistic to each other, but historically supplementary: Social Democracy and fascism. In the person of the social democracy, the petty bourgeoisie, which follows finance capital, leads behind it millions of workers.

The *big German bourgeoisie* is vacillating at present; it is split up. Its disagreements are exhausted by the question: which of the two methods of cure for the social crisis shall be applied at present? The Social Democratic therapy repels one part of the big bourgeoisie with the indefiniteness of its results, and with the danger of too great levies (taxes, social legislation, wages).

The surgical intervention of fascism seems to the other part to be uncalled for by the situation and too risky. In other words, the finance bourgeoisie as a whole vacillates in the evaluation of the situation, not seeing sufficient basis as yet for the proclamation of an offensive of its own 'third period', when the social democracy is unconditionally replaced by fascism, when, generally speaking, it undergoes a general annihilation for its services rendered. The vacillations of the big bourgeoisie—with a weakening of its basic parties—between the Social Democracy and fascism are an extraordinarily clear symptom of a pre-revolutionary situation. With the approach of the real revolutionary situation, these vacillations, it is understood, will come to an end immediately.

4: The Petty Bourgeoisie and Fascism

In order that the social crisis may bring about the proletarian revolutions, it is necessary that, besides other conditions, a decisive shift of the petty bourgeois classes occurs in the direction of the proletariat. This gives the proletariat a chance to put itself at the head of the nation as its leader.

The last election revealed—and this is where its principal symptomatic significance lies—a shift in the opposite direction. Under the blow of the crisis, the petty bourgeoisie swung, not in the direction of the proletarian revolution, but in the direction of the most extreme imperialist reaction, pulling behind it considerable sections of the proletariat.

The gigantic growth of National Socialism is an expression of two factors: a deep social crisis, throwing the petty bourgeois masses off balance, and the lack of a revolutionary party that would be regarded by the masses of the people as an acknowledged revolutionary leader. If the Communist Party is the *party of revolutionary hope*, then fascism, as a mass movement, is the *party of counter-revolutionary despair*. When revolutionary hope embraces the whole proletarian mass, it inevitably pulls behind it on the road of revolution considerable and growing sections of the petty bourgeoisie. Precisely in this sphere, the election revealed the opposite picture: counter-revolutionary despair embraced the petty bourgeois mass with such a force that it drew behind it many sections of the proletariat.

How is this to be explained? In the past, we have observed (Italy, Germany) a sharp strengthening of fascism, victorious or at least threatening, as a result of a spent or missed revolutionary situation, at the conclusion of a revolutionary crisis in which the proletarian vanguard revealed its inability to put itself at the head of the nation and change the fate of all its classes, the petty bourgeoisie included. This is precisely what gave fascism its peculiar strength in Italy. But at present, the problem in Germany does not arise at the conclusion of a revolutionary crisis but only at its approach. From this, the leading Communist Party officials, optimists *ex-officio*, draw the conclusion that fascism, having come 'too late', is doomed to inevitable and speedy defeat (**Rote Fahne**).

These people do not want to learn anything. Fascism comes 'too late' in relation to old revolutionary crises. But it appears sufficiently early—at the dawn—in relation to the new revolutionary crisis. The fact that it gained the possibility to take up such a powerful starting position *on the eve* of a revolutionary period, and not at its conclusion, is not the weak side of fascism but the weak side of Communism. The petty bourgeoisie does not wait—as a consequence of new disappointments in the ability of the party to improve its fate—it bases itself upon the experiences of the past, it remembers the lesson of 1923, the capricious leaps of the ultra-left course of Maslow-Thälmann, the opportunist impotence of the same Thälmann, the clatter of the 'third period', etc.[4] Finally—and this is the most important—its lack of faith in the proletarian revolution is nourished by the lack of faith in the Communist party on the part of millions of Social Democratic workers. The petty bourgeoisie, even when completely thrown off the conservative road by circumstances, can turn to the social revolution only when the sympathies of the majority of the working class are for the social revolution. Precisely this most important condition is still lacking in Germany, and not by accident.

The programmatic declaration of the German Communist Party before the elections was completely and exclusively devoted to fascism, as the main enemy. Nevertheless, fascism came out the victor, gathering not only millions of semi-proletarian elements, but also many hundreds of thousands of industrial workers. This is an expression of the fact that in spite of the parliamentary victory of the Communist Party, the proletarian revolution as a whole suffered a serious defeat in this election, it is understood, of a preliminary, warning, and not decisive character. It can become decisive and will inevitably become decisive, if the Communist Party is unable to evaluate its partial parliamentary victory in connection with this 'preliminary' character of the defeat of the revolution as a whole, and draw from this all the necessary conclusions.

Fascism in Germany has become a real danger, as an acute expression of the helpless position of the bourgeois regime, the conservative role of the Social Democracy in this regime, and the accumulated powerlessness of the Communist Party to abolish it. Whoever denies this is either blind or a braggart.

In 1923, Brandler, in spite of all our warnings, monstrously exaggerated the forces of fascism. From the wrong evaluation of the relationship of forces grew a hesitating, evasive, defensive cowardly policy. This destroyed the revolution. Such events do not pass without leaving traces in the consciousness of all the classes of the nation. The overestimation of fascism by the Communist leadership created one of the conditions for its further strengthening. The contrary mistake, this very underestimation of fascism by the present leadership of the Communist Party, may lead the revolution to a more severe crash for many years to come.

The danger acquires particular acuteness in connection with the question of the *tempo* of development, which does not depend upon us alone. The malarial character of the political curve revealed by the election speaks for the fact that the tempo of development of the national crisis may turn out to be very speedy. In other words, the course of events in the very near future may resurrect in Germany, on a new historical plane, the old tragic contradiction between the maturity of a revolutionary situation, on the one hand, and the weakness and strategical impotence of the revolutionary party on the other. This must be side clearly, openly, and above all, in time.

5: The Communist Party and the Working Class

It would be a monstrous mistake to console oneself with the

fact, for instance, that the Bolshevik Party in April 1917, after the arrival of Lenin, when the party first began to prepare for the seizure of power, had less than 80,000 members and led behind itself, even in Petrograd, not more than a third of the workers and a far smaller part of the soldiers. The situation in Russia was altogether different.

The revolutionary parties came out of the underground only in March, after an almost three-year interruption of even that strangled political life which existed prior to the war. The working class during the war renewed itself approximately 40 per cent. The overwhelming mass of the proletariat did not know the Bolsheviks, had not even heard of them. The voting for the Mensheviks and Social Revolutionaries in March-June was simply an expression of the first hesitating steps after the awakening. In this voting there was not even a shadow of disappointment with the Bolsheviks or accumulated lack of faith in them, which may result from the mistakes of the party, checked up by the experience of the masses. On the contrary. Every day of revolutionary experience in 1917 pushed the masses away from the conciliators and to the side of the Bolsheviks. From this followed the stormy, inexorable growth of the ranks of the party, and particularly of its influence.

The situation in Germany has at its root a different character, in this respect as well as in others. The German Communist Party did not come upon the scene yesterday, nor the day before. In 1923 it had behind it, openly or in a semi-concealed form, the majority of the working class. In 1924, on the ebbing wave, it received 3,600,000 votes, a greater percentage of the working class than at present. This means that those workers who remained with the Social Democracy, as well as those who voted this time for the National Socialists, did so not out of simple ignorance, not because they awakened only yesterday, not because they have as yet had no chance to know what the Communist Party is, but because they have *no faith*, on the basis of their own experience in the recent years.

Let us not forget that in February 1928, the Ninth Plenum of the Executive Committee of the Comintern gave the signal for an intensified, extraordinary, irreconcilable struggle against 'social fascism'. The German Social Democracy was in power almost all this time, revealing to the masses at every step its criminal and shameful role. And all this was supplemented by an enormous economic crisis. It would be difficult to invent circumstances more favourable for the weakening of the Social Democracy. Nevertheless, it retained its basis positions. How is this striking fact to be explained? Only by the fact that the leadership of the Communist Party, by its whole policy, assisted the Social Democracy, supporting it from the left.

This does not at all mean that by voting for the Social Democracy, five to six million working men and women expressed their full and unlimited confidence in it. The Social Democratic workers should not be considered blind. They are not at all so naive about their own leaders, but they do not see a different way out for themselves in the given situation. Of course, we are not speaking of the labour aristocracy and bureaucracy, but of the rank and file workers. The policy of the Communist Party does not inspire them with confidence, not because the Communist Party is not a revolutionary party but because they do not believe in its ability to gain a revolution victory, and do not wish to risk their heads in vain. Voting reluctantly for the Social Democracy, these workers do not express confidence in it, but for that they express their lack of confidence in the Communist Party. This is where the great difference lies between the present position of the German Communists and the position of the Russian Bolsheviks in 1917.

But by this alone, the difficulties are not exhausted: inside the Communist Party itself, and particularly in the circle of its supporters and the workers voting for it, is a great reserve of vague lack of faith in the leadership of the party. From this grows what is called the 'disparity' between the general influence of the party and its numerical strength, and particularly with its role in the trade unions—in Germany such a disparity undoubtedly exists. The official explanation of the disparity is that the party has not been able to 'strengthen' its influence organisationally. Here the mass is looked upon as purely passive material, which enters or does not enter the party, depending exclusively upon whether the secretary can grab every worker by the throat. The bureaucrat does not understand that workers have their own mind, their experience, their will and their active or passive policy toward the party. The worker votes for the party—for its banner, for the October revolutions, for his own future revolution. But by refusing to join the Communist Party or to follow it in the trade union struggle, he says that he has no faith in its daily policy.

The 'disparity' is consequently, in the final analysis, an expression of the lack of confidence of the masses in the present leadership of the Communist International. And this lack of confidence, created and strengthened by mistakes, defeats, fictions, and direct deception of the masses from 1923 to 1930, is one of the greatest hindrances on the road to the victory of the proletarian revolution.

Without an internal confidence in itself, the party will not conquer the class. Not to conquer the proletariat means not to break the petty bourgeois masses away from fascism. One is inextricably bound up with the other.

6: Back to the 'Second' Period or once more towards the 'Third'?

If we were to use the official terminology of centrism, we would formulate the problem in the following form: the leadership of the Comintern foisted the tactic of the 'third period' upon the national sections, that is, the tactic of an immediate revolutionary upsurge, at a time (1928) when the features of the 'second period' were most clearly visible, that is, the stabilisation of the bourgeoisie and the ebb and decline of the revolution. The turn from this, which came in 1930, meant a rejection of the tactic of the 'third period' in favour of the tactic of the 'second period'. In the meantime, this turn made its way through the bureaucratic apparatus at a moment when the most important symptoms began, at any rate in Germany, to signal plainly the real approach of a 'third period'. Does the need for a new tactical turn flow from all this—in the direction of the recently abandoned tactic of the 'third period'?

We use these designations so as to make the posing of this problem more accessible to those circles whose minds are clogged up by the methodology and terminology of the centrist bureaucracy. But we have no intention whatever to adopt this terminology, which conceals a combination of Stalinist bureaucratism and Bukharinist metaphysics. We reject the apocalyptic presentation of the 'third' period as the final one: how many periods there will be before the victory of the proletariat is a question of the relation of forces and the changes in the situation; all this can be tested only through action. We reject the very essence of this strategic schematicism with its numbered periods; there is no abstract tactic established in advance for the 'second' and 'third' periods.

It is understood that we cannot achieve victory and the seizure of power without an armed uprising. But how shall we reach this uprising? By what methods? And at what tempo shall we mobilise the masses? This depends not only upon the objective situation in general, but in the first place, upon the state in which the arrival of the social crisis in the country finds the proletariat, upon the relation between the party and the class, the proletariat and the petty bourgeoisie, etc. The state of the proletariat at the threshold of the 'third period' depends in its turn upon the tactic the party applied in the period preceding it.

The normal, natural change of tactics, with the present turn of the situation in Germany, should have been the *acceleration of tempo, the sharpening of slogans and methods of struggle*. This tactical turn would have been normal and natural only if the tempo and slogans of struggle of yesterday had corresponded to the conditions of the preceding period. But this never occurred. The sharp discordance of the ultra-left policy and the stabilised situation is precisely the reason for the tactical turn. What has resulted is that at the moment when the new turn of the objective situation, along with the unfavourable general regrouping of the political forces, brought Communism a big gain in votes, the party turns out to be strategically and tactically more disorientated, entangled, and off the track than ever before.

To make clearer the contradiction fallen into by the German Communist Party, like most of the other sections of the Comintern, only far deeper than the rest of them, let us take the simplest comparison. In order to jump over a barrier, a preliminary running start is necessary. The higher the barrier, the more important it is to start the run on time, not too late and not too early, in order to approach the obstruction with the necessary reserve of strength. Beginning with February 1928, and especially since July 1929, however, the German Communist Party did nothing but take the running start. It is no wonder that the party began to lose its wind and drag its feet. The Comintern finally gave the command: 'Single quick time!' But no sooner had the winded party started to change to a more normal step than before it began to appear not an imaginary but an actual barrier, which might require a revolutionary jump.

Will there be enough distance for taking the run? Shall the turn be rejected and changed to a counter-turn? These are the tactical and strategic questions which appear before the German party in all their acuteness.

In order that the leading cadres of the party should be able to find a correct reply to these questions they must have the chance to judge the closest section of the road in connection with the strategy of the past years and its consequences, as revealed in this election. If, in opposition to this, the bureaucracy should succeed, by cries of victory, to drown the voice of political self-criticism, this would inevitably lead the proletariat to a catastrophe more terrible than that of 1923.

7: The possible variations of the further development

A revolutionary situation, confronting the proletariat with the immediate problem of seizing power, is made up of objective and subjective elements, each bound with the other, and to a large extent conditioning each other. But this mutual dependence is relative. The law of uneven development applies fully also to the factors of a revolutionary situation. An insufficient development of one of them may produce a condition in which the revolutionary situation either does not come to an explosion and spends itself, or, coming to an explosion, ends in defeat for the revolutionary working class. What is the situation in Germany in this respect?

1. A deep national crisis (economy, international situation) is unquestionable at hand. There appears to be no way out along the normal road of the bourgeois parliamentary regime.

2. The political crisis of the ruling class and its system of government is absolutely indubitable. This is not a parliamentary crisis, but a crisis of class rule.

3. The revolutionary class, however, is still deeply split by internal contradictions. The strengthening of the revolutionary party at the expense of the reformists is as yet at its inception, and has been proceeding thus far at a tempo which is far from corresponding with the depth of the crisis.

4. The petty bourgeoisie, at the very beginning of the crisis, has already assumed a position antagonistic to the *present system* of capitalist rule, but at the same time mortally hostile to the proletarian revolution.

In other words: there are at hand the basic objective conditions for a proletarian revolution; there is one of its political conditions (the state of the ruling class); the other political condition (the state of the proletariat) has first begun to change in the direction of revolution, and because of the heritage of the past, cannot change rapidly; finally, the third political condition (the state of the petty bourgeoisie) is not directed towards the proletarian revolution but towards a bourgeois counter-revolution. The change of this last condition into a favourable one cannot be accomplished without radical changes in the proletariat itself, that is, without the political liquidation of the Social Democracy.

We have, thus, a deeply contradictory situation. Some of its factors put the proletarian revolution on the order of the day; others, however, exclude the possibility of its victory in the next period, that is, without a previous deep change in the political relation of forces.

Theoretically, several variations of the further development of the present situation in Germany can be considered, depending upon objective factors, the policy of the class enemies included, as well as the conduct of the Communist Party itself. Let us note schematically four possible variations of development.

1. The Communist Party, frightened by its own strategy of the 'third period', moves ahead gropingly, with extreme caution, avoiding risky steps, and—without giving battle—misses a revolutionary situation. This would mean a repetition of the policy of Brandler in 1921-23, only changed in form. Reflecting the pressure of the social democracy, the Brandlerists and semi-Brandlerists, outside the party as well as inside of it, will drive

in this direction.

2. Under the influence of the election success, the party, on the contrary, makes a new sharp turn to the left, in the direction of a direct struggle for power, and being a party of the active minority, suffers a catastrophic defeat. Driving in this direction are: fascism, the clamorous, senseless agitation of the apparatus which does not weigh anything, which does not enlighten, but stupefies; the despair and impatience of a part of the working class, particularly the unemployed youth.

3. It is further possible that the leadership, rejecting nothing, will attempt empirically to find a middle course between the dangers of the first two variations, and in this connection, will commit a series of new mistakes and, in general, will so slowly eliminate the lack of confidence of the proletarian and semi-proletarian masses, that by that time the objective conditions will have changed in a direction unfavourable for a revolution, giving way to a new period of stabilisation. It is chiefly in this eclectic direction, combining *chvostism* in general with adventurism in particular, that the Moscow Stalinist top is pushing the German Party, fearing to take a clear position and preparing an alibi for itself beforehand, that is, the possibility to throw responsibility over to the 'executors'—at the right or at the left, depending upon the results. This policy, with which we are familiar enough, sacrifices the international-historical interests of the proletariat to the interests of the 'prestige' of the bureaucratic top. Intimations of such a course are already given in **Pravda** of 16 September.

4. Finally, the most propitious, or more correctly, the only propitious variation: the Germany party, through the efforts of its best and most conscious elements, takes a careful survey of the whole present contradictory situation. By a correct, audacious and flexible policy, the party, on the basis of the present situation, still succeeds to unite the majority of the proletariat and to secure a change of front of the semi- proletarian and most oppressed petty bourgeois masses. The proletarian vanguard, as the leader of the nation of the toiling and oppressed, comes to victory. To help the party change its policy towards this course is the task of the Bolshevik-Leninists (Left Opposition).

It would be fruitless to guess which of these variations has more chances to happen in the next period. Such questions are not decided by guesses but by struggle.

One of its necessary elements in an irreconcilable ideological struggle against the centrist leadership of the Comintern. From Moscow, the signal has already been given for a policy of bureaucratic prestige which covers up the mistakes of yesterday and prepares tomorrow's by the false cries about the new triumph of the line. Monstrously exaggerating the victory of the party, monstrously underestimating the difficulties, interpreting even the success of fascism as a positive factor for the proletarian revolution, *Pravda* nevertheless explains briefly: 'The successes of the party should not make us dizzy.' The treacherous policy of the Stalinist leadership is true to itself even here. The analysis of the situation is given in the spirit of uncritical ultra-leftism. In this way the party is consciously pushed on the road of adventurism. At the same time, Stalin prepares his alibi in advance with the aid of the ritualistic phrase about 'dizziness'. It is precisely this policy, short-sighted, unscrupulous, that may ruin the Germany revolution.

8: Where is the Way Out?

We have given above, without any glossing over or embellishment, an analysis of the difficulties and dangers which are related fully to the political and subjective sphere, which grew primarily out of the mistakes and crimes of the epigone leadership,[5] and which now definitely threaten to demolish a new revolutionary situation developing before our very eyes. The officials will either close their eyes to our analysis or else they will replenish their stock of slander. But it is not a matter of hopeless officials; it concerns the fate of the Germany proletariat. In the party, as well as in the apparatus, there are not a few people who observe and think, and who will be compelled tomorrow by sharp circumstances to think with doubled intensity. It is to them we direct our analysis and our conclusions.

Every critical situation has great sources of indefiniteness. Moods, views and forces, hostile and friendly, are formed in the very process of the crisis. They cannot be foreseen mathematically. They must be measured in the process of the struggle, through struggle, and on the basis of these living measurements, necessary corrections must be made in the policy.

Can the strength of the conservative resistance of the Social Democratic workers be calculated beforehand? It cannot. In the light of the events of the past year, this strength seems to be gigantic. But the truth is that what helped most of all to weld together Social Democracy was the wrong policy of the Communist Party, which found its highest generalisation in the absurd theory of social fascism. To measure the real resistance of the Social Democratic ranks, a different measuring instrument is required, that is, a correct Communist tactic. With this condition—and it is not a small condition—the degree of internal unity of the Social Democracy can be revealed in a comparatively brief period.

In a different form, what has been said above also applies to fascism: it emanated, aside from the other conditions present, in the tremblings of the Zinoviev-Stalin strategy. What is its force for offensive? What is its stability? Has it reached its culminating point as the optimists *ex officio* assure us, or is it only on the first step of the ladder? This cannot be foretold mechanically. It can be determined only through action. Precisely in regard to fascism, which is a razor in the hands of the class enemy, the wrong policy of the Comintern may produce fatal results in a brief period. On the other hand, a correct policy—not in such a short period, it is true—can undermine the positions of fascism.

A revolutionary party, at the time of a crisis in the regime, is much stronger in the extra-parliamentary mass struggles than within the framework of parliamentarism. Again, on only one condition: if it can correctly estimate the situation and connect in practice the living needs of the masses with the task of seizing power. Everything is now reduced to this. It would therefore be the greatest mistake to see in the present situation in Germany only difficulties and dangers. No. The situation also reveals tremendous possibilities, providing it is clearly and thoroughly understoood and correctly utilised.

What is needed for this?

1. A forced turn to the 'right', at a time when the circumstances turn 'leftward', demands a particularly attentive, scrupulous and capable viewing of the further changes of all the factors in the situation.

The abstract contrasting of the methods of the second and third periods must be immediately rejected. The situation must be taken as it is, with all its contradictions and the live dynamics of its development. We must keep vigilantly abreast of the real changes in the situation and influence it in the direction of its real development, and not to fit into the patterns of Molotov and Kuusinen.

To be oriented in the situation—that is the most important and most difficult part of the task. By bureaucratic methods, it cannot be solved at all. Statistics, important though they are by themselves, are insufficient for this purpose. It is necessary to sound the very deepest mass of the proletariat and the toilers in general. Not only must live and attractive slogans be advanced but we must trace the hold they get on the masses. This can be achieved only by an active party which puts out tens of thousands of feelers everywhere, which gathers their testimony, considers all the questions and actively works out its collective viewpoint.

2. The question of the party regime is inextricably bound up with this. People appointed by Moscow, independent of the confidence of lack of confidence of the party, will not be able to lead the masses in an assault upon capitalist society. The more artificial the present regime, the deeper will be its crisis in the days and hours of decision. Of all the 'turns', the most important and urgent one applies to the party regime. It is a question of life and death.

3. The change in the regime is the precondition for a change in the course, and together with it, its consequences. One is inconceivable without the other. The party must break away from the atmosphere of deceit, reservations, silence over real calamities, the praising of spurious values—in a word, from the disastrous atmosphere of Stalinism, which is not created by ideological and political influence but by the crude, material dependence of the apparatus and the methods of commanding based upon it.

One of the necessary conditions for the liberation of the party from bureaucratic bondage is a general examination of the 'general line' of the German leadership, beginning with 1923, and even with the March days of 1921. The Left Opposition, in a number of documents and theoretical works, has given its evaluation of all the stages of the unfortunate official policy of the Comintern. This criticism must become the property of the party. To avoid it or to be silent about it will not be possible. The party will not rise to the height of its great tasks if it does not freely evaluate its present in the light of its past.

If the Communist Party, in spite of the exceptionally favourable circumstances, has proved powerless seriously to shake the structure of the Social Democracy with the aid of the formula of 'social fascism', then real fascism now threatens this structure, no longer with wordy formulae of so-called radicalism, but with the chemical formulae of explosives. No matter how true it is that the Social Democracy by its whole policy prepared the blossoming of fascism, it is not less true that fascism comes as a deadly threat primarily to that same Social Demo-cracy, all of whose magnificence is inextricably bound with parliamentary democratic-pacifist forms and methods of government.

There can be no doubt that at the crucial moment, the leaders of the Social Democracy and a thin layer of labour aristocrats will prefer the triumph of fascism to the revolutionary dictatorship of the proletariat. It is precisely the approach of such a choice that creates exceptional difficulties for the Social Democratic leaders among their own workers. The policy of a united front of the workers against fascism flows from this situation. It opens up tremendous possibilities to the Communist Party. A condition for success, however, is the rejection of the theory and practice of 'social fascism', the harm of which becomes a positive menace under the present circumstances.

The social crisis will inevitably produce deep cleavages within the Social Democracy. The radicalisation of the masses will affect the Social Democratic workers long before they cease to be Social Democrats. We will inevitably have to make agreements with the various Social Democratic organisations and factions against fascism, putting definite conditions to the leaders, in this connection, before the eyes of the masses. Only frightened opportunists, yesterday's allies of Purcell and Cook, of Chiang Kai-Shek and Wang Chin Wei, can bind themselves beforehand by formal obligations against such agreements. We must return from the empty official's phrase about the united front to the policy of the united front as it was formulated by

Lenin and always applied by the Bolsheviks in 1917.

4. The problem of unemployment is one of the most important elements of the political crisis. The struggle against capitalist rationalisation and for the seven-hour working day remains entirely on the order of the day. But only the slogan of an extensive, planned collaboration with the Soviet Union can raise this struggle to the height of the revolutionary tasks. In the programmatic declaration for the election, the central committee of the German party states that *after achieving power* the Communists will establish economic collaboration with the Soviet Union. There is no doubt of this. But a historical perspective cannot be set up against the political tasks of the day. The workers, and the unemployed in the first place, must be mobilised right now under the slogan of extensive economic collaboration with the Soviet republic. The State Planning Commission of the Union of Soviet Socialist Republics should work out a plan of economic collaboration with the participation of the German Communists and trade unionists, which, using the present unemployment as its point of departure, is developed into an all-sided collaboration embracing all the basic branches of the economy.

The problem does not lie in promising to reconstruct the economy after the seizure of power; it lies in seizing power. The problem is not to promise the collaboration of Soviet Germany with the USSR, but to win the working masses for this collaboration today, connecting it closely with the crisis and unemployment, and developing it further on in a gigantic plan for the socialist reconstruction of both countries.

5. The political crisis in Germany brings into question the Versailles regime in Europe. The Central Committee of the Germany Communist Party declares that, having taken power, the Germany proletariat will liquidate the Versailles documents. Is that all? The abolition of the Versailles Treaty as the highest achievement of the proletarian revolution! What is to be put in its place? There is not a word about this. Such a negative way of putting the question brings the party close to the National Socialists (fascists). The *Soviet United States of Europe*—that is the only correct slogan which points the way out of the dismemberment of Europe, which threatens not only Germany but the

whole continent with complete economic and cultural decline.

The slogan of the proletarian unification of Europe is at the same time a very important weapon in the struggle against the abomination of fascist chauvinism, the baiting of France, and so forth. The most incorrect, the most dangerous policy is that of passive adaptation to the enemy by painting oneself to look like him. The slogans of national madness must be opposed by the slogans of international liberation. For this, the party must be purged of national socialism, the principal element of which is the theory of socialism in one country...

We have examined the question of the tactical turn in the Communist International exclusively in the light of the German situation because, in the first place, the German crisis now puts the German Communist Party once more in the centre of attention of the world proletarian vanguard, and because in the light of this crisis all the problems are brought out in sharpest relief. It would not be difficult, however, to show that what has been said here also holds good, to one degree or another, for other countries.

In France, all the forms of class struggle after the war bear an immeasurably less sharp and less decisive character than they do in Germany. But the general tendencies of development are the same, not to speak of the direct dependence of the fate of France upon the fate of Germany. At any rate, the turns of the Communist International have a universal character. The French Communist Party, which was declared by Molotov back in 1928 to be the first candidate for power, has conducted an absolutely suicidal policy in the last two years. It especially overlooked the economic crisis. The tactical turn was proclaimed in France at the very moment when the crisis began to take the place of the industrial revival. In this way, the same contradictions, difficulties and tasks about which we speak in reference to Germany, are on the order of the day in France as well.

The turn in the Communist International, combined with the turn in the situation, puts new and exceptionally important tasks before the Left Communist Opposition. Its forces are not big. But every current grows together with the growth of its tasks. To understand them clearly is to possess one of the most important guarantees of victory.

Part Two | **1931**

Chris Harman

1931: Background

THE ELECTIONS of 1930 had failed to produce a majority for any government. Brüning was only able to continue in office by ruling most of the time by presidential decree without reference to parliament. He was not, however, able to offer any solution to the crisis. In foreign affairs an attempt to form a customs union with Austria so as to alleviate some of the economic consequences of the Treaty of Versailles had to be abandoned under pressure from France. In July two major banks failed. Unemployment continued to grow. Unable to solve the crisis in any way, the government reduced wages, cut social security payments, curtailed the rights of parliament and the press. Among the mass of the population it was the 'most hated government'. Both Nazis and Communists spoke of the 'Hunger Chancellor'. Yet Brüning was able to survive for two years. On the one hand he had the support of the major sections of big business and the army; on the other the mass fascist opposition on the right and the mass Communist opposition of the left effectively balanced, to form an unstable equilibrium.

The Nazi support continued to grow. By the end of 1930 there were more than 100,000 in the para-military SA struggling for control of the streets. The few leading industrialists (notably the coal baron Kirdof and the head of the steel trust, Thyssen) who had previously supported Hitler, were now joined by many more, although some influential figures still held back.

The Social Democrats were aware of the danger threatening them, but hardly made an adequate response. They had their own para-military organisation, the Reichsbanner. They also, through their control of the Prussian government, controlled the police force responsible for two-thirds of Germany. This had 80,000 members, armed with machine guns, armoured cars, tear gas, grenades etc. The intention in the event of a coup by the fascists or Reichswehr was to use these to arm the Reichsbanner. Thus the defensive strategy was to rely upon Prussia as a Social Democratic fortress. At the same time the Social Democrats 'tolerated' the Brüning government. However unpopular it was, they argued it was the 'lesser evil' to the fascists.

But even had this strategy provided means of physical defence, it did not begin to offer any solution to the social and economic problems that were driving the millions to support the fascists. All the Social Democratic leaders could do was to wait and hope that the crisis would pass of its own accord. This might seem a good policy to the estimated three or four thousand members of the huge bureaucracies under Social Democratic control (in the SPD or the free trade unions, working for Social Democrat-controlled provincial governments, etc), but could offer no way out to the unemployed and poverty stricken masses.

A section of the SPD became increasingly impatient with this sit-and-wait attitude. After fighting for a leftward turn in party policy throughout 1931, these split under the leadership of the Reichstag deputy Seydewitz to form a left socialist party, the SAP. This failed, however, to gather mass support around it.

The inability of the Social Democrats to deal with the crisis presented huge opportunities to the KPD. Yet it too hardly seemed capable of taking advantage of them. The line imposed from Moscow made it incapable of dealing with the situation. For it still defined the 'social fascists', not the Nazis, as the major danger. Thus when whole sections of the Social Democratic workers were beginning to have serious doubts about the policies of their leaders, Thälmann called the demand they were making for a defensive united front of Social Democrats and Communists as 'the latest manoeuvre of social fascism'.[1] The worst 'social fascists' he argued, were those who had gone so far as to break from the SPD to the left.

But the worst example of this fatal Moscow-inspired sectarianism was the so-called 'red referendum'. For some time the Nazis and extreme nationalists (united in the 'Harzburg Front') had been trying to remove the Social Democratic regime in

Prussia as an obstacle in their path to power. It was clear that the Nazis would be the chief beneficiaries of any new elections. Therefore they attempted to use a clause in the constitution that would enable a referendum to be held on whether the Prussian government should remain in office. The immediate response of the entire KPD leadership was to oppose the referendum. They argued vigorously in this direction until only three weeks before the day of voting. Then suddenly, under Comintern directions, the whole line changed. The referendum was supported and the whole energies of the party used in that direction. A united front with the 'social fascists' was ruled out by Stalin, but not apparently with the real fascists. Nevertheless, the referendum was defeated by the refusal of the mass of workers to support it.

During this period, the KPD often attempted to win support from the Nazis by outbidding them using their own phraseology. It spoke of 'people's revolution against the Treaty of Versailles' and fraternised with extreme nationalist officers, such as Schleringer and Count Sternback-Fermoy.

There was, however, little consistency to its policy. Thus it did briefly suggest a United Front to Social Democrat leaders in July 1931, but upon receiving a refusal reverted immediately to its previous line of denouncing any united front 'from above'. It favoured only a 'united front from below' in which Social Democrat supporters marched behind Communist banners.

To justify this whole policy various arguments were used. The most notorious was that a Nazi victory would be short-lived, and by destroying Social Democratic influence prepare the way for a Communist one. As Remmele put it in the Reichstag:

> Once they [the Nazis] are in power, then the united front of the proletariat will be established and it will make a clean sweep of everything... We are not afraid of the fascist gentlemen. They will shoot their bolt quicker than any other government.[2]

The Communist Party remained the force that could have altered the situation. Its members were prepared to fight in the present, not in some hypothetical future. But it continued to fight ineffectually, without clear direction. Its leaders, under direction from Stalin's Comintern apparatus, continued to insist that Hitler was not the main danger. Thälmann warned of 'an opportunist exaggeration of Hitler Fascism'.[3] In the earlier period the natural hatred felt by militant Communist leaders towards the murderers of Luxemburg, Liebknecht and others no doubt played an important part in making such a line acceptable. Now however, it was known that to accept any alternative line would lead to removal from office by Moscow. Of the three major KPD leaders, one, Heinz Neumann, did call for a modification of policy; he was immediately ordered by the Comintern apparatus to leave Germany for Spain.

Trotsky wrote **Germany: Key to the International Situation** in November 1931. Because of shortage of space we have had to cut out some of the early paragraphs. These deal with the overall international situation, touching for instance upon the overthrow of the monarchy in Spain, the tempo of development in France and Britain, problems facing Russia. This selection is taken from the second English edition published by the Revolutionary Communist Party in 1944.

What Next? was written in the first part of 1932. In it Trotsky is chiefly concerned with examining the various forces that exist within the working-class movement and arguing that they can still fight successfully if the right strategy is accepted. This leads him into a long, and still very relevant, discussion on the question of the united front. The translation here is that by Joseph Vanzler, published in the United States in 1932.

Leon Trotsky

Germany: Key to the International Situation

ON THE hardly peaceful political background of the world there stands out in bold relief, the situation in Germany. The economic and political contradictions have here reached unheard-of acuteness. The solution is approaching. The moment has come in which the pre-revolutionary situation must be transformed into the revolutionary or—the counter-revolutionary. On the direction in which the solution of the German crisis will develop will depend the fate not only of Germany herself but the fate of Europe, the fate of the entire world for very many years to come.

Socialist construction in the USSR, the course of the Spanish revolution, the development of the pre-revolutionary situation in England, the future of French imperialism, the fate of the revolutionary movement in China and India—all this directly and immediately rests upon the question of who will be victorious in Germany in the course of the next few months: Communism or fascism?

After last year's September elections to the Reichstag, the leadership of the German Communist Party declared that fascism has reached its culmination point, that in the future it would rapidly disintegrate and clear the road for the proletarian revolution. The Communist Left Opposition (Bolshevik-Leninists) at that time ridiculed this giddy optimism. Fascism is a product of two conditions: a sharp social crisis on the one hand, the revolutionary weakness of the German proletariat on the other. The weakness of the proletariat in itself is composed of two elements: of the particular historical role of the Social Democracy, this still powerful capitalist agency in the ranks of the proletariat, and of the inability of the centrist leadership of the

Communist Party to unite the workers under the banner of the revolution.

For us, the Communist Party represents the subjective factor, for the Social Democracy is an objective obstacle that must be swept away. Fascism would in reality fall to pieces if the Communist Party was able to unite the working class and by that alone transform it into a powerful revolutionary magnet for all the oppressed masses of the people. But the policy of the Communist Party since the September elections has only made its inconsistencies more profound: the empty talk of 'social fascism', the flirtations with chauvinism, the imitation of genuine fascism for the purpose of petty market competition with the latter, the criminal adventurism of the 'Red Referendum'— all this prevents the Communist Party from becoming the leader of the proletariat and of the people. During the last few months it has brought under its banner only those new elements whom the great crisis pushed into its ranks almost by force.

Despite the disastrous political conditions existing for it, the Social Democracy has, thanks to the aid rendered it by the Communist Party, been able to retain the greatest bulk of its following and has up to the present escaped with considerable, to be sure, but nevertheless only secondary losses. In so far as the fascists are concerned, they have, despite the petty bragging of Thälmann, Remmele and others and in complete conformity with the prognosis of the Bolshevik-Leninists, made new important advances since September of last year. The Comintern leadership has been unable either to foresee or forestall anything. It can only register the defeats. Its resolutions and other documents are, unfortunately, only snapshots of the rear end of the historical process.

The decisive hour is very close. But the Comintern does not want, or rather fears, to give itself an account of the actual character of the present world situation. The presidium of the Comintern resorts to hollow agitational scraps of paper. The leading party of the Comintern, the CPSU, has taken no position whatsoever. As if the 'leaders of the world proletariat' had their mouths full of water! They prefer to keep silent. They are disposed to mark time. They mean to wait. They have substituted for the policy of Lenin ... the policy of the ostrich. One of these decisive moments in history is closely approaching in which the Comintern, after a series of big but still 'partial' mistakes which have undermined and shaken up the forces accumulated in the first five years of its existence, is risking the capital, fatal error which may wipe out the Comintern as a revolutionary factor for an entire historic epoch from the political map.

Let blind men and cowards refuse to notice this. Let slanderers and hired journalists accuse us of being in league with the counter-revolution! Has counter-revolution become not that which entrenches world imperialism, but that which interferes with the digestion of Communist bureaucrats? The Bolshevik-Leninists cannot be intimidated by calumnies nor restrained from fulfilling their revolutionary duties. Nothing must be concealed, nothing minimised. We must tell the advanced workers in loud and audible tones: after the 'third period' of adventurism and boasting, the 'fourth period'—of panic and capitulation—has set in.

The silence of the present leaders of the CPSU signifies when translated into articulate language: 'Leave us in peace!' The internal difficulties of the USSR are extraordinarily great. The uncontrollable economic and social contradictions are growing more and more acute. The demoralisation of the apparatus, as the inevitable product of the plebiscitary regime, has taken on veritably menacing proportions. The political relationships and above all the relationships inside the party, the relationships between the demoralised apparatus and the dispersed mass are as tense as a taut wire. All the wisdom of the bureaucrats consists of waiting, of *postponing*. The situation in Germany quite obviously threatens with convulsions. But the Stalinist apparatus fears convulsions precisely more than anything. 'Leave us in peace! Let us first disentangle ourselves from our extremely sharp inner contradictions and then ... we shall see.' This is the sentiment in the higher spheres of the Stalinist faction. It is precisely this sentiment that is concealed behind the silence of the 'leaders' at a moment in which it is their most elementary revolutionary duty to speak out clearly and distinctly.

It is not at all astonishing that the disloyal silence of the Moscow leadership has become a panic signal for the Berlin leaders. Now, when it is necessary to prepare to lead the masses in decisive struggle, the leadership of the German Communist Party reveals confusion, evades all this with phrases. These people are not accustomed to independent responsibility. Above everything else, they are now dreaming of a way of proving that 'Marxism-Leninism' demands a retreat in the face of struggle.

In this connection they have not as yet created a complete theory, but it is already in the air. It is carried from mouth to mouth and glimpses of it are to be found in articles and speeches. The sense of the theory is the following: fascism is growing unrestrained; its victory is inevitable in any case: instead of 'blindly' throwing ourselves into the struggle and permitting ourselves to be crushed, it is better to retreat cautiously and to allow fascism to seize power and to compromise itself. Then— oh! then—we will show what we can do.

Adventurism and light-mindedness give way, according to laws of political psychology, to prostration and capitulation. The victory of the fascists, held impossible the year before, is looked upon as certain today. Some Kuusinen or other, inspired behind the scenes by some sort of Radek, is already preparing for Stalin the genial strategic formula: retreat in time, lead the revolutionary troops out of the firing line, and set up a trap for fascism in the form of the state power.

Were this theory to entrench itself in the German Communist Party, determine its course within the next few months, it would signify on the part of the Comintern a betrayal of no lesser historical proportions than the betrayal of the Social Democracy on 4 August 1914,[1] and at that, with much more frightful consequences.

It is the duty of the Left Opposition to sound the alarm: the leadership of the Comintern is leading the German proletariat toward an enormous catastrophe, the core of which is the panicky capitulation before fascism!

The coming into power of the German 'National Socialists' would mean above all the extermination of the flower of the German proletariat, the disruption of its organisations, the extirpation of its belief in itself and in its future. Considering the far greater maturity and acuteness of the social contradictions in Germany, the hellish work of Italian fascism would probably appear as a pale and almost humane experiment in comparison with the work of the German National Socialists.

Retreat, you say, you who were yesterday the prophets of the 'third period'? Leaders and institutions can retreat. Individual persons can hide. But the working class will have no place to retreat to in the face of fascism and nowhere to hide. If one were really to assume the monstrous and improbable to happen: that the party will actually evade the struggle and thus deliver the proletariat to the mercy of its mortal enemy, this would signify only one thing: the gruesome battles would unfold not *before* the seizure of power by the fascists but *after* it, that is, under conditions ten times more favourable for fascism than those of today. The struggle of the proletariat, taken unawares, disoriented, disappointed and betrayed by its own leadership, against the fascist regime would be transformed into a series of frightful bloody and futile convulsions. Ten proletarian insurrections, ten defeats one on top of the other, could not debilitate and enfeeble the German working class as much as a retreat before fascism would weaken it at the given moment, when the decision is still impending as to the question of who is to become master in the German household.

Fascism is not yet in power. The road to power has not yet opened up for it. The leaders of fascism still fear to risk it. They realise that there is too much at stake, that their necks are in danger. Under these circumstances the mood of capitulation among the Communist chiefs can only unexpectedly simplify and facilitate their tasks for them.

If at present even influential layers of the bourgeoisie fear the fascist experiment, precisely because they want no convulsions, no long and severe civil war, the capitulation policy of official Communism — clearing the road to power for the fascists—would completely push the middle classes and the as yet vacillating sections of the petty bourgeoisie, as well as considerable sections of the proletariat itself, to the side of fascism.

It goes without saying that some day triumphant fascism will fall as a victim to the objective contradictions and to its own inadequacy. But for the immediate, perceptible future, for the next ten to twenty years, a victory of fascism in Germany would mean a suspension in the development of revolutionary progress, collapse of the Comintern and the triumph of world imperialism in its more heinous and bloodthirsty forms.

A victory for fascism in Germany would signify inevitable war against the USSR.

In fact it would really be sheer political stupidity to believe that once they came into power, the German National Socialists would begin with a war against France or even against Poland. The inevitable civil war against the German proletariat will bind the fascist foreign policy hand and foot in the first period of their rule. Hitler will need Pilsudski just as much as Pilsudski will need Hitler. Both alike will become tools of France. Just as the French bourgeoisie fears the seizure of power by the German fascists at the present moment as a leap into the unknown, so will French reaction, in its 'nationalist' as well as in its radical-socialist form, stake all on fascism the day of Hitler's victory.

None of the 'normal' bourgeois parliamentary governments can at the present time risk a war against the USSR: for it would bring with it the threat of imperceptible internal complications. But once Hitler comes into power and proceeds to crush the vanguard of the German workers, pulverising and demoralising the whole proletariat for many years to come, the fascist government alone will be the only government capable of waging war against the USSR. Naturally, it will act under such circumstances in a common front with Poland and Rumania, with the other border states as well as with Japan in the Far East. In this enterprise, the Hitler government would only be the executive organ of world capitalism as a whole. Clemenceau, Millerand, Lloyd George, Wilson could not directly carry on war against the Soviet government; but they were able, in the course of three years, to support the armies of Kolchak, Wrangel and Denikin.[2] In case he is victorious, Hitler will become the super-Wrangel of the world bourgeoisie.

It is needless to say, yes and impossible to predict today, how such a gigantic duel would end. But it is absolutely clear: if the war of the world bourgeoisie against the Soviets will break out after the seizure of power by the fascists in Germany, then that will mean frightful isolation and a life-and-death struggle under the hardest and most dangerous conditions for the USSR. The crushing of the German proletariat at the hands of the fascists would already comprise at least half of the collapse of the Soviet republic.

But before this question can enter the arena of European battles, it must be decided in Germany. That is why we say that the key to the world situation lies in Germany. In whose hands? For the present, still in the hands of the Communist Party. It has not lost it yet. But it may. The leadership is steering it in that direction.

Everyone who preaches the 'strategical retreat', that is, capitulation, everyone who tolerates such preaching, is a traitor. The propagators of the retreat before the fascists must be considered as unconscious agents of the enemy in the ranks of the proletariat.

The most elementary revolutionary duty of the German Communist Party demands that it say: fascism can come into power only after a merciless, annihilating civil war to the bitter end. First of all, all the worker-Communists must know this. The social democratic workers must know it, the non-party workers, the whole proletariat. The whole international proletariat must know it. The Red Army must know it in time.

But is not the struggle really hopeless? In 1923, Brandler enormously over-estimated the power of fascism and by this covered up his capitulation. The international labour movement is still suffering the consequences of that strategy today. The historical capitulation of the German Communist Party and the Comintern in 1923 served as the basis for the subsequent rise of fascism. At present, German fascism represents an immeasurably greater political force than eight years ago. We have continually warned against underestimating the fascist danger and it is not for us to deny its existence at present. It is precisely for this reason that we can and must say to the revolutionary German workers today: your leaders are falling from one extreme to another.

In the meantime, the main strength of the fascists is their strength in numbers. Yes, they have received many votes. But in the social struggle votes are not decisive. The main army of fascism still consists of the petty bourgeoisie and the new middle class: the small artisans and shopkeepers of the cities, the petty officials, the employees, the technical personnel, the *intelligentsia*, the impoverished peasantry. On the scales of election statistics, one thousand fascist votes weigh as much as a thousand Communist votes. But on the scales of the revolutionary struggle, a thousand workers in one big factory represent a force a hundred times greater than a thousand petty officials, clerks, their wives and their mothers-in-law. The great bulk of the fascists consists of human rubbish.

The Social Revolutionaries were the party of the greatest numbers in the Russian revolution. In the first period, everyone who was not either a conscious bourgeois or a conscious worker voted for them. Even in the Constituent Assembly, that is, after the October revolution, the Social Revolutionaries formed the majority. They therefore considered themselves a great national party. They turned out to be a great national zero.

We do not want to draw an equation sign between the Russian Social Revolutionaries and the German National Socialists. But there are, undoubtedly, features of similarity between them that are very important in clarifying the question under discussion. The Social Revolutionaries were a party of hazy popular hopes. The National Socialists are a party of national despair. The petty bourgeoisie has always shown the greatest ability of passing over from hope to despair, dragging a part of the proletariat along with it. The great bulk of the National Socialists is, as was the case with the Social Revolutionaries—human rubbish.

Seized with panic, the strategists of distress are forgetting the chief thing: the great social and fighting advantages of the proletariat. Its forces are not spent. It is capable not only of struggle, but of victory. The stories about the sentiment of despondency in the factories reflect, in most cases, the despondent sentiments of the observers, that is, of the party functionaries who have lost their heads. But we must also take into consideration the fact that the complicated situation and the confusion among the leading circles cannot but alarm the workers. The workers understand that the great battle requires firm leadership. The workers are not frightened by the strength of fascism nor by the necessity of a ruthless struggle, they are disturbed only by the uncertainty and wavering of the leadership, by the vacillations in the moment of greatest responsibility. Not a trace of depression and downheartedness will remain in the factories just as soon as the party raises its voice firmly, clearly and confidently.

No doubt the fascists have serious fighting cadres, experienced shock brigades. We must not take a light attitude in this respect: the 'officers' play a big part even in the civil war army. Still, it is not the officers, but the soldiers who decide. The soldiers of the proletarian army, however, are immeasurably higher types, more trustworthy, more steadfast than the soldiers of the Hitler army.

After the conquest of power fascism will easily find its soldiers. With the aid of the state apparatus, an army of the pet sons of the bourgeoisie, of intellectuals, counter-clerks, demoralised workers, lumpen proletarians, etc, is easily created. Example: Italian fascism. And yet, here too, it should be mentioned: the Italian fascist militia has not as yet gone through a serious historical test of its fighting value. But German fascism is not yet in power. It has still to conquer power in the struggle with the proletariat. Will the Communist Party enter this struggle with worse troops than those of fascism? And can we assume, even if only for a moment, that the German workers who have the powerful means of production and transportation in their hands, who have been knitted together by the conditions of their work into an army of iron, of coal, of railroads, of electrical works, will not prove to be immeasurably superior in the decisive struggle to Hitler's human rubbish?

An important element in the strength of a party or a class is also the conception which the party or the class has of the relationship of forces in the country. In every war the enemy strives to create an exaggerated idea of his strength. That was one of the secrets of Napoleon's strategy. In lying, Hitler can hold his own against Napoleon. But his boasting becomes a military factor only at the moment the Communists begin to believe him. More than anything else, a realistic inventory of strength is immediately necessary. What do the National Socialists dispose of in the factories, on the railroads; in the army, how many organised and armed officers have they? A clear social analysis of the composition of both camps, persistent and watchful accounting of forces—these are the unfailing sources of revolutionary optimism.

At present the strength of the National Socialists lies not so much in their own army as in the schism within the army of their mortal enemy. But it is precisely the reality of the fascist danger, its growth and proximity, the consciousness of the necessity of averting it at any cost, that must inevitably push the workers toward unity in the name of self-defence. The concentration of the proletarian forces will take place all the more quickly and successfully, the more reliable the axis of this process will prove to be, that is, the Communist Party. The key to the situation still rests in its hands. Woe to it if it loses it!

In the course of the last few years, the functionaries of the Comintern have shouted on all and every occasion, often unwarrantedly, of the immediate war danger threatening the USSR. Today this danger is taking on real character and concrete outlines. This must be made an axiom for every revolutionary worker: the attempt of the fascists to seize power in Germany can bring in its trail nothing less than the mobilisation of the Red Army. For the proletarian state, it will be a matter of revolutionary self-defence in a most direct and immediate sense. Germany is not only Germany. It is the heart of Europe. Hitler is not only Hitler. He is the candidate for the post of a super-Wrangel. But the Red Army is not only the Red Army. It is the arm of the proletarian world revolution.

Leon Trotsky

What Next?
Vital Questions for the German Proletariat

CAPITALISM IN RUSSIA proved to be the weakest link in the chain of imperialism, because of its extreme backwardness. In the present crisis, German capitalism reveals itself as the weakest link for the diametrically opposite reason: precisely because it is the most advanced capitalist system in the conditions of the European *impasse*. As the productive forces of Germany become more and more highly geared, the more dynamic power they gather, the more they are strangled within the state system of Europe—a system that is akin to the 'system' of cages within an impoverished provincial zoo. At every turn in the conjuncture of events German capitalism is thrown up against those problems which it had attempted to solve by means of war. Acting through the Hohenzollern government, the German bourgeoisie girded itself to 'organise Europe'. Acting through the regime of Brüning-Curtius,[1] it attempted... to form a customs union with Austria. It is to such a pathetic level that its problems, potentialities, and perspectives have been reduced! But even the customs union was not to be attained. Like the witch's house in fairy tales, the entire European system stands on a pair of hen's legs. The great and salutary hegemony of France is in danger of toppling over, should a few million Austrians unite with Germany.

For Europe in general and primarily for Germany, no advance is possible along the capitalist road. The temporary resolution of the present crisis to be achieved by the automatic interplay of the forces of capitalism itself—on the bones of the workers—would signify only the resurrection of all the contradictions at the next stage, only in still more acute and concentrated form.

The specific weight of Europe in world economy can only diminish. Already the forehead of Europe is plastered beyond removal with American labels: the Dawes Plan, the Young Plan, Hoover's moratorium. Europe is placed thoroughly on American rations.

The decay of capitalism results in social and cultural decomposition. The road is barred for further normal differentiation within nations, for the further growth of the proletariat at the expense of the diminution of intermediate classes. Further prolongation of the crisis can bring in its trail only the pauperisation of the petty bourgeoisie and the transformation of ever larger groups of workers into the lumpen proletariat. In its most acute form, it is this threat that grips advanced capitalist Germany by the throat.

The rottenest portion of putrefying capitalist Europe is the Social Democratic bureaucracy. It entered upon its historical journey under the banner of Marx and Engels. It set for its goal the overthrow of the rule of the bourgeoisie. The powerful upsurge of capitalism caught it up and dragged it in its wake. In the name of reform, the Social Democracy betrayed the revolution, at first by its actions and later by its words. Kautsky, it is true, for a long time still defended the phraseology of revolution, making it serve as a handmaiden to the requirements of reformism. Bernstein, on the contrary, demanded the renunciation of revolution: for capitalism was entering the period of peaceful development without crises, and without wars. Exemplary prophecy! Apparently, between Kautsky and Bernstein there was an irreconcilable divergence. Actually, however, they symmetrically complemented one another as the right and left boots on the feet of reformism.

The war came. The Social Democracy supported the war in the name of future prosperity. Instead of prosperity, decay set in. Now the task no longer consisted in deducing from the inadequacy of capitalism the necessity for revolution, nor in reconciling the workers to capitalism by means of reforms. The new task of the Social Democracy now consisted in making society safe for the bourgeoisie at the cost of sacrificing reforms.

But even this was not the last stage of degeneracy. The present crisis that is convulsing capitalism obliged the Social

Democracy to sacrifice the fruits achieved after protracted economic and political struggles and thus to reduce the German workers to the level of existence of their fathers, grandfathers, and great-grandfathers. There is no historical spectacle more tragic and at the same time more repulsive than the fetid disintegration of reformism amid the wreckage of all its conquests and hopes. The theatre is rabid in its straining for modernism. Let it stage more often Hauptmann's **The Weavers**: this most modern of modern dramas. And let the director of the theatre also remember to reserve the front rows for the leaders of the Social Democracy.

However, these leaders are in no mood for drama: they have reached the utmost limits of their adaptability. There is a level beneath which the working class of Germany cannot drop willingly nor for any length of time. Moreover, the bourgeois regime, fighting for its existence, is in no mood to recognise this level. The emergency decrees of Brüning are only the beginning, only feelers to get the lay of the land. Brüning's regime rests upon the cowardly and perfidious support of the Social Democratic bureaucracy which in its turn depends upon the sullen, halfhearted support of a section of the proletariat. The system based on bureaucratic decrees in unstable, unreliable, temporary. Capitalism requires another, more decisive policy. The support of the Social Democrats, keeping a suspicious watch on their own workers, is not only insufficient for its purposes, but has already become irksome. The period of halfway measures has passed. In order to try to find a way out, the bourgeoisie must absolutely rid itself of the pressure exerted by the workers' organisations; these must be eliminated, destroyed, utterly crushed.

At this juncture, the historic role of fascism begins. It raises to their feet those classes that are immediately above the proletariat and that are ever in dread of being forced down into its ranks; it organises and militarises them at the expense of finance capital, under the cover of the official government, and it directs them to the extirpation of proletarian organisations, from the most revolutionary to the most conservative.

Fascism is not merely a system of reprisals, of brutal force, and of police terror. Fascism is a particular governmental system based on the uprooting of all elements of proletarian democracy within bourgeois society. The task of fascism lies not only in destroying the Communist vanguard but in holding the entire class in a state of forced disunity. To this end the physical annihilation of the most revolutionary section of the workers does not suffice. It is also necessary to smash all independent and voluntary organisations, to demolish all the defensive bulwarks of the proletariat, and to uproot whatever has been achieved during three-quarters of a century by the Social Democracy and the trade unions. For, in the last analysis, the Communist Party also bases itself on these achievements.

The Social Democracy has prepared all the conditions necessary for the triumph of fascism. But by this fact it has also prepared the stage for its own political liquidation. It is absolutely correct to place on the Social Democrats the responsibility for the emergency legislation of Brüning as well as for the impending danger of fascist savagery. It is absolute balderdash to identify Social Democracy with fascism.

By its policies during the revolution of 1848, the liberal bourgeoisie prepared the stage for the triumph of counter-revolution, which in turn emasculated liberalism. Marx and Engels lashed the German liberal bourgeoisie no less sharply than Lassalle did, and their criticism was more profound than his. But when the Lassalleans lumped the liberal bourgeoisie together with the feudal counter-revolution into 'one reactionary mass', Marx and Engels were justly outraged by this false ultra-radicalism. The erroneous position of the Lassalleans turned them on several occasions into involuntary aides of the monarchy, despite the general progressive nature of their work, which was infinitely more important and consequential than the achievements of liberalism.

The theory of 'social fascism' reproduces the basic error of the Lassalleans on a new historical background. After dumping National Socialists and Social Democrats into one fascist pile, the Stalinist bureaucracy flies headlong into such activities as backing the Hitler referendum, which in its own fashion is in no way superior to Lassalle's alliances with Bismarck.

In the present phase, German Communism in its struggle against the Social Democracy must lean on two separate facts: (a) the political responsibility of the Social Democracy for the strength of fascism; (b) the absolute irreconcilability between fascism and those workers' organisations on which the Social Democracy itself depends.

The contradictions within German capitalism have at present reached such a state of tension that an explosion is inevitable. The adaptability of the Social Democracy has reached that limit beyond which lies self-annihilation. The mistakes of the Stalinist bureaucracy have reached that limit beyond which lies catastrophe. Such is the threefold formula that characterises the situation in Germany. Everything is now poised on the razor edge of a knife.

When of necessity one must follow conditions in Germany through newspapers that arrive almost a week late; when one must allow another week before manuscripts may bridge the gap between Constantinople and Berlin,[1] after which additional weeks must pass before the pamphlet reaches its public, involuntarily the question arises: 'Won't it be altogether too late?' And each time one answers oneself: No! The armies that are drawn up for battle are so colossal that one need not fear a lightning-quick settlement of the issue. The strength of the German proletariat has not been drained. Its powers have not as yet been brought into play. The logic of facts will make itself heard more imperiously with every passing day. And this justifies the author's attempt to add what he has to say even if it is delayed a few weeks, i.e., an entire historical period.

The Stalinist bureaucracy came to the conclusion that it would be able to complete its labours more peacefully were the author of these pages confined in Prinkipo. It obtained from the government of Hermann Müller, the Social Democrat, a refusal of a visa for the ... 'Menshevik': in this instance the united front was established without any wavering or delay. Today, in official Soviet publications, the Stalinists are broadcasting the news that I am 'defending' Brüning's government in accordance with an agreement made with the Social Democracy, which in return is pulling strings to allow me the right of entry into Germany. Instead of becoming indignant over such viciousness, I permit myself to laugh at its stupidity. But I must cut short my laughter, for time is pressing.

There cannot be the slightest doubt that the course of events will demonstrate the correctness of our position. But in what manner will history demonstrate its proof: through the catastrophe of the Stalinist faction, or through the victory of Marxist policies?

Therein lies at present the crux of the entire question. This question is the question of the fate of the German nation, and not of its fate alone.

The problems that are analysed in this pamphlet did not originate yesterday. For nine years now the leadership of the Comintern has busied itself with the revaluation of values and with disorganising the vanguard of the international proletariat by means of tactical convulsions which in their totality fall under the label of 'the general line'. The Russian Left Opposition (Bolshevik-Leninists) was formed not only because of Russian problems but also because of international ones. Among these, the problems of the revolutionary development in Germany occupied by no means the last place. Sharp divergences on this subject date back to 1923. During the succeeding years the author of these pages spoke more than once on these controversial questions. A considerable portion of my critical works has been published in German. The present pamphlet is in its turn a contribution to the theoretical and political work of the Left Opposition. Much that is mentioned hereafter only in passing was in its time submitted to detailed analysis. Therefore I must refer my readers for particulars to my books, **The Third International After Lenin, The Permanent Revolution**, etc. Now, when these differences confront everyone in the form of a great historical problem, it is possible to estimate their origins much better and more profoundly. For the serious revolutionary, for the true Marxist, such a study is absolutely essential. Eclectics live by means of episodic thoughts and improvisations that originate under the impact of events. Marxist cadres capable of leading the proletarian revolution are trained only by the continual and successive working out of problems and disputes.

1. The Social Democracy

The 'Iron Front' is essentially a bloc of numerically powerful Social Democratic trade unions with impotent groups of bourgeois 'republicans' which have lost entirely the support of the people and all confidence in themselves. When it comes to fighting, cadavers are worthless, but they come in handy to keep the living from fighting. Their bourgeois allies serve the Social Democratic leaders as a bridle around the necks of the workers' organisations. We must fight! We must fight! ... but that is only empty talk. With God's help, everything will be settled ultimately without any bloodshed. Is it possible that the fascists will really decide to stop talking and get down to business? They, the Social Democrats, never so much as ventured on such a course, and they, the Social Democrats, are no worse than other people.

In case of actual danger, the Social Democracy banks not on the 'Iron Front' but on the Prussian police. It is reckoning without its host! The fact that the police was originally recruited in large numbers from among Social Democratic workers is absolutely meaningless. Consciousness is determined by environment even in this instance. The worker who becomes a policeman in the service of the capitalist state is a bourgeois cop, not a worker. Of late years these policemen have had to do much more fighting with revolutionary workers than with Nazi students. Such training does not fail to leave its effect. And above all: every policeman knows that though governments may change, the police remain.

In its New Year's issue, the theoretical organ of the Social Democracy, **Das Freie Wort** (what a wretched sheet!), prints an article in which the policy of 'toleration' is expounded in its highest sense. Hitler, it appears, can never come into power against the police and the Reichswehr. Now, according to the Constitution, the Reichswehr is under the command of the president of the Republic. Therefore fascism, it follows, is not dangerous so long as a president faithful to the Constitution remains at the head of the government. Brüning's regime must be supported until the presidential elections, so that a constitutional president may then be elected through an alliance with the parliamentary bourgeoisie; and thus Hitler's road to power will be blocked for another seven years. The above is, as given, the literal content of the article. A mass party, leading millions (towards socialism!) holds that the question as to which class will come to power in present-day Germany, which is shaken to its very foundations, depends not on the fighting strength of the

German proletariat, not on the shock troops of fascism, not even on the personnel of the Reichswehr, but on whether the pure spirit of the Weimar Constitution (along with the required quantity of camphor and naphthalene) shall be installed in the presidential palace. But suppose the spirit of Weimar, in a certain situation, recognises together with Bethmann-Hollweg, that 'necessity knows no law'; what then? Or suppose the perishable substance of the spirit of Weimar falls asunder at the most untoward moment, despite the camphor and naphthalene, what then? And what if ... but there is no end to such questions.

The politicians of reformism, these dextrous wirepullers, artful intriguers and careerists, expert parliamentary and ministerial manoeuvrists, are no sooner thrown out of their habitual sphere by the course of events, no sooner placed face to face with momentous contingencies, than they reveal themselves to be— there is no milder expression for it—utter and complete fools.

To rely upon a president is to rely upon 'the state'! Faced with the impending clash between the proletariat and the fascist petty bourgeoisie—two camps which together comprise the crushing majority of the German nation—these Marxists from the **Vorwärts** yelp for the night watchman to come to their aid. They say to the state 'Help! Intervene!' (*Staat, greif zu!*). Which means 'Brüning, please don't force us to defend ourselves with the might of workers' organisations, for this will only arouse the entire proletariat; and then the movement will rise above the bald pates of our party leadership: beginning as anti-fascist, it will end Communist'.

To this Brüning could reply, unless he preferred silence: 'With the police force I could not handle fascism even if I wanted to; but I wouldn't even if I could. Setting the Reichswehr in motion means only splitting the Reichswehr, if not throwing it altogether against us. But what is most important is that the turning of the bureaucratic apparatus against the fascists would mean untying the hands of the workers, restoring their full freedom of action: the consequence would be precisely those which you, Social Democrats, dread so much, and which I accordingly dread twice as much'.

The effect which the appeals of the Social Democracy produce on the state apparatus, on the judges, the Reichswehr, and the police cannot fail to be just the opposite to the one desired. The most 'loyal' functionary, the most 'neutral', the least bound to the Social Democracy, can reason only thus: 'Millions are behind the Social Democrats; enormous resources are in their hands: the press, the parliament, the municipalities; their own hides are at stake; in the struggle against the fascists, they are assured of the support of the Communists; and even so these mighty gentlemen beg me, a functionary, to save them from the attack of another party comprising millions whose leaders may become my bosses tomorrow; things must be pretty bad for the gentlemen of the Social Democracy, probably quite hopeless ... it is time for me (the functionary), to think about my own hide'. And as a result, the 'loyal', 'neutral' functionary, who vacillated yesterday, will invariably reinsure himself, i.e., tie up with the National Socialists to safeguard his own future. In this manner the reformists who have outlived their own day work for the fascists along bureaucratic lines.

The Social Democracy, the hanger-on of the bourgeoisie, is doomed to wretched ideological parasitism. One moment it catches up ideas of bourgeois economists, and the next, it tries to utilise bits of Marxism. After citing from my pamphlet the reasons against the participation of the Communist Party in Hitler's referendum, Hilferding concludes: 'Truly, there is nothing to add to these lines in order to explain the tactics of the Social Democracy as regards the Brüning government'.

Remmele and Thalheimer step forward: 'Please take note, Hilferding relies on Trotsky'. A fascist yellow sheet steps forward in turn: 'Trotsky is paid for this job by the promise of a visa'. Next a Stalinist journalist comes to the fore and wires the communication of a fascist paper to Moscow. The editorial board of *Izvestia*, which includes the unfortunate Radek, prints the telegram. This chain deserves only to be mentioned and passed by.

Let us return to more serious questions. If Hitler can afford himself the luxury of fighting against Bruening, it is only because the bourgeois regime as a whole leans for its support on the back of that half of the working class which is led by Hilferding & Co. If the Social Democracy had not put through its policy of class betrayal, then Hitler, not to mention the fact that he would have never attained his present power, would have been clutching at Brüning's government as a lifesaving anchor. If the Communists together with the Social Democracy had overthrown Brüning, that would have been a fact of the greatest political significance. The consequences, in any case, would have risen over the heads of the leaders of the Social Democracy. Hilferding attempts to find justification for his betrayal in our criticism, which demands that the Communists take Hilferding's betrayal into account as an accomplished fact.

Although Hilferding has 'nothing to add' to Trotsky's words, he nevertheless does add something: the correlation of forces, he says, is such that even in the event of united action of Social Democratic and Communist workers, there would be no possibility 'by forcing the fight, to overthrow the enemy and to seize power'. In this remark, glossed over in passing without any evidence, lies the very crux of the question. According to Hilferding, in Germany today, where the proletariat composes the majority of the population and the deciding productive force of society, the united front of the Social Democracy and the Communist Party could not place the power in the hands of the proletariat!

When is the precise moment, then, that the power can pass into the hands of the proletariat? Prior to the war was the perspective of the automatic growth of capitalism, of the growth of the proletariat, and of the equal growth of the Social Democracy. This process was cut short by the war, and no power in the world will restore it. The decay of capitalism means that the question of power must be decided on the basis of the now existing productive forces. By prolonging the agony of the capitalist regime, the Social Democracy leads only to the further decline of economic culture, to the disorganisation of the proletariat, to social gangrene. No other perspectives lie ahead; tomorrow will be worse than today; the day after tomorrow worse than tomorrow. But the leaders of the Social Democracy no longer dare to look into the future. Theirs are all the vices of the ruling class doomed to destruction; they are lightminded, their will is paralysed, they are given to blubbering over events and hoping for miracles. Come to think of it, Tarnow's economic researches fulfil now the same function as did once the consoling revelations of a Rasputin...

The Social Democrats together with the Communists would not be able to seize power. There he stands, the snobbish, educated, petty bourgeois, an utter coward, soaked from head to foot with distrust and contempt for the masses. The Social Democracy and the Communist Party together hold about 40 per cent of the votes, despite the fact that the betrayals of the Social Democracy and the mistakes of the Communist Party drive millions into the camp of indifferentism and even National Socialism. Once a fact, the joint action of these two parties alone, by opening before the masses new perspectives, would incommensurably increase the strength of the proletariat. But let us limit ourselves to 40 per cent. Has Brüning perhaps more, or Hitler? But there are only these three groups that can rule Germany: the proletariat, the Centre Party, or the fascists. But a notion is firmly implanted in the heads of the educated petty bourgeois: for the representatives of capital to rule, 20 per cent of the votes suffice, because the bourgeoisie, you see, has the banks, the trusts, the syndicates, the railroads. True, our educated petty bourgeois made ready to 'socialise' all these twelve years ago. But enough is too much! A programme of socialisation—yes; the expropriation of the expropriators—no, that is already Bolshevism.

We have taken the correlation of forces in their parliamentary cross section. But that's a trick mirror. In parliamentary representation the strength of an oppressed class is way below its actual strength and contrariwise: the representation of the bourgeoisie even the day before its downfall will still be a masquerade of its supposed strength. Only revolutionary struggle tears away all the covers from the actual relation of forces. During a direct and immediate struggle for power, the proletariat, unless paralysed by sabotage from within, by Austro-Marxism and by all other forms of betrayal, develops a force incommensurably superior to its parliamentary expression.

Let us recall once again the invaluable lessons of history. Even after the Bolsheviks had seized power, and firmly seized it, they had less than one-third of the votes in the Constituent Assembly; together with the Left Social Revolutionaries, less than 40 per cent. Yet despite a fearful economic collapse, despite the war, despite the betrayal of the European and, first of all, of the German Social Democracy, despite the post-war reaction of weariness, despite the growth of Thermidorean tendencies, the first workers' government stands on its feet fourteen years. And what can be said of Germany? At the moment the Social Democratic worker together with the Communist arises to seize power, the task will be nine-tenths completed.

Nevertheless, says Hilferding, had the Social Democracy voted against Brüning's government and thereby overthrown it, the consequence would have been the coming of the fascists to power. That is the way, perhaps, the matter may appear on a parliamentary plane; but the matter itself does not rest on a parliamentary plane. The Social Democracy could refuse to support Brüning only in the event that it decided to enter upon the road of revolutionary struggle. Either support Brüning, or fight for the dictatorship of the proletariat. No third course is given. The Social Democracy, by voting against Brüning, would change at once the correlation of forces—not on the parliamentary chessboard, whose chess pieces might surprisingly enough be found underneath the table—but on the arena of the revolutionary struggle of the classes.

After such an about-face, the forces of the working class would increase not twofold but tenfold, for the moral factor holds by no means the last place in the class struggle, particularly during great historical upheavals. Under the impact of this moral force, the masses of the people, one stratum after another, would be charged to the point of highest intensity. The proletariat would say to itself, with assurance, that it alone was called to give a different and a higher direction to the life of this great nation. Disintegration and decomposition in Hitler's army would set in before the decisive battles. Battles of course could not be avoided; but with a firm resolution to fight to victory, by attacking boldly, victory might be achieved infinitely more easily than the most extreme revolutionary optimist now imagines.

Only a trifle is lacking for this: the about-face of the Social Democracy, its taking the road of revolution. To hope for a voluntary shift on the part of the leaders after the experiences of 1914-1922 would be the most ludicrous of all illusions. But the majority of Social Democratic workers—that is something else again; they can make the turn, and they will make it; it is only necessary to help them. And this turn will be not only against the bourgeois government, but against the upper layers of their own party.

At this point, our Austro-Marxist, who has 'nothing to add' to our words, will try once more to bring against us citations from our own books: didn't we write point blank that the policies of the Stalinist bureaucracy represent a chain of errors; didn't we stigmatise the participation of the Communist Party in the Hitler referendum? We did write, we did stigmatise. But we wage battle with the Stalinist leadership in the Comintern precisely because it is incapable of breaking up the Social Democracy, of tearing the masses from under its influence, of freeing the locomotive of history from its rusty brake. By its convulsions, its mistakes, its bureaucratic ultimatism, the Stalinist bureaucracy preserves the Social Democracy, permits it again and again to regain its foothold.

The Communist Party is a proletarian, anti-bourgeois party, even if erroneously led. The Social Democracy, though composed of workers, is entirely a bourgeois party, which under 'normal conditions' is led quite expertly from the point of view of bourgeois aims, but which is good for nothing at all under the conditions of a social crisis. The leaders of the Social Democracy are themselves forced to recognise, though unwillingly, the bourgeois character of the party. Referring to the crisis and the unemployment situation, Tarnow mouths moth-eaten phrases about the 'disgrace of capitalist civilisation', quite in the manner of a Protestant minister preaching on the sinfulness of wealth; referring to socialism, Tarnow talks after the manner of this same minister when the latter preaches about rewards beyond the grave; but when it comes to concrete questions he assumes another tone: 'If on 14 September [1930], this spectre [unemployment] had not hovered over the ballot box, this day would have been written differently into the pages of German history'. (Report at the Leipzig Congress). The Social Democracy lost votes and seats because capitalism, on account of the crisis, had revealed its authentic visage.

The crisis did not strengthen the party of 'socialism', on the contrary, it weakened it, just as it depressed the trade turnover, the resources of banks, the self-assurance of Hoover and Ford, the profits of the Prince of Monaco, etc. Today, one is obliged to look, not in bourgeois papers, but in the Social Democratic press for the most optimistic evaluations of the conjuncture. Can more undebatable proofs of the bourgeois character of this party be produced? If the atrophy of capitalism produces the atrophy of the Social Democracy, then the approaching death of capitalism cannot but denote the early death of the Social Democracy. The party that leans upon the workers but serves the bourgeoisie, in the period of the greatest sharpening of the class struggle, cannot but sense the smells wafted from the waiting grave.

2. Democracy and Fascism

The eleventh plenum of the Executive Committee of the Communist International (ECCI)came to the decision that it was imperative to put an end to those erroneous views which originate in 'the liberal interpretation of the contradictions between fascism and bourgeois democracy and the outright fascist forms...'

The gist of this Stalinist philosophy is quite plain: from the Marxist denial of the *absolute* contradiction it deduces the *general* negation of the contradiction, even of the *relative* contradiction. This error is typical of vulgar radicalism. For if there be no contradiction *whatsoever* between democracy and fascism—even in the sphere of the *form* of the rule of the bourgeoisie—then these two regimes obviously enough must be equivalent. Whence the conclusion: Social Democracy equals fascism. For some reason, however, Social Democracy is dubbed *social* fascism. And the meaning of the term 'social' in this connection has been left unexplained to this very moment.*

Nevertheless, the nature of things does not change in

* Metaphysicians (people who do not reason dialectically) assign to one and the same abstraction two, three, or more designations, often directly contradictory. 'Democracy' ingeneral and 'fascism' in general, so we are told, are in no way distinguished from one another. But in addition there must also exist in the world, on his account, 'the dictatorship of workers and peasants' (for China, India, Spain). Proletarian dictatorship? No! Capitalist dictatorship, perhaps? No! What then? A **democratic** one! Somewhere in the universe, it appears, there exists a pure classless democracy. Yet according to the eleventh plenum of the ECCI, democracy

accordance with the decisions of the ECCI plenums. A contradiction does exist between democracy and fascism. It is not at all 'absolute', or, putting it in the language of Marxism, it doesn't at all denote the rule of two irreconcilable classes. But it does denote different systems of the domination of one and the same class. These two systems: the one parliamentary-democratic, the other fascist, derive their support from different combinations of the oppressed and exploited classes; and they unavoidably come to a sharp clash with each other.

The Social Democracy, which is today the chief representative of the parliamentary-bourgeois regime, derives its support from the workers. Fascism is supported by the petty bourgeoisie. The Social Democracy without the mass organisations of the workers can have no influence. Fascism cannot entrench itself in power without annihilating the workers' organisation. Parliament is the main arena of the Social Democracy. The system of fascism is based upon the destruction of parliamentarism. For the monopolistic bourgeoisie, the parliamentary and fascist regimes represent only different vehicles of dominion; it has recourse to one or the other, depending upon the historical conditions. But for both the Social Democracy and fascism, the choice of one or the other vehicle has an independent significance; more than that, for them it is a question of political life or death.

At the moment that the 'normal' police and military resources of the bourgeois dictatorship, together with their parliamentary screens, no longer suffice to hold society in a state of equilibrium—the turn of the fascist regime arrives. Through the fascist agency, capitalism sets in motion the masses of the crazed petty bourgeoisie, and bands of the declassed and demoralised lumpen proletariat; all the countless human beings whom finance capital itself has brought to desperation and frenzy. From fascism the bourgeoisie demands a thorough job; once it has

---

differs in no wise from fascism. That being so, wherein does 'the democratic dictatorship' differ from ... the fascist dictatorship?
Only a person utterly naive will expect to get a serious and honest answer to this fundamental question from the Stalinists. They will let loose a few more choice epithets—and that's all. And meanwhile the fate of the revolutions in the Orient is tied up with this question.

resorted to methods of civil war, it insists on having peace for a period of years. And the fascist agency, by utilising the petty bourgeoisie as a battering ram, by overwhelming all obstacles in its path, does a thorough job.

After fascism is victorious, finance capital gathers into its hands, as in a vice of steel, directly and immediately, all the organs and institutions of sovereignty, the executive, administrative, and educational powers of the state: the entire state apparatus together with the army, the municipalities, the universities, the schools, the press, the trade unions, and the cooperatives. When a state turns fascist, it doesn't only mean that the forms and methods of government are changed in accordance with the patterns set by Mussolini—the changes in this sphere ultimately play a minor role—but it means, primarily and above all, that the workers' organisations are annihilated; that the proletariat is reduced to an amorphous state; and that a system of administration is created which penetrates deeply into the masses and which serves to frustrate the independent crystallisation of the proletariat. Therein precisely is the gist of fascism.

The above is not at all contradicted by the fact that during a given period, between the democratic and the fascist systems, a transitional regime is established, which combines the features of both: such, in general, is the law that governs the displacement of one social system by another, even though they are irreconcilably inimical to each other. There are periods during which the bourgeoisie leans upon both the Social Democracy and fascism, that is, during which it simultaneously manipulates its electoral and terroristic agencies. Such, in a certain sense, was the government of Kerensky during the last months of its existence, when it leaned partly on the Soviets and at the same time conspired with Kornilov. Such is the government of Brüning as it dances on a tightrope between two irreconcilable camps, balancing itself with the emergency decrees instead of a pole. But such a condition of the state and of the administration is temporary in character. It signalises the transition period, during which the Social Democracy is on the verge of exhausting its mission, while in that same period, neither Communism nor fascism is ready as yet to seize power.

The Italian Communists, who have had to study the problems of fascism for a long time, have protested time and again against the widespread abuse of these concepts. Formerly, at the Sixth Congress of the Comintern, Ercoli was still formulating views on the question of fascism which are now credited as 'Trotskyist'. Ercoli at that time defined fascism as being the most thorough and uncompromising system of reaction, and he explained:

> This administration supports itself not by the cruelty of its terroristic acts, not by murdering large numbers of workers and peasants, not by applying on a large scale varied methods of brutal torture, not by the severity of its law courts; but it depends upon the systematic annihilation of each and every form of the independent organisation of the masses.

In this Ercoli is absolutely correct: the gist of fascism and its task consist in a complete suppression of all workers' organisations and in the prevention of their revival. In a developed capitalist society this goal cannot be achieved by police methods alone. There is only one method for it, and that is directly opposing the pressure of the proletariat—the moment it weakens—by the pressure of the desperate masses of the petty bourgeoisie. It is this particular system of capitalist reaction that has entered history under the name of fascism.

'All questions as to the relation between fascism and Social Democracy,' wrote Ercoli,

> belong to the same sphere [the irreconcilability of fascism with the existence of the workers' organisation]. It is in this relation that fascism clearly differentiates itself from all other reactionary regimes established hitherto in the contemporary capitalist world. It rejects all compromise with the Social Democracy; it persecutes it relentlessly; it deprives it of all legal means of existence; it forces it to emigrate.

So reads an article published in the leading organs of the Comintern! Subsequently, Manuilsky buzzed in Molotov's ear the great idea of the 'third period', France, Germany and Poland were assigned to 'the front rank of the revolutionary offensive'.

The seizure of power was proclaimed to be the immediate task. And since, in the face of the uprising of the proletariat, all parties, except the Communist, are counter-revolutionary, it was no longer necessary to distinguish between fascism and Social Democracy. The theory of social fascism was ordained. And the functionaries of the Comintern lost no time in realigning themselves. Ercoli made haste to prove that, precious as truth was to him, Molotov was more precious, and ... he wrote a report in defence of the theory of social fascism. 'The Italian Social Democracy,' he announced in February 1930, 'turns fascist with the greatest readiness'. Alas, the functionaries of official Communism turn flunkeys even more readily.

As to be expected, our criticism of the theory and application of the 'third period' was decreed counter-revolutionary. Nevertheless, the cruel experiences that cost the proletarian vanguard dearly forced an about-face in this sphere also. The 'third period' was pensioned off, and so was Molotov himself—from the Comintern. But the theory of social fascism remained behind as the lone ripe fruit of the third period. No changes could take place here: only Molotov was tied up with the third period; but Stalin himself was enmeshed in social fascism.

Die Rote Fahne begins its researches into social fascism with Stalin's words:

> Fascism is the military organisation of the bourgeoisie which leans upon the Social Democracy for active support. The Social Democracy, objectively speaking, is the moderate wing of fascism.

Objectively speaking, it is a habit with Stalin, when he attempts to generalise, to contradict the first phrase by the second and to conclude in the second what doesn't at all follow from the first. There is no debating that the bourgeoisie leans on the Social Democracy, and that fascism is a military organisation of the bourgeoisie; and this has been remarked upon a long time ago. The only conclusion which follows from this is that the Social Democracy as well as fascism are the tools of the big bourgeoisie. How the Social Democracy becomes thereby also a 'wing' of fascism is incomprehensible. Equally profound is another observation by the same author: fascism and Social

Democracy are not enemies, they are twins. Now twins may be the bitterest enemies; while on the other hand allies need not be born necessarily on one and the same day and from identical parents. Stalin's constructions lack even formal logic, to say nothing of dialectics. Their strength lies in the fact that none dares challenge them.

'As regards "the class content" there are no distinctions between democracy and fascism,' lectures Werner Hirsch, echoing Stalin.[2] The transition from democracy to fascism may take the character of 'an organic process,' that is, it may occur 'gradually' and 'bloodlessly'. Such reasoning might dumbfound anyone, but the epigones have inured us to becoming dumbfounded.

There are no 'class distinctions' between democracy and fascism. Obviously this must mean that democracy as well as fascism is bourgeois in character. We guessed as much even prior to January 1932. The ruling class, however, does not inhabit a vacuum. It stands in definite relations to other classes. In a developed capitalist society, during a 'democratic' regime, the bourgeoisie leans for support primarily upon the working classes, which are held in check by the reformists. In its most finished form, this system finds its expression in Britain during the administration of the Labour government as well as during that of the Conservatives. In a fascist regime, at least during its first phase, capital leans on the petty bourgeoisie, which destroys the organisations of the proletariat. Italy, for instance! Is there a difference in the 'class content' of these two regimes? If the question is posed only as regards the *ruling class*, then there is no difference. If one takes into account the position and the interrelations of *all* classes, from the angle of the proletariat, then the difference appears to be quite enormous.

In the course of many decades, the workers have built up within the bourgeois democracy, by utilising it, by fighting against it, their own strongholds and bases of *proletarian democracy*: the trade unions, the political parties, the educational and sport clubs, the co-operatives, etc. The proletariat cannot attain power within the formal limits of bourgeois democracy, but can do so only by taking the road of revolution: this has been proved both by theory and experience. And these bulwarks of workers' democracy within the bourgeois state are absolutely essential for taking the revolutionary road. The work of the Second International consisted in creating just such bulwarks during the epoch when it was still fulfilling its progressive historic labour.

Fascism has for its basic and only task the razing to their foundations of all institutions of proletarian democracy. Has this any 'class meaning' for the proletariat, or hasn't it? The lofty theoreticians had better ponder over this. After pronouncing the regime to be bourgeois—which no one questions—Hirsch, together with his master, overlooks a mere trifle: the position of the proletariat in this regime. In place of the historical process they substitute a bald sociological abstraction. But the class war takes place on the soil of history, and not in the stratosphere of sociology. The point of departure in the struggle against fascism is not the abstraction of the democratic state, but the living organisations of the proletariat, in which is concentrated all its past experience and which prepare it for the future.

The statement that the transition from democracy to fascism may take on an 'organic' and a 'gradual' character can mean one thing and one thing only and that is: without any fuss, without a fight, the proletariat may be deprived not only of all its material conquests—not only of its given standard of living, of its social legislation, of its civil and political rights—but also even of the basic weapon whereby these were achieved, that is, its organisations. The 'bloodless' transition to fascism implies, under this terminology, the most frightful capitulation of the proletariat that can be conceived.

Werner Hirsch's theoretical discussions are not accidental; while they serve to develop still further the theoretical soothsayings of Stalin, they also serve to generalise the entire present agitation of the Communist Party. The party's chief resources are in fact being strained only to prove that there is no difference between Brüning's regime and Hitler's regime. Thälmann and Remmele see in this the quintessence of Bolshevik policy.

Nor is the matter restricted to Germany only. The notion that nothing new will be added by the victory of fascists is being zealously propagated now in all sections of the Comintern. In the January issue of the French periodical **Cahiers du Bolchevisme** we read:

The Trotskyists behave in practice like Breitscheid; they accept the famous Social Democratic theory of the 'lesser evil', according to which *Brüning is not as bad as Hitler,* according to which it is not so unpleasant to starve under Brüning as under Hitler, and infinitely more preferable to be shot down by Gröner than by Frick.

This is not the most stupid passage, although—to give it due credit—stupid enough. Unfortunately, however, it expresses the gist of the political philosophy of the leaders of the Comintern.

The fact of the matter is that the Stalinists compare the two regimes from the point of view of vulgar democracy. And indeed, were one to consider Brüning's regime from the criterion of 'formal' democracy, one would arrive at a conclusion which is beyond argument: nothing is left of the proud Weimar Constitution save the bones and the skin. But this does not settle the question so far as we are concerned. The question must be approached from the angle of *proletarian* democracy. This criterion is also the only reliable one on which to consider the question as to when and where the 'normal' police methods of reaction under decaying capitalism are replaced by the fascist regime.

Whether Brüning is 'better' than Hitler (better looking perhaps?) is a question which, we confess, doesn't interest us at all. But one need only glance at the list of workers' organisations to assert: fascism has not conquered yet in Germany. In the way of its victory there still remain gigantic obstacles and forces.

The present Brüning regime is the regime of bureaucratic dictatorship, or more definitely, the dictatorship of the bourgeoisie enforced by means of the army and the police. The fascist petty bourgeoisie and the proletarian organisations seem to counterbalance one another. Were the workers united by soviets, were factory committees fighting for the control of production, then one could speak of *dual power*. Because of the split within the proletariat, because of the tactical helplessness of its vanguard, *dual power* does not exist as yet. But the very fact that mighty organisations of workers do exist, which *under certain conditions* are capable of repelling fascism with crushing force, that is what keeps Hitler from seizing power and imparts a certain 'independence' to the bureaucratic apparatus.

Brüning's dictatorship is a caricature of Bonapartism. His dictatorship is unstable, unreliable, short-lived. It signalises not the initiation of a new social equilibrium but the early crash of the old one. Supported directly only by a small minority of the bourgeoisie, tolerated by the Social Democracy against the will of the workers, threatened by fascism, Brüning can bring down the thunder of paper decrees but not real thunderbolts. Brüning is fit for dissolving parliament with its own assent; he'll do to promulgate a few decrees against the workers; to proclaim a Christmas truce and to make a few deals under its cover; to break up a hundred meetings, close down a dozen papers, exchange letters with Hitler worthy of a village druggist—that is all. But for greater things his arms were too short.

Brüning is compelled to tolerate the existence of workers' organisations because he hasn't decided to this very day to hand the power over to Hitler, and inasmuch as he himself has no independent means of liquidating them. Brüning is compelled to tolerate the fascists and to patronise them inasmuch as he mortally fears the victory of the workers. Brüning's regime is a transitional, short-lived regime, preceding the catastrophe. The present administration holds on only because the chief camps have not as yet pitted their strength. The real battle has not begun. It is still to come. The dictatorship of bureaucratic impotence fills in the lull before the battle, before the forces are openly matched.

The wiseacres who boast that they do not recognise any difference 'between Brüning and Hitler', are saying in reality: it makes no difference whether our organisations exist, or whether they are already destroyed. Beneath this pseudo-radical phraseology there hides the most sordid passivity: we can't escape defeat anyway! Read over carefully the quotation from the French Stalinist periodical. They reduce the question to whether it is better to starve under Hitler or Brüning. To them it is a question of under whom to starve. To us, on the contrary, it is not a question of under which conditions it is better to die. We raise the question of how to fight and win. And we conclude thus: the major offensive must be begun before the bureaucratic dictatorship is replaced by the fascist regime, that is, before the workers' organisations are crushed. The general offensive should be prepared for by deploying, extending, and sharpening the sectional clashes. But for this one must have a correct perspective and, first of all, one should not proclaim victorious the enemy who is still a long way from victory.

Herein is the crux of the problem; herein is the strategical key to the background; herein is the operating base from which the battle must be waged. Every thinking worker, the more so every Communist, must give himself an accounting and plumb to the bottom the empty and rotten talk of the Stalinist bureaucracy about Brüning and Hitler being one and the same thing. You are muddling! we say in answer. You muddle disgracefully because you are afraid of the difficulties that lie ahead, because you are terrified by the great problems that lie ahead; you throw in the sponge before the fighting is begun, you proclaim that we have already suffered defeat. You are lying! The working class is split; it is weakened by the reformists and disorientated by the vacillations of its own vanguard, but it is not annihilated yet, its forces are not yet exhausted. No. The proletariat of Germany is powerful. The most optimistic estimates will be infinitely surpassed once its revolutionary energy clears the way for it to the arena of action.

Brüning's regime is the preparatory regime. Preparatory to what? Either to the victory of fascism, or to the victory of the proletariat. This regime is preparatory because both camps are only preparing for the decisive battle. If you identify Brüning with Hitler, you identify the conditions before the battle with the conditions after defeat; it means that you admit defeat beforehand; it means that you appeal for surrender without a battle.

The overwhelming majority of the workers, particularly the Communists, does not want this. The Stalinist bureaucracy, of course, does not want it either. But one must take into account not one's good intentions, with which Hitler will pave the road to his Hell, but the objective meaning of one's policies, of their direction and their tendencies. We must disclose in its entirety the passive, timidly hesitant, capitulating and declamatory character of the politics of Stalin-Manuilsky-Thälmann-Remmele. We must teach the revolutionary workers to understand that the key to the situation is in the hands of the Communist Party; but the

Stalinist bureaucracy attempts to use this key to lock the gates to revolutionary action.

3. Bureaucratic Ultimatism

When the newspapers of the new Socialist Workers Party (the SAP) criticise 'the party egoism' of the Social Democracy and of the Communist Party; when Seydewitz assures us that so far as he is concerned, 'the interests of the class come before the interests of the party', they only fall into political sentimentalism, or, what is worse, behind this sentimental phraseology they screen the interests of their own party. This method is no good. Whenever reaction demands that the interests of 'the nation' be placed before class interests, we Marxists take pains to explain that under the guise of 'the whole', the reaction puts through the interests of the exploiting class. The interests of the nation cannot be formulated otherwise than from the point of view of the ruling class, or of the class pretending to sovereignty. The interests of the class cannot be formulated otherwise than in the shape of a programme; the programme cannot be defended otherwise than by creating the party.

The class, taken by itself, is only material for exploitation. The proletariat assumes an independent role only at that moment when from a social class *in itself* it becomes a political class *for itself*. This cannot take place otherwise than through the medium of a party. The party is that historical organ by means of which the class becomes class conscious. To say that 'the class stands higher than the party' is to assert that the class in the raw stands higher than the class which is on the road to class consciousness. Not only is this incorrect; it is reactionary. There isn't the slightest need for this smug and shallow theory in order to establish the necessity for a united front.

The progress of a class toward class consciousness, that is, the building of a revolutionary party which leads the proletariat, is a complex and a contradictory process. The class itself is not homogeneous. Its different sections arrive at class consciousness by different paths and at different times. The bourgeoisie participates actively in this process. Within the working class, it creates its own institutions, or utilises those already existing, in order to oppose certain strata of workers to others. Within the proletariat several parties are active at the same time. Therefore, for the greater part of its historical journey, it remains split politically. The problem of the united front—which arises during certain periods most sharply— originates therein.

The historical interests of the proletariat find their expression in the Communist Party—when its policies are correct. The task of the Communist Party consists in winning over the majority of the proletariat; and only thus is the socialist revolution made possible. The Communist Party cannot fulfil its mission except by preserving, completely and unconditionally, its political and organisational independence apart from other parties and organisations within and without the working class.

To transgress this basic principle of Marxist policy is to commit the most heinous of crimes against the interests of the proletariat as a class. The Chinese Revolution of 1925-1927 was wrecked precisely because the Comintern, under the leadership of Stalin and Bukharin, forced the Chinese Communist Party to enter into the party of the Chinese bourgeoisie, the Kuomintang, and to obey its discipline. The experience resulting from the application of Stalinist policies as regards the Kuomintang will enter forever into history as an example of how the revolution was ruinously sabotaged by its leaders. The Stalinist theory of 'two-class workers' and peasants' parties' for the Orient is the generalisation and authorisation of the practice employed with the Kuomintang; the application of this theory in Japan, India, Indonesia and Korea has undermined the authority of the Comintern and has set back their revolutionary development for a number of years. This same policy—perfidious in its essence— was applied, though not quite so cynically, in the United States, in Britain, and in all countries of Europe up to 1928.

The struggle of the Left Opposition for the maintenance of the complete and unconditional independence of the Communist Party and of its policies, under each and every historical condition, and on all stages of the development of the proletariat, strained the relations between the Opposition and the Stalinist faction to the breaking point during the period of Stalin's bloc with Chiang Kai-shek, Wang Chin-wei, Purcell, Radich, LaFollette, etc. It is quite unnecessary to recall that both Thälmann and Remmele as well as Brandler and Thalheimer, during this struggle, were completely on Stalin's side against the Bolshevik-Leninists. It is not we, therefore, who have to go to school and learn from Stalin and Thälmann about the independent policies of the Communist Party!

But the proletariat moves toward revolutionary consciousness not by passing grades in school but by passing through the class struggle, which abhors interruptions. To fight, the proletariat must have unity in its ranks. This holds true for partial economic conflicts, within the walls of a single factory, as well as for such 'national' political battles as the one to repel fascism. Consequently the tactic of the united front is not something accidental and artificial—a cunning manoeuvre—not at all; it originates, entirely and wholly, in the objective conditions governing the development of the proletariat. The words in the **Communist Manifesto** which state that the Communists are not to be opposed to the proletariat, that they have no interests separate and apart from those of the proletariat as a whole, carry with them the meaning that the struggle of the party to win over the majority of the class must in no instance come into opposition with the need of the workers to keep unity within their fighting ranks.

Die Rote Fahne is completely justified in condemning all discussions concerning the contention that 'the class interests must be placed above party interests'. In reality, the correctly understood interests of the class are identical with the correctly formulated problems of the party. So long as the discussion is limited to this historico-philosophical assertion, the position of *Die Rote Fahne* is unassailable. But the political conclusions which it deduces therefrom are nothing short of a mockery of Marxism.

The identity, in principle, of the interests of the proletariat and of the aims of the Communist Party does not mean either that the proletariat as a whole is, even today, conscious of its class interests, or that the party under all conditions formulates them *correctly*. The very need for the party originates in the plain fact that the proletariat is not born with the innate understanding of its historical interests. The task of the party consists in *learning*, from experience derived from the struggle, how to demonstrate to the proletariat its right to leadership. And yet the

Stalinist bureaucracy, on the contrary, holds to the opinion that it can demand outright obedience from the proletariat, simply on the strength of a party passport, stamped with the seal of the Comintern.

Every united front that doesn't first place itself under the leadership of the Communist Party, reiterates *Die Rote Fahne*, is directed against the interests of the proletariat. Whoever doesn't recognise the leadership of the Communist Party is himself a 'counter-revolutionary'. The worker is obliged to trust the Communist organisation in advance, on its word of honour. From the identity, in principle, of the aims of the party and of the class, the functionary deduces his right to lay down the law to the class. The very historical problem which the Communist Party is yet to solve—that of uniting the overwhelming majority of the workers under its banner—is turned by the bureaucrat into an ultimatum, into a pistol which he holds against the temple of the working class. Formalistic, administrative, and bureaucratic thinking supplants the dialectic.

The historical problem that must be solved is decreed as solved already. The confidence yet to be won is announced as won already. That, it goes without saying, is the easiest way out. But very little is achieved that way. In politics one must proceed from facts as they are, and not as one would like them to be, or as they will be eventually. The position of the Stalinist bureaucracy drawn to its conclusion leads, in fact, to the negation of the party. For what is the net result of all its historical labour, if the proletariat is obliged beforehand to accept the leadership of Thälmann and Remmele?

From the worker desirous of joining the ranks of the Communists, the party has a right to demand: you must accept our programme and obey our regulations and the authority of our electoral institutions. But it is absurd and criminal to present the same *a priori* demand, or even a part of it, to the working masses of workers' organisations when the matter of joint action for the sake of definite aims of struggle is broached. Thereby the very foundations of the party are undermined; for the party can fulfil its task only by maintaining correct relations with the class. Instead of issuing such a one-sided ultimatum, which irritates and insults the workers, the party should submit a definite programme for joint action: that is the surest way of achieving leadership in reality.

Ultimatism is an attempt to rape the working class after failing to convince it: workers, unless you accept the leadership of Thälmann-Remmele-Neumann, we will not permit you to establish the united front. The bitterest foe could not devise a more unsound position than the one in which the leaders of the party place themselves. That is the surest way to ruin.

The leadership of the German Communist Party stresses its ultimatism all the more sharply by the casuistic circumlocution in its proclamations: 'We make no demands that you accept our Communist view beforehand.' This rings like an apology for policies for which there is no apology. When the party proclaims its refusal to enter into any kind of negotiations with other organisations but offers to take in under the party leadership those Social Democratic workers who want to break with their organisations without their being obliged to call themselves Communists, then the party is using the language of pure ultimatism.

The reservation as regards 'our Communist views' is absolutely ludicrous; the worker who is at this very moment ready to break with his party and to participate in the struggle under Communist leadership would not be deterred by the fact that he must call himself a Communist. Jugglery with labels and subtleties of diplomacy are foreign to the worker. He takes politics and organisations as they are. He remains with the Social Democracy so long as he does not trust the Communist leadership. We can say with assurance that the majority of Social Democratic workers remain in their party to this day not because they trust the reformist leadership but because they do not as yet trust that of the Communists. But they do want to fight against fascism even now. Were they shown the first step to take in a common struggle, they would insist upon their organisations taking that step. If their organisations balked, they might reach the point of breaking with them.

Instead of aiding the Social Democratic workers to find their way through experience, the CEC (Central Executive Committee) of the Communist Party abets the leaders of the Social Democracy against the workers. The Welses and the Hilferdings are enabled to mask successfully their own unwillingness to fight, their dread of fighting, their inability to fight by citing the aversion of the Communist Party to participation in a common struggle. The stubborn, doltish, and insensate rejection by the Communist Party of the policies of the united front provides the Social Democracy, under the present conditions, with its most important political weapon. This is just the reason why the Social Democracy—with the parasitism inherent in its nature—snaps up our criticism of the ultimatistic policies of Stalin-Thälmann.

The official leaders of the Comintern are now expatiating with an air of profundity upon the need to elevate the theoretical level of the party and to study 'the history of Bolshevism'. Actually 'the level' is falling constantly, the lessons of Bolshevism are forgotten, distorted and trampled underfoot. In the meantime, it is by no means difficult to find in the history of the Russian party the precursor of the present policy of the German CEC: he is none other than the deceased Bogdanov, the founder of ultimatism. As far back as 1905 he deemed it impossible for the Bolsheviks to participate in the Petrograd Soviet, unless the Soviet recognised beforehand the leadership of the Social Democrats. Under Bogdanov's influence, the Petrograd Bureau of the CEC (Bolsheviks) passed a resolution in October 1905: to submit before the Petrograd Soviet the demand that it recognise the leadership of the party; and in the event of refusal—to walk out of the Soviet. Krassikov, a young lawyer, in those days a member of the CEC (Bolsheviks), read this ultimatum at the plenary session of the Soviet. The worker deputies, among them Bolsheviks also, exchanged surprised looks and then passed on to the business on the order of the day. Not a man walked out of the Soviet. Shortly after than Lenin arrived from abroad, and he raked the ultimatists over the coals mercilessly. 'You can't,' he lectured them, 'nor can anyone else by means of ultimatums force the masses to skip the necessary phases of their own political development.'

Bogdanov, however, did not discard his methodology, and he subsequently founded an entire faction of 'ultimatists' or 'up and outers', called *Otzovists*. They received the latter nickname because of their tendency to call upon the Bolsheviks to get up and get out from all those organisations that refused to accept the ultimatum laid down from above: 'you must first accept our leadership'. The ultimatists attempted to apply their policy not only to the Soviets but also to the parliamentary sphere and to the trade unions, in short, to all legal and semi-legal organisations of the working class.

Lenin's fight against ultimatism was a fight for the correct interrelation between the party and the class. The ultimatists in the old Bolshevik Party never played a role of the slightest importance, otherwise the victory of Bolshevism would not have been possible. The strength of Bolshevism lay in its wide-awake and sensitive relation to the class. Lenin continued his fight against ultimatism even when he was in supreme command, in particular and especially as regards the attitude to the trade unions.

'Indeed, if now in Russia,' he wrote,

> after two and a half years of unheard-of victories over the bourgeoisie of Russia and of the Entente, we were to place before the trade unions as a condition for their joining us that they 'recognise the dictatorship' we would be guilty of stupidity, we would impair our influence over the masses, we would aid the Mensheviks. For the task of the Communists consists in being able to convince the backward; to know how to work among them and not to fence ourselves off from them by a barrier of fictitious and puerile 'left' slogans.[3]

This holds all the more for the Communist Parties of the West, which represent only a minority of the working class.

During the last few years, however, the situation in the USSR has changed rapidly. The arming of the Communist Party with sovereignty means the introduction of a new element into the interrelation between the vanguard and the class: into this relation there enters the element of *force*. Lenin's struggle against party and Soviet bureaucracy was in its essence a struggle not against the faulty organisation of departments, nor against departmental red tape and inefficiency, but against the apparatus laying down the law to the class, against the transformation of the party bureaucracy into a new 'ruling' clique. Lenin's counsel, from his deathbed, that a proletarian Control Commission be created, independent of the CEC, and that Stalin and his faction be removed from the party apparatus, was aimed against the bureaucratic degeneration of the party. For various reasons, which cannot be dealt with here, the party ignored this counsel. Of recent years the bureaucratic degeneration of the party has reached the extreme limit. Stalin's apparatus simply lays down the law. The language of command is the language of ultimatism. Every worker must perforce and forthwith accept as infallible all the past, present, and future decisions of the CEC. The more erroneous the policies become, the greater are the pretensions to infallibility.

After gathering into its hands the apparatus of the Comintern, the Stalinist faction naturally transferred its methods to the foreign sections also, i.e., to the Communist Parties in the capitalist nations. The policy of the Germany leaders has for its counterpart the policy of the Moscow leadership. Thälmann observes how Stalin's bureaucracy rules the roost, by condemning as counter-revolutionary all those who do not recognise its infallibility. Wherein is Thälmann worse than Stalin? If the working class does not willingly place itself under his leadership, that is only because the working class is counter-revolutionary. Double-dyed counter-revolutionaries are those who point out the balefulness of ultimatism. The collected works of Lenin are among the most counter-revolutionary publications. There is sufficient reason why Stalin should—as he does—submit them to such rigid censorship, particularly on their publication in foreign languages.

As baleful as ultimatism is under all conditions, if in the USSR it dissipates the moral capital of the party—it breeds double disaster for the Western parties, which must yet begin accumulating their moral capital. Within the Soviet Union, at least, the victorious revolution has created the material grounds for bureaucratic ultimatism in the shape of an apparatus for repression, whereas in capitalist countries, including Germany, ultimatism becomes converted into an important caricature, and interferes with the movement of the Communist Party to power. Above all, the ultimatism of Thälmann-Remmele is ridiculous. And whatever is ridiculous is fatal, particularly in matters concerning a revolutionary party.

Let us for a moment transfer the problem to Great Britain, where the Communist Party (as a consequence of the ruinous mistakes of Stalinist bureaucracy) still comprises an insignificant portion of the proletariat. If one accepts the theory that every type of the united front, except the Communist, is 'counter-revolutionary', then obviously the British proletariat must put off its revolutionary struggle until that time when the Communist Party is able to come to the fore. But the Communist Party cannot come to the front of the class except on the basis of its own revolutionary experience. However, its experience cannot take on a revolutionary character in any other way than by drawing mass millions into the struggle. Yet non-Communist masses, the more so if organised, cannot be drawn into the struggle except through the policy of the united front.

We fall into a vicious circle, from which there is no way out by means of bureaucratic ultimatism. But the revolutionary dialectic has long since pointed the way out and has demonstrated it by countless examples in the most diverse spheres: by correlating the struggle for power with the struggle for reforms; by maintaining complete independence of the party while preserving the unity of the trade unions; by fighting against the bourgeois regime and at the same time utilising its institutions; by relentlessly criticising parliamentarism—from the parliamentary tribunal; by waging war mercilessly against reforms, and at the same time making practical agreements with the reformists in partial struggles.

In Britain, the incompetence of ultimatism hits one in the eye because of the extreme weakness of the party. In Germany, the balefulness of ultimatism is masked somewhat by the considerable numerical strength of the party and by its growth. But the German party is growing on account of the pressure of events and not thanks to the policies of the leadership; not because of ultimatism, but despite it. Moreover, the numerical growth of the party does not play the decisive role; what does decide is the political interrelation between the party and the class. Along this line, which is fundamental, the situation is not improving, because the German party has placed between itself and the class the thorny hedge of ultimatism.

4. Stalinist zigzags on the question of the United Front

The former Social Democrat Torhorst (from Düsseldorf), who has come over to the Communist Party, spoke in the name of the party in mid-January, in Frankfurt. In her official report she said: 'The leaders of the Social Democracy are sufficiently exposed, and it would be only a waste of energy to continue our efforts in this direction, with unity from above'. We quote from a Frankfurt Communist newspaper which lauds the report highly. 'The leaders of the Social Democracy are sufficiently exposed'. Sufficiently—so far as the spokeswoman herself is concerned, who came over from the Social Democracy to the Communists (which, of course, does her honour); but insufficiently—so far as those millions of workers are concerned who vote for the Social Democrats and who put up with the reformist bureaucracy of the trade unions.

It is hardly necessary, however, to cite an isolated report. In the latest proclamation to reach me, *Die Rote Fahne* (28 January 1932) argues once again that the united front can be established only against the Social Democratic leaders, and without them. Proof: 'None will believe them who has lived through and has experienced the handiwork of these "leaders" for the last eighteen years.' And what, may we ask, is to be done about those who have participated in politics fewer than eighteen years, and even fewer than eighteen months? Since the outbreak of the war, several political generations have matured who must recapitulate the experience of older generations, even though within a much smaller space of time. 'The whole point of the matter is,' Lenin coached the ultra-leftists, 'that we must not assume whatever is obsolete for us to be obsolete for the class, for the masses.'

Moreover, even the older generation that did pass through the experience of eighteen years hasn't at all broken with the leaders. On the contrary, it is just the Social Democracy that still retains many 'old-timers', who are bound to the party by long-standing traditions. It's sad, surely, that the masses learn so slowly. But in a goodly measure to blame for this are the Communist 'pedagogues' who have been palpably unable to expose the criminal nature of reformism. The least that can be done now is to utilise the situation; and at the same time when the attention of the masses is strained to its highest pitch by mortal danger, to subject the reformists to a new and this time, perhaps, really decisive test.

Without hiding or mitigating our opinion of the Social Democratic leaders in the slightest, we may and we must say to the Social Democratic workers: 'Since, on the one hand, you are still unwilling to break with your leaders, here is what we suggest: force your leaders to join us in a common struggle for such and such practical aims, in such and such a manner; as for us, we Communists are ready.' Can anything be more plain, more palpable, more convincing?

In precisely this sense I wrote—with the conscious intention of arousing the sincere horror of blockheads and the fake indignation of charlatans—that in the war against fascism we were ready to conclude practical military alliances with the devil and his grandmother, even with Noske and Zorgiebel.*

The official party, itself, violates its stillborn policy at every step. In its appeals for the 'Red United Front' (with its own self), it invariably puts forward the demand for 'the unconditional freedom of the *proletarian* press and the right to demonstrate, meet, and organise'. This slogan is clear-cut through and through. But when the Communist Party speaks of *proletarian* and not only of Communist papers, meetings, etc, it thereby, in fact, puts forward the slogan of the united front with that very Social Democracy that publishes workers' papers, calls meetings, etc. To put forward political slogans that in themselves include the idea of the united front with the Social Democracy, and to reject the making of practical agreements to fight for these slogans—that is the height of absurdity.

Münzenberg, whose practical horse-sense occasionally falls foul of 'the general line', wrote in November in **Der Rote Aufbau**: 'It's true that National Socialism is the most reaction-

* The French periodical **Cahiers du Bolchevisme**, the most preposterous and illiterate of all Stalinist publications, pounced greedily upon this reference to the devil's grandmother, never suspecting, of course, that she has a long history in the Marxist press. The hour is not distant, we hope, when the revolutionary workers will send their ignorant and unscrupulous teachers to serve their apprenticeship with the above-mentioned grandmother.

ary, the most chauvinistic, and the most bestial wing of the fascist movement in Germany; and that all true left circles [!] are most vitally concerned in interfering with the growth in influence and power of this wing of German fascism.' If Hitler's party is 'the *most* reactionary and *most* bestial' wing, then Brüning's regime is, at least, *less* bestial and *less* reactionary. Münzenberg, here, is stealthily flirting with the theory of the 'lesser evil'. To preserve a semblance of piety, he goes on to differentiate between different kinds of fascism: mild, medium and strong, as if it were a question of Turkish tobacco. However, if all 'the left circles' (and have they no names?) are interested in the victory over fascism, then isn't it imperative to put these 'left circles' to a practical test?

Isn't it self-evident that Breitscheid's diplomatic and equivocal offer should have been grabbed with both hands; and that from one's own side, one should have submitted a concrete, carefully detailed, and practical programme for a joint struggle against fascism and demanded joint sessions of the executives of both parties, with the participation of the executives of the Free Trade Unions? Simultaneously, one should have carried this same programme energetically down through all the layers of both parties and of the masses. The negotiations should have been carried on openly before the eyes of the entire nation: daily accounts should have appeared in the press without distortions and absurd fabrications. Such an agitation by its directness and incisiveness would tell with far greater effect on the worker than the incessant din on the subject of 'social fascism'. Under such conditions, the Social Democracy could not hide for a single day behind the pasteboard pageant of 'the Iron Front'.

Everyone should read **Left-Wing Communism: An Infantile Disorder**; today it is the timeliest of timely books. It is in reference to just such situations as the present one in Germany that Lenin speaks of (we quote verbatim):

> the absolute necessity for the vanguard of the proletariat, for its class-conscious section, for the Communist Party to resort to tacking and veering in its course, to agreements and compromises with different proletarian groups, with different parties of workers and small proprietors... The whole matter lies in being able to apply this tactic for the

sake of raising and now lowering the common level of proletarian class consciousness, revolutionary spirit, and the capacity to fight and to win.

But what steps does the Communist Party take? Day in and day out, it reiterates in its newspapers that the only united front it will accept 'is the one directed against Brüning, Severing, Leipart, Hitler and their ilk'. In the face of a proletarian uprising, there is no gainsaying it, there will be no difference between Brüning, Severing, Leipart, and Hitler. Against the October Bolshevik uprising, the Social Revolutionaries and the Mensheviks united with the Cadets and Kornilov; Kerensky led the Black Hundreds and the Cossacks of General Krasnov against Petrograd; the Mensheviks supported Kerensky and Krasnov; the Social Revolutionaries engineered the uprising of the *junkers* under the leadership of monarchist officers.

But this doesn't at all mean that Brüning, Severing, Leipart, and Hitler *always* and *under all conditions* belong to the same camp. Just now their interests diverge. At the *given* moment the question that is posed before the Social Democracy is not so much one of defending the foundations of capitalist society against proletarian revolution as of defending the semi- parliamentarian bourgeois system against fascism. The refusal to make use of the antagonism would be an act of gross stupidity.

'To wage war for the purpose of overthrowing the international bourgeoisie,' Lenin wrote in **Left-Wing Communism,**

> and to refuse beforehand to tack and veer in one's course and to make good use of the antagonism (*no matter how temporary* in interests between the enemies; to eschew agreements and compromises with possible (*no matter how temporary, vacillating, and adventitious*) allies—isn't that too ridiculous for words?

Again we quote verbatim; the words we italicise in parentheses are Lenin's.

We quote further:

> It is possible to vanquish a more powerful enemy only by straining one's forces to their utmost; and it is imperative that one make use, most painstakingly, carefully, cautiously

and expertly, of any 'rift' between the enemies, no matter how tiny.

But what are Thälmann and Remmele under Manuilsky's guidance doing? With might and main they are striving to cement, with the theory of social fascism and with the practice of sabotage against the united front, the rift—and what a rift—between the Social Democracy and fascism.

Lenin enjoined that use be made of 'every opportunity to gain a mass ally, no matter how temporary, vacillating, unreliable, and adventitious. Whoever hasn't been able to get that into his head,' he said, 'doesn't understand an iota of Marxism, and of contemporary scientific socialism in general.' Prick up your ears, prophets of the new Stalinist school: it is written here in black and white that you don't understand an iota of Marxism. It's you Lenin spoke of. Please let us hear from you.

But, the Stalinists reply, without a victory over the Social Democracy, victory over fascism is impossible. Is this true? In a *certain* sense it is. Yet the converse theorem is also true: without victory over Italian fascism, victory over the Italian Social Democracy is impossible. Both fascism and the Social Democracy are tools in the hands of the bourgeoisie. So long as capital rules, fascism and Social Democracy will exist in divers combinations. All the questions, therefore, are reduced to the same denominator: the proletariat must overthrow the bourgeois regime.

But just now, when this regime is tottering in Germany, fascism steps forward in its defence. To knock down this defender, we are told, it is first necessary to finish off the Social Democracy... Thus we are led into a vicious circle by schematism dead as a herring. The only conceivable way out is in the domain of action. And the character of this action is determined not by juggling abstract categories but by the real interrelations between the living historic forces.

'Oh, no!' the functionaries keep drumming, 'we shall 'first' liquidate the Social Democracy. How? Very simply, we shall order our party organisations to recruit 100,000 new members within such and such a period.' Instead of political struggle— merely propaganda; instead of dialectic strategy— departmental plans. And what if the real development of the class struggle, at this very moment, has posed the question of fascism before the working class, as a life and death question? Then the working class must be wheeled about with its back to the question; it must be lulled; it must be convinced that the task of fighting against fascism is a minor task; that it will wait and solve itself; that fascism in reality rules already; that Hitler will add nothing new; that there is no cause to fear Hitler; that Hitler will only clear the road for the Communists.

Is that exaggerating, perhaps? No, this is the exact and indubitable idea that motivates the leaders of the Communist Party. They do not always follow it to its ultimate conclusion. On coming in contact with the masses they recoil often from the ultimate conclusions; they make a hodgepodge of diverse policies, confusing themselves and the workers; but on all those occasions when they try to make both ends meet, they proceed from the inevitability of the victory of fascism.

On 14 October 1931, Remmele, one of the three official leaders of the Communist Party, said in the Reichstag:

Herr Brüning has put it very plainly: once they [the fascists] are in power, then the united front of the proletariat will be established and it will make a clean sweep of everything. (Violent applause from the Communists).

Brüning's scaring the bourgeoisie and the Social Democracy with such a perspective—that is intelligible: he thus safeguards his sovereignty. Remmele's solacing the workers with such a perspective—that is infamous: he thus prepares the way for Hitler's domination, for this perspective in its entirety is false to the core and bears witness to an utter misunderstanding of mass psychology and of the dialectics of revolutionary struggle.

Should the proletariat of Germany, before whose eyes the development of events now proceeds openly, permit fascism to come into power, i.e., should it evince a most fatal blindness and passivity, then there are no reasons whatever for the assumption that *after* the fascists are in power, this same proletariat will shake off its passivity immediately and 'make a clean sweep'. Nothing like this, for instance, happened in Italy. Remmele reasons completely after the manner of the French petty-bourgeois phrasemongers of the nineteenth century who proved themselves entirely incapable of leading the masses, but who were quite firmly convinced, nevertheless, that should Louis Bonaparte plant himself over the republic, the people would rise, on the instant, in their defence and 'make a clean sweep'. However, the people that had permitted the adventurer Louis Bonaparte to seize the power proved, sure enough, incapable of sweeping him away thereafter. Before this happened, new major events, historical quakes, and a war had to occur.

The united front of the proletariat is achievable—for Remmele, as he has told us—only after Hitler assumes power. Can a more pathetic confession of one's own impotence be made? Since we, Remmele & Co, are incapable of uniting the proletariat, we place the burden of this task upon Hitler's shoulders. After he has united the proletariat for us, then we will show ourselves in our true stature. Remmele follows this up with a boastful announcement:

> We are the victors of the coming day; and the question is no longer one of who shall vanquish whom. This question is already answered. (Applause from the Communists). The question now reads only, 'At what moment shall we over-throw the bourgeoisie?'

Right to the point! As we say in Russian, that's pointing one's finger and hitting the sky. We are the victors of the *coming* day. All we lack today is the united front. Herr Hitler will supply us with it tomorrow, when he assumes power. Which still means that the victor of the *coming* day will be not Remmele but Hitler. And then, you might as well carve it on your nose, the moment for the victory of the Communists will not arrive so soon.

Remmele feels himself that his optimism limps on its left leg, and he attempts to bolster it up. 'We are not afraid of the fascist gentlemen. They will shoot their bolt quicker than any other government. ("Right you are!" from the Communists).' And for proof: the fascists want paper-money inflation, and that means ruin for the masses of the nation; consequently, everything will turn out for the best. Thus the verbal inflation of Remmele leads the German workers astray.

Here we have before us a programmatic speech of an official leader of the party; it was issued in immense numbers and was used in the Communist membership drive: appended to the speech is a printed blank for enrolment in the party. And this very programmatic speech is based part and parcel upon capitulation to fascism. 'We are not afraid' of Hitler's assuming power. What is this, if not the formula of cowardice turned inside out. 'We' don't consider ourselves capable of keeping Hitler from assuming power; worse yet: the bureaucrats, have so degenerated as not to dare think seriously of fighting Hitler. Therefore, 'we are not afraid'. What don't you fear: fighting against Hitler? On, no! they are not afraid of... Hitler's victory. They are not afraid of refusing to fight. They are not afraid to confess their own cowardice. For shame!

In one of my previous pamphlets I wrote that the Stalinist bureaucracy was baiting a trap for Hitler—in the guise of state power. The Communist journalists, who flit from Münzenberg to Ullstein and from Mosse to Münzenberg,[4] announced immediately that 'Trotsky vilifies the Communist Party'. Isn't it really self-evident that Trotsky, out of his aversion for Communism, out of his hatred for the German proletariat, out of his passionate desire to save German capitalism—yes, Trotsky foists a plan of capitulation upon the Stalinist bureaucracy. But in reality I only gave a brief summary of Remmele's programmatic speech and of a theoretical article by Thälmann. Where does the vilification come in?

Moreover both Thälmann and Remmele are only holding steadfastly to the Stalinist gospel. Let us recall once again what Stalin propounded in the autumn of 1923 when everything in Germany was—as now—poised on the razor edge of a knife. 'Should the Communists (on the given plane),' wrote Stalin to Zinoviev and Bukharin,

> strive to seize power without the Social Democracy? Are they sufficiently mature for this?—that's the question as I see it ... Should the power in Germany at this moment fall, so to speak, and should the Communists catch it up, they'll fall through with a crash. That's 'at best'. If it comes to the worst—they'll be smashed to pieces and beaten back... Of course, the fascists aren't asleep, but it serves our purposes better to let them be the first to attack: that will solidify the

entire working class around the Communists... In my opinion the Germans should be restrained and not encouraged'.

In his pamphlet **The Mass Strike**, Langner writes:

> The assertion [Brandler's] that a battle in October [1923] would have resulted only in a 'decisive defeat', is nothing but an attempt to gloss over opportunistic mistakes and the opportunistic capitulation without a fight.

That is absolutely correct. But who was the instigator of 'the capitulation without a fight'? Who was it that 'restrained' instead of 'encouraging'? In 1931, Stalin only amplified his formula of 1923: let the fascists assume the power, they'll only be clearing the road for us. Naturally it is much safer to attack Brandler than Stalin: the Langners understand that quite well...

In point of fact, in the last two months—not without the influence of the outspoken protests from the left—a certain change has occurred: the Communist Party no longer says that Hitler must assume power in order to shoot his bolt quickly; now it lays more stress on the converse side of the question: the battle against fascism cannot be postponed until after Hitler assumes the power; the battle must be waged now by arousing the workers against Brüning's decrees and by widening and deepening the strife on the economic and political arenas. That is absolutely correct. Everything that the representatives of the Communist Party have to say within this sphere is not to be gainsaid. Here we have no disagreements whatever. Still the most important question remains: how to get down from words to business?

The overwhelming majority of the members of the Communist Party as well as a considerable portion of the officialdom—we haven't the slightest doubt—sincerely want to fight. But the facts must be faced openly: there's no fighting being done, there is no sign of fighting in sight. Brüning's decrees passed by scot-free. The Christmas truce was not broken. The policy of calling sectional and improvised strikes, judging by the accounts of the Communist Party itself, has not achieved any serious successes to date. The workers see this. Shrieking alone will not convince them.

The Communist Party places on the shoulders of the Social Democracy the responsibility for the passivity of the masses. In a historical sense that is indubitable. But we are not historians, we are revolutionary politicians. Our task is not one of conducting historical researches, but of finding the way out.

The SAP, which during the first period of its existence took up formally the question of fighting fascism (especially in articles by Rosenfeld and Seydewitz) made a certain step forward by timing the counterattack coincidentally with Hitler's assumption of power. Its press now demands that the fight to repel fascism be begun immediately by mobilising the workers against hunger and the police yoke. We admit readily that the change in the policy of the SAP was brought about under the influence of Communist criticism: one of the tasks of Communism precisely consists in pushing centrism forward by criticising its dual tendencies. But that alone does not suffice: one must exploit politically the fruits of one's own criticism by proposing to the SAP to pass from words to action. One must subject the SAP to a public and clear test; not by analysing isolated quotations—that's not enough—but by offering to make an agreement towards taking specified practical steps against the foe. Should the SAP lay bare its incompetence, the higher the authority of the Communist Party would rise, the sooner an intermediate party would be liquidated. What's there to fear?

However, it is not true that the SAP does not seriously want to fight. There are various tendencies within it. For the moment, so long as the matter is reduced to abstract propaganda for a united front, the inner contradictions lie dormant. Once the battle is begun, they will become apparent. The Communist Party alone stands to gain thereby.

But there still remains the most important question as regards the SPD. Should it reject those practical propositions which the SAP accepts, a new situation would arise. The centrists, who would prefer to straddle the fence between the KPD and the SPD in order to complain first about one and then about the other, and to gain in strength at the expense of both (such is the philosophy evolved by Urbahns)—these centrists would find themselves suspended in midair, because it would immediately become apparent that the SPD itself is sabotaging the revolutionary struggle. Isn't that an important gain? The workers within the SAP from then on would definitely lean towards the KPD.

Moreover, the refusal of Wels & Co to accept the programme of joint action, agreed to by the SAP, would not let the Social Democrats go scot-free either. The *Vorwärts* would be deprived immediately of the chance to complain about the passivity of the KPD. The gravitation of the Social Democratic workers towards the united front would increase immediately; and that would be equivalent to their gravitation towards the KPD. Isn't that plain enough?

At each one of these stages and turns the KPD would tap new resources. Instead of monotonously repeating the same ready-made formulas before one and the same audience, it would be enabled to set new strata into motion, to teach them through actual experience, to steel them, and to strengthen its hegemony among the working class.

Not for a moment should one even discuss that the KPD must thereby renounce its independent leadership of strikes, demonstrations, and political campaigns. It reserves to itself complete freedom of action. It waits for nobody. But on the basis of its new activities, it puts through an active political manoeuvre in relation to other workers' organisations; it breaks down the conservative barriers between the workers; it drives out into the open the contradictions in reformism and in centrism: it hastens the revolutionary crystallisation of the proletariat.

5. A Historical Review of the United Front

The contentions regarding the policies of the united front take their origin from such fundamental and inexorable exigencies of the struggle of *class against class* (in the Marxist and not the bureaucratic sense of these words) that one cannot read the refutations of the Stalinist bureaucracy without a feeling of shame and indignation. It is one thing to keep on explaining, from day to day, the most rudimentary ideas to the most backward and benighted workers or peasants. One can do it without any feeling of exhaustion; for here it is a matter of enlightening fresh strata. But woe to him who is perforce obliged to explain and to prove elementary propositions to people whose brains have been flattened out by the bureaucratic steamroller. What can one do with 'leaders' who have no logical arguments at their disposal and who make up for that by referring to the handbook of international epithet. The fundamental propositions of Marxism they parry by one and the same epithet, 'counter-revolution!' This word has become inordinately cheapened on the lips of those who have in no manner as yet proved their capacity to achieve a revolution. Still, what about the decisions passed by the first four congresses of the Comintern? Does the Stalinist bureaucracy accept them, or not?

The documents still survive and still preserve their significance to this day. Out of a large number, I have chosen the theses worked out by me, between the Third and Fourth Congresses; they relate to the French Communist Party. They were approved by the Politburo of the CPSU and the Executive Committee of the Comintern and were published, in their time, in various foreign Communist publications. Below is reprinted verbatim that part of the theses which is devoted to the formulation and the defence of the policy of the united front:

> It is perfectly self-evident that the class life of the proletariat is not suspended during this period preparatory to the revolution. Clashes with industrialists, with the bourgeoisie, with the state power, on the initiative of one side or the other, run their due course.
>
> In these clashes—insofar as they involve the vital interests of the entire working class, or its majority, or this or that section—the working masses sense the need of unit in action... Any part which mechanically counterposes itself to this need... will unfailingly be condemned in the minds of the workers...
>
> The problem of the united front—despite the fact *that a split is inevitable in this epoch between the various political organisations basing themselves on the working class*—grows out of the urgent need to secure for the working class the possibility of a united front in the struggle against capitalism.
>
> For those who do not understand this task, the party is only

a propaganda society and not an organisation for mass action...

If the Communist Party had not broken drastically and irrevocably with the Social Democrats, it would not have become the party of the proletarian revolution...

If the Communist Party did not seek for organisation avenues to the end that at every given moment joint, co-ordinated action between the Communist and the non-Communist (including the Social Democratic) working masses were made possible, it would have thereby laid bare its own incapacity to win over—on the basis of mass action—the majority of the working class ...

After separating the Communists from the reformists it is not enough to fuse the Communists together by means of organisational discipline; it is necessary that this organisation should learn how to guide all the collective activities of the proletariat in all spheres of its living struggle.

This is the second letter of the alphabet of Communism.

Does the united front extend only to the working masses or does it also include the opportunist leaders?

The very posing of this question is a product of misunderstanding.

If we were able simply to unite the working masses around our own banner .. and skip over the reformist organisations, whether party or trade union, that would of course be the best thing in the world. But then the very question of the united front would not exist in its present form...

...we are, apart from all other considerations, interested in dragging the reformists from their asylums and placing them alongside ourselves before the eyes of the struggling masses. With a correct tactic we stand only to gain from this. A Communist who doubts or fears this resembles a swimmer who has approved the theses on the best method of swimming but dares not plunge into the water...

In entering into agreements with other organisations, we naturally obligate ourselves to a certain discipline in action. But this discipline cannot be absolute in character. In the event that the reformists begin putting brakes on the struggle to the obvious detriment of the movement and act counter to the situation and the moods of the masses, we as an independent organisation always reserve the right to lead the struggle to the end, and this without our temporary semi-allies...

It is possible to see in this policy a rapprochement with the reformists only from the standpoint of a journalist who believes that he rids himself of reformism by ritualistically criticising it without ever leaving his editorial office, but who is fearful of clashing with the reformists before the eyes of the working masses and giving the latter an opportunity to appraise the Communist and the reformist on the equal plane of the mass struggle. Behind this seemingly revolutionary fear of 'rapprochement' there really lurks a political passivity which seeks to perpetuate an order of things wherein the Communists and reformists each retain their own rigidly demarcated spheres of influence, their own audiences at meetings, their own press, and all this together creates an illusion of serious political struggle...

On the question of the united front we see the very same passive and irresolute tendency, but this time masked by verbal irreconcilability. At the very first glance, one is hit between the eyes by the following paradox: the rightist party element s with their centrist and pacifist tendencies, who... come simultaneously to the forefront as the most irreconcilable opponents of the united front... In contrast, those elements who have... held in the most difficult hours the position of the Third International are today in favour of the tactic of the united front.

As a matter of fact, the mask of pseudo-revolutionary intransigence is now being assumed by the partisans of the dilatory and passive tactic.[5]

Doesn't it seem as if these lines were written today against Stalin-Manuilsky-Thälmann-Neumann? Actually, they were written ten years ago, against Frossard, Cachin, Charles Rappoport, Daniel Renoult, and other French opportunists disguising themselves with ultra-leftism. We put this question point-blank to the Stalinist bureaucracy: were the theses we quoted 'counter-revolutionary' even during that time when they expressed the policies of the Russian Politburo, with Lenin at its head, and when they defined the policy of the Comintern? We warn them duly not to attempt in answer to reply that conditions have changed since that period: the matter does not concern questions of conjuncture; but, as the text itself puts it, of *the ABC of Marxism.*

And so, ten years ago, the Comintern explained that the gist of the united-front policy was in the following: the Communist Party proves to the masses and their organisations its readiness in action to wage battle in common with them for aims, no matter how modest, so long as they lie on the road of the historical development of the proletariat; the Communist Party in this struggle takes into account the actual condition of the class at each given moment; it turns not only to the masses, but also to those organisations whose leadership is recognised by the masses; it confronts the reformist organisations before the eyes of the masses with the real problems of the class struggle. The policy of the united front hastens the revolutionary development of the class by revealing in the open that the common struggle is undermined not by the disruptive acts of the Communist Party but by the conscious sabotage of the leaders of the Social Democracy. It is absolutely clear that these conceptions could in no sense have become obsolete.

Then how explain the rejection of the policy of the united front by the Comintern? By the miscarriages and the failures of this policy in the past. Were these failures, the causes of which reside not in the policy but in the politicians, examined and analysed and studied in their time, the German Communist Party would be strategically and tactically excellently equipped for the present situation. But the Stalinist bureaucracy chose to behave like the nearsighted monkey in the fable; after adjusting the spectacles on its tail and licking them to no result, the monkey concluded that they were no good at all and dashed them against a rock. Put it as you please, but the spectacles are not at fault.

The mistakes made in the policy of the united front fall into two categories. In most cases the leading organs of the Communist Party approached the reformists with an offer to join in a common struggle for radical slogans which were alien to the situation and which found no response in the masses. These proposals had the character of blank shots. The masses remained indifferent; the reformist leaders interpreted these proposals of the Communists as a trick to destroy the Social Democracy. In each of these instances only a purely formal, declamatory application of the policy of united front was inaugurated; whereas, by its very nature, it can prove fruitful only on the basis of a realistic appraisal of the situation and of the condition of the masses. The weapon of 'open letters' became outworn from too frequent and hence faulty application, and had to be given up.

The second type of perversion bore a much more fatal character. In the hands of the Stalinist bureaucracy, the policy of the united front became a hue and cry after allies at the cost of sacrificing the independence of the party. Backed by Moscow and deeming themselves omnipotent, the functionaries of the Comintern seriously esteemed themselves to be capable of laying down the law to the classes and of prescribing their itinerary; of checking the agrarian and strike movements in China; of buying an alliance with Chiang Kai-shek at the cost of sacrificing the independent policies of the Comintern; of re-educating the trade-union bureaucracy, the chief bulwark of British imperialism, through educational courses at banquet tables in London, or in Caucasian resorts; of transforming Croatian bourgeois of Radich's type into Communists, etc. All this was undertaken, of course, with the best of intentions, in order to hasten developments by accomplishing for the masses what the masses weren't mature enough to do for themselves.

It is not beside the point to mention that in a number of countries, Austria in particular, the functionaries of the Comintern tried their hand, during the past period, at creating artificially and 'from above' a 'left' Social Democracy—to serve as a bridge to Communism. Nothing but failures were produced by this tomfoolery also. Invariably these experiments and filibusterings ended catastrophically. The revolutionary movement in the world was flung back for many years.

Thereupon Manuilsky decided to break the spectacles; and as for Kuusinen—to avoid further mistakes, he decreed everyone except himself and his cronies to be fascists. Whereupon the matter was clarified and simplified; no more mistakes were possible. What kind of a united front can there be with 'social fascists' against national fascists, or with the 'left social fascists' against the 'rights' Thus by describing over our heads an arc of 180 degrees, the Stalinist bureaucracy found itself compelled to announce the decisions of the first four congresses as counter-revolutionary.

6. Lessons of the Russian Experience

In one of our earlier pamphlets, we made reference to the Bolshevik experience in the struggle against Kornilov; the official leaders answered with bellows of disapproval. We shall recapitulate here once again the gist of the matter, in order to show more clearly and in greater detail how the Stalinist school draws lessons from the past.

During July and August 1917, Kerensky, then head of the government, was in fact fulfilling the programme of Kornilov, the commander-in-chief of the army. He reinstated at the front military court-martials and the death penalty. He deprived the duly elected soviets of all influence upon government matters; he repressed the peasants; he doubled the price of bread (under the state trade monopoly of the foodstuffs); he prepared for the evacuation of revolutionary Petrograd; with Kornilov's consent, he moved up counter-revolutionary troops towards the capital; he promised the Allies to initiate a new attack at the front, etc. Such was the general political background.

On 26 August, Kornilov broke with Kerensky because of the latter's vacillation, and threw his army against Petrograd. The status of the Bolshevik Party was semilegal. Its leaders from Lenin down were either hiding underground or committed to prison, being indicted for affiliation with the General Staff of the Hohenzollerns. The Bolshevik papers were being suppressed. These persecutions emanated from Kerensky's government, which was supported from the left by the coalition of Social Revolutionary and Menshevik deputies.

What course did the Bolshevik Party take? Not for an instant did it hesitate to conclude a practical alliance to fight against Kornilov with its jailers—Kerensky, Tseretelli, Dan, etc. Everywhere committees for revolutionary defence were organised, into which the Bolsheviks entered as a minority. This did not hinder the Bolsheviks from assuming the leading role: in agreements projected for revolutionary mass action, the most thoroughgoing and the boldest revolutionary party stands to gain always. The Bolsheviks were in the front ranks; they smashed down the barriers blocking them from the Menshevik workers and especially from the Social Revolutionary soldiers, and carried them along in their wake.

Perhaps the Bolsheviks took this course of action only because they were caught unawares? No. During the preceding months, the Bolsheviks tens and hundreds of times demanded that the Mensheviks join them in a common struggle against the mobilising forces of the counter-revolution. Even on 27 May, while Tseretelli was clamouring for repressions against Bolshevik sailors, Trotsky declared during the session of the Petrograd Soviet:

> When the time comes and the counter-revolutionary general will try to slip the noose around the neck of the revolution, the Cadets will be busy soaping the rope, but the sailors of Kronstadt will come to fight and to die side by side with us.

These words were fully confirmed. In the midst of Kornilov's campaign, Kerensky appealed to the sailors of the cruiser *Aurora*, begging them to assume the defence of the Winter Palace. These sailors were, without exception, Bolsheviks. They hated Kerensky. Their hatred did not hinder them from vigilantly guarding the Winter Palace. Their representatives came to the Kresty Prison for an interview with Trotsky, who was jailed there, and they asked: 'Why not arrest Kerensky?' But they put the query half in jest: the sailors understood that it was necessary first to smash Kornilov and after that to attend to Kerensky. Thanks to a correct political leadership, the sailors of the *Aurora* understood more than Thälmann's central committee.

Die Rote Fahne refers to our historical review as 'fraudulent'. Why? Vain question. How can one expect reasoned refutations from these people? They are under orders from Moscow, on the pain of losing their jobs, to set up a howl at the mention of Trotsky's name. They fulfil the command, as best they can. Trotsky produced, in their words, 'a fraudulent comparison' between the struggle of the Bolsheviks during Kornilov's reactionary mutiny, at the beginning of September 1917—at the time when the Bolsheviks were fighting with the Mensheviks for a majority within the soviets, immediately before an acutely revolutionary situation; at the time when the Bolsheviks, armed in the struggle against Kornilov, were simultaneously carrying on a flank attack on Kerensky—with the present 'struggle' of Brüning 'against' Hitler. 'In this manner, Trotsky paints the support of Brüning and of the Prussian government as "the lesser evil".'

It is quite a task to refute this barrage of words. A pretence is made that I compare the Bolshevik struggle against Kornilov with Brüning's struggle against Hitler. I don't overestimate the mental capacities of the editors of **Die Rote Fahne**, but these gentlemen could not be so stupid as not to understand what I meant. Brüning's struggle against Hitler I compared with Kerensky's struggle against Kornilov; the struggle of the Bolsheviks against Kornilov I compared with the struggle of the German Communist Party against Hitler. Wherein is this comparison 'fraudulent'? The Bolsheviks, says **Die Rote Fahne,** were fighting at the time with the Mensheviks for the majority in the soviets. But the German Communist Party, too, is fighting against the Social Democracy for the majority of the working class. In Russia they were faced with 'an acute revolutionary situation'. Quite true! If, however, the Bolsheviks had adopted Thälmann's position in August 1917, then instead of a revolutionary situation a counter- revolutionary situation could have ensued.

During the last days of August, Kornilov was crushed, in reality not by force of arms but by the singleness of purpose with which the masses were imbued. Then and there, after 3 September, Lenin offered through the press to compromise with the Social Revolutionaries and the Mensheviks: you compose the majority in the soviets, he said to them. Take over the state; we shall support you against the bourgeoisie. Guarantee us complete freedom of agitation and we shall assure you of a peaceful struggle for the majority in the soviets. Such an opportunist was Lenin! The Mensheviks and the Social Revolutionaries rejected the compromise, i.e., the new offer of a united front against the bourgeoisie. In the hands of the Bolsheviks, this rejection became a mighty weapon in preparation for the armed uprising, which within seven weeks swept away the Mensheviks and the Social Revolutionaries.

Up to now there has been only one victorious proletarian revolution in the world. I do not at all hold that we committed no errors on our road to victory; but nevertheless, I maintain that our experience has some value for the German Communist Party. I cite the closest and the most pertinent historical analogy. How do the leaders of the German Communist Party reply? With profanity.

Only the ultra-left group, *Der Rote Kämpfer*, attempted to refute our comparison 'seriously', accoutred in the complete armour of erudition. It holds that the Bolsheviks behaved correctly in August,

> because Kornilov was the standard-bearer of the Tsarist counter-revolution, which means that he was waging the battle of the feudal reaction against the bourgeois revolution. Under these conditions the tactical coalition of the workers with the bourgeoisie and its Social Revolutionary-Menshevik appendage was not only correct but necessary and unavoidable as well, because the interests of both classes coincided in the matter of repelling the feudal counter-revolution.

But since Hitler represents not the feudal but the bourgeois counter-revolution, the Social Democracy which supports the bourgeoisie cannot take the field against Hitler. That's why the united front does not exist in Germany, and that's why Trotsky's comparison is erroneous.

All this has a very imposing sound. But coming down to actual facts, not a word of it is true. In August 1917, the Russian bourgeoisie was not at all opposed to the feudal reaction; all the landowners supported the Cadet Party, which fought against the expropriation of the landowners. Kornilov proclaimed himself a Republican, 'the son of a peasant' and the supporter of agrarian reform and of the constitutional assembly. *The entire bourgeoisie supported Kornilov.* The alliance of the Bolsheviks with the Social Revolutionaries and Mensheviks was made possible only because the conciliationists *broke with the bourgeoisie temporarily* they were compelled to, from fear of Kornilov. The representatives of these parties knew that the moment Kornilov was victorious the bourgeoisie would no longer need them, and would allow Kornilov to strangle them. Within these limits there is, as we see, a complete analogy with the interrelations between the Social Democracy and fascism.

The distinctions begin not at all where the theoreticians of *Der Rote Kämpfer* see them. In Russia, the masses of the petty bourgeoisie, above all the peasants, gravitated to the left and not to the right. Kornilov did not lean upon the petty bourgeoisie. And just because of this, his movement was not fascists. The counter-revolution was bourgeois—not at all feudal—in conspiracy with the generals. Therein lay its weakness. Kornilov leaned upon the moral support of the entire bourgeoisie and the military support of the officers and junkers, i.e., the younger generation of the same bourgeoisie. This proved to be insufficient. But had Bolshevik policies been false, the victory of Kornilov was by no means excluded.

As we see, the arguments in *Der Rote Kämpfer* against the united front in Germany are based on the fact that its theoreticians understand neither the Russian nor the German situations.*

Since **Die Rote Fahne** doesn't feel secure on the slippery ice of Russian history, it attempts to tackle the question from the opposite direction:

> To Trotsky, only the National Socialists are fascists. The declaration of the state of emergency, the dictatorial wage reductions, the effective prohibition of strikes... all this is not fascism to Trotsky. All this our party must put up with.

These people almost disarm one with the impotence of their spleen. When and where did I suggest anyone's 'putting up with'

---

* All the other views of this group rest on the same plane and are only a rehash of the grossest blunders of the Stalinist bureaucracy, but accompanied by even more exaggerated ultra-left grimaces. Fascism is enthroned already; there is no independent danger in Hitler; and besides, the workers don't want to fight. If that's the way matters stand; if there's still plenty of time left, then the theoreticians of *Der Rote Kämpfer* might as well put their leisure to some use; and instead of scribbling bad articles they ought better to read a few good books. Marx long since explained to Weitling that ignorance never did anyone any good.

Brüning's government? And just what does this 'putting up with' mean? If it's a matter of parliamentary or extraparliamentary support of the Brüning regime, then you should be ashamed of even bringing up such a topic for discussion among Communists. But in another and a wide historical sense you, raucously bleating gentlemen, are nevertheless compelled to 'put up with' Brüning's government, because you lack the thews and sinews to overthrow it.

All the arguments which *Die Rote Fahne* musters against me in relation to the German situation might have been used with equal justification against the Bolsheviks in 1917. One might have said: 'For Bolsheviks, Kornilovism begins only with Kornilov. But isn't Kerenksy a Kornilovite? Aren't his policies aimed toward strangling the revolution? Isn't he crushing the peasants by means of punitive expeditions? Doesn't he organise lock-outs? Doesn't Lenin have to hide underground? And all this we must put up with?'

So far as I recall, I can't think of a single Bolshevik rash enough to have advanced such arguments. But were he to be found, he would have been answered something after this fashion. 'We accuse Kerensky of preparing for and facilitating the coming of Kornilov to power. But does this relieve us of the duty of rushing to repel Kornilov's attack? We accuse the gatekeeper of leaving the gates ajar for the bandit. But must we therefore shrug our shoulders and let the gates go hang?' Since, thanks to the toleration of the Social Democracy, Bruening's government has been able to push the proletariat up to its knees in capitulation to fascism, you arrive at the conclusion that up to the knees, up to the waist, or over the head—isn't it all one thing? No, there is some difference. Whoever is up to his knees in a quagmire can still drag himself out. Whoever is in over his head, for him there is no returning.

Lenin wrote about the ultra-lefts:

They say many flattering things about us Bolsheviks. At times one feels like saying, "Please, praise us a little less, and try your hand a little more at investigating the tactics of the Bolsheviks, and become a little better acquainted with them".

7. Lessons of the Italian Experience

Italian fascism was the immediate outgrowth of the betrayal by the reformists of the uprising of the Italian proletariat. From the time the war ended, there was an upward trend in the revolutionary movement in Italy, and in September 1920, it resulted in the seizure of factories and industries by the workers. The dictatorship of the proletariat was an actual fact; all that was lacking was to organise it, and to draw from it all the necessary conclusions. The Social Democracy took fright, and sprang back. After its bold and heroic exertions, the proletariat was left facing the void. The disruption of the revolutionary movement became the most important factor in the growth of fascism. In September, the revolutionary advance came to a standstill; and November already witnessed the first major demonstration of the fascists (the seizure of Bologna).

True, the proletariat, even after the September catastrophe, was capable of waging defensive battles. But the Social Democracy was concerned with only one thing: to withdraw the workers from under fire at the costs of one concession after the other. The Social Democracy hoped that the docile conduct of the workers would restore the 'public opinion' of the bourgeoisie against the fascists. Moreover, the reformists even banked strongly upon the help of Victor Emmanuel. To the last hour, they restrained the workers with might and main from giving battle to Mussolini's bands. It availed them nothing. The Crown, along with the upper crust of the bourgeoisie, swung over to the side of fascism. Convinced at the last moment that fascism was not to be checked by obedience, the Social Democrats issued a call to the workers for a general strike. But their proclamation suffered a fiasco. The reformists had dampened the powder so long, in their fear lest it should explode, that when they finally and with a trembling hand applied a burning fuse to it, the powder did not catch.

Two years after its inception, fascism was in power. It entrenched itself thanks to the fact that the first period of its overlordship coincided with a favourable economic conjuncture, which followed the depression of 1921-1922. The fascists crushed the retreating proletariat beneath the offensive power of the petty bourgeoisie. But this was not achieved at a single blow. Even after he assumed power, Mussolini proceeded on his course with due caution: he lacked as yet ready-made models. During the first two years, not even the constitution was altered. The fascist government took on the character of a coalition. In the meantime the fascist bands were busy at work with clubs, knives and pistols. Thus, slowly, the fascist government was created that meant the complete strangulation of all independent mass organisations.

Mussolini attained this at the cost of bureaucratising the fascist party itself. After utilising the onrushing forces of the petty bourgeoisie, fascism strangled it within the vice of the bourgeois state. He couldn't have done otherwise, for the disillusionment of the masses he had united was transforming itself into the most immediate danger ahead. Fascism, become bureaucratic, approaches very closely to other forms of military and police dictatorship. It no longer possesses its former social support. The chief reserve of fascism—the petty bourgeoisie—has been spent. Only historical inertia enables the fascist government to keep the proletariat in a state of dispersion and helplessness. The correlation of forces is changing automatically in favour of the proletariat. This change must lead to a revolution. The downfall of fascism will be one of the most catastrophic events in European history. But all these processes, as the facts bear out, need time. The fascist government has maintained itself for ten years already. How much longer will it hold on? Without venturing into the risky business of setting dates, one can still say with assurance that Hitler's victory in Germany would mean a new and a long lease of life for Mussolini. Hitler's crash will mean the beginning of the end for Mussolini.

In its politics as regards Hitler, the German Social Democracy has not been able to add a single word: all it does is repeat more ponderously whatever the Italian reformists in their own time performed with greater flights of temperament. The latter explained fascism as a post-war psychosis; the German Social Democracy sees in it a 'Versailles' or crisis psychosis. In both, the reformists shut their eyes to the organic character of fascism as a mass movement growing out of the collapse of capitalism.

Fearful of the revolutionary mobilisation of the workers, the Italian reformists banked all their hopes on 'the state'. Their slogan was 'Victor Emmanuel! Help! Intervene!' The German Social Democracy lacks such a democratic bulwark as a monarch loyal to the constitution. So they must be content with a president. 'Hindenburg! Help! Intervene!'

While waging battle against Mussolini, that is, while retreating before him, Turati let loose his dazzling motto, 'One must have the manhood to be a coward'. The German reformists are less frisky with their slogans. They demand 'Courage under unpopularity' (*Mut zur Unpopularität*). Which amounts to the same thing. One must not be afraid of the unpopularity which has been aroused by one's own cowardly temporising with the enemy.

Identical causes produce identical effects. Were the march of events dependent upon the Social Democratic Party leadership, Hitler's career would be assured.

One must admit, however, that the German Communist Party has also learned little from the Italian experience.

The Italian Communist Party came into being almost simultaneously with fascism. But the same conditions of revolutionary ebb tide which carried the fascists to power served to deter the development of the Communist Party. It did not take account of the full sweep of the fascist danger; it lulled itself with revolutionary illusions; it was irreconcilably antagonistic to the policy of the united front; in short, it ailed from all the infantile diseases. Small wonder! It was only two years old. In its eyes fascism appeared to be only 'capitalist reaction'. The *particular* traits of fascism which spring from the mobilisation of the petty bourgeoisie against the proletariat, the Communist Party was unable to discern. Italian comrades inform me that with the sole exception of Gramsci, the Communist Party wouldn't even allow of the possibility of the fascists' seizing power. Once the proletarian revolution had suffered defeat, and capitalism had kept its ground, and the counter-revolution had triumphed, how could there be any further kind of counter-revolutionary upheaval? The bourgeoisie cannot rise up against itself! Such was the gist of the political orientation of the Italian Communist Party. Moreover, one must not let out of sight the fact that Italian fascism was then a new phenomenon, and only in the process of formation; it wouldn't have been an easy task even for a more experienced party to distinguish its specific traits.

The leadership of the German Communist Party reproduces today almost literally the position from which the Italian Communists took their point of departure: fascism is nothing else but capitalist reaction; from the point of view of the proletariat, the differences between diverse types of capitalist reaction are meaningless. This vulgar radicalism is the less excusable because the German party is much older than the Italian was at a corresponding period; and in addition, Marxism has been enriched now by the tragic experience in Italy. To insist that fascism is already here, or to deny the very possibility of its coming to power—amounts politically to one and the same thing. By ignoring the specific nature of fascism, the will to fight against it becomes inevitably paralysed.

The brunt of the blame must be borne, of course, by the leadership of the Comintern. Italian Communists above all others were duty-bound to raise their voices in alarm. But Stalin, with Manuilsky, compelled them to disavow the most important lessons of their own annihilation. We have already observed with what diligent alacrity Ercoli switched over to the position of social fascism, i.e., to the position of passively waiting for the fascist victory in Germany.

For a long time, the international Social Democracy solaced itself with the notion that Bolshevism was conceivable only in a backward country. It found refuge in the same solace afterwards as regards fascism. The German Social Democracy is now compelled to experience on its own back the falseness of this comforting notion: its fellow travellers from the petty bourgeoisie have gone and are going over to the fascist camp; the workers are leaving it for the Communist Party. Only these two groups are growing in Germany: fascism and Bolshevism. Even though Russia on the one hand and Italy on the other are countries incomparably more backward than Germany, nevertheless they have both served as arenas for the development of political movements which are inherent in imperialist capitalism as such. Advanced Germany must recapitulate the processes which reached their fulfilment in Russia and Italy. The fundamental problem of German development may be at present formulated thus: which way out—the way of Russia or the way of Italy?

Obviously, this does not mean that the highly developed social structure is of no significance from the point of view of the development of the destinies of Bolshevism and fascism. Italy is a petty-bourgeois and peasant country to a much greater degree than Germany. One need only recall that to 9.8 million engaged in farming and forestry in Germany there are 18.5 million employed in industry and trade; that is, almost twice as many. Whereas in Italy, to 10.3 million engaged in farming and forestry there are 6.4 million employed in industry and trade. These bare totals do not by far give an adequate representation of the preponderant relative weight of the proletariat in the life of the German nation. Even the tremendous number of the unemployed is only a proof, turned inside out, of the social might of the German proletariat. The whole question consists in how to translate this might into the language of revolutionary politics.

The last major defeat of the German party, which can be placed on the same historical board with the September days in Italy, dates back to 1923. During the more than eight years that have elapsed since, many wounds have been healed and a new generation has risen to its feet. The German party represents an incomparably greater force than did the Italian Communists in 1922. The relative weight of the proletariat; the considerable time elapsed since its last defeat; the considerable strength of the Communist Party—these are the three advantages, which bear a great significance for the general summation of the background and of the perspectives.

But to make the best of one's advantages, one must understand them. That is lacking. Thälmann's position in 1932 reproduces Bordiga's in 1922. In this direction, the danger takes on a particularly acute character. But here too there exists one supplementary advantage which was non-existent ten years ago. Within the revolutionary ranks in Germany there is a Marxist opposition, which leans upon the experience of the preceding decade. This opposition is weak numerically, but the march of events adds extraordinary strength to its voice. Under certain conditions a slight shock may bring down an avalanche. The critical shock of the Left Opposition can aid in bringing about a timely change in the politics of the proletarian vanguard. In this lies our task at present!

8. Through the United Front—to the Soviets as the highest organs of the United Front

Verbal genuflections before the soviets are equally as fashionable in the 'left' circles as the misconception of their historical function. Most often the soviets are defined as the organs of struggle for power, as the organs of insurrection, and finally as the organs of dictatorship. Formally these definitions are correct. But they do not at all exhaust the historical function of the soviets. First of all they do not explain why, in the struggle for power, precisely the soviets are necessary. The answer to this question is: just as the trade union is the rudimentary form of the united front in the economic struggle, so *the soviet is the highest form of the united front* under the conditions in which the proletariat enters the epoch of fighting for power.

The soviet in itself possesses no miraculous powers. It is the class representation of the proletariat, with all of the latter's strong and weak points. But precisely and only because of this does the soviet afford to the workers of diverse political trends the organisational opportunity to unite their efforts in the revolutionary struggle for power. In the present pre-revolutionary environment it is the duty of the most advanced German workers to understand most clearly the historical function of the soviets as the organs of the united front.

Could the Communist Party succeed, during the preparatory epoch, in pushing all other parties out of the ranks of the workers by uniting under its banner the overwhelming majority of the workers, then there would be no need whatever for soviets. But historical experience bears witness to the fact that there is no basis whatever for the expectation that in any single country—in countries with an old capitalist culture even less than in backward ones—the Communist Party can succeed in occupying such an undisputed and absolutely commanding position in the workers' ranks, prior to the proletarian overturn.

Precisely in Germany today are we shown that the proletariat is faced with the task of a direct and immediate struggle for power, long before it has been completely united under the banner of the Communist Party. The revolutionary situation itself, if approached on the political plane, arises from the fact that all groups and layers of the proletariat, or at least their overwhelming majority, are seized with the urge to unite their efforts in changing the existing regime. This does not mean, however, that they all understand how to do it; and still less that they are ready at the very moment to break with their parties and to join the ranks of the Communists. The political conscience of the class does not mature so methodically and uniformly; deep inner divergences remain even in the revolutionary epoch, when all processes develop by leaps and bounds.

But, at the same time, the need for an organisation above parties and embracing the entire class becomes extremely urgent. To crystallise this need into a form—that is the historic destiny of the soviets. That is their great function. Under the conditions of a revolutionary situation they arise as the highest organised expression of proletarian unity. Those who haven't understood this, have understood nothing in matters relating to the problem of the soviets. Thälmann, Neumann, and Remmele may keep on writing articles and uttering speeches about the future 'Soviet Germany' without end. By their present policies they are sabotaging the inception of the soviets in Germany.

Removed from the actual sphere of action, unable to gather direct impressions from the masses or to place a hand daily on the pulse of the working class, it is very difficult to forecast the transitional forms which lead in Germany to the creation of soviets. In another connection I offered the hypothesis that the German soviets may arise as an expanded form of the factory committees: in this, I leaned chiefly on the experience in 1923. But of course that is not the only way. Under the pressure of want and unemployment on the one hand and the onset of the fascists on the other, the need for revolutionary unity may all at once come to the surface in the form of soviets, skipping the factory committees. But whichever way the soviets arise, they cannot become anything save the organisational expression of the strong and weak sides of the proletariat, of its inner contradictions and the general urge to overcome them; in short, the organs of the united front.

The Social Democracy and the Communist Party divide in Germany the influence over the working class. The Social Democratic leadership does its best to repel the workers from itself. The leadership of the Communist Party strives with all its might to counteract the influx of the workers. As a consequence we get the formation of a third party and a comparatively slow change in the correlation of forces in favour of the Communists. But even if Communist Party policies were entirely correct, the workers' need for a revolutionary unification of the class would have grown incomparably faster than the preponderance of the Communist Party within the class. The need of creating soviets would thus remain in its full scope.

The creation of the soviets presupposes that the different parties and organisations within the working class, beginning with the factories, become agreed, both as regards the very necessity for the soviets and as regards the time and methods of their formation. Which means: since the soviets, in themselves, represent the highest form of the united front in the revolutionary epoch, therefore their inception must be preceded by the policy of the united front in the preparatory period.

Is it necessary to recall once again that in the course of six months in 1917, the soviets in Russia had a conciliationist Social Revolutionary-Menshevik majority? Without renouncing for one moment its revolutionary independence as a party, the Bolshevik Party observed, within the framework of soviet activities, discipline in relation to the majority. There isn't the slightest doubt that in Germany, from the very first day on which the first soviet is formed, the Communist Party will occupy in it a place much more important than that of the Bolsheviks in the soviets of March 1917. Nor is the possibility excluded that the Communists would very shortly receive the majority in the soviets. This would not in any way deprive the soviets of their significance as the apparatus of the united front, because the minority—the Social Democratic, non-party, Catholic workers, etc—would at first still number millions; and any attempt to hurdle such a minority is the best conceivable method of breaking one's neck under the most revolutionary conditions obtainable. But this is all the music of the future. Today, the Communist Party is in the minority. And that must serve as our point of departure.

What has been said above doesn't mean, of course, that the infallible means of achieving the soviets lies in preliminary agreements with Wels, Hilferding, Breitscheid, etc. If in 1918 Hilferding cudgelled his brain for ways of including the soviets in the Weimar Constitution without injuring the latter, then one must assume that his brain is now at work over the problem of how to include fascist barracks in the Weimar Constitution without damaging the Social Democracy... One must begin creating the soviets at the moment when the general condition of the proletariat permits soviets to be created, even against the will of the upper crust of the Social Democracy. But to do so, it is necessary to tear away the Social Democratic mass from the leading clique; and the way to do that is not by pretending it is already done. In order to separate the millions of Social Democratic workers from their reactionary leaders we must begin by showing these workers that we are ready to enter the soviets even with these 'leaders.'

One must not, however, discount entirely beforehand the possibility that top layers of the Social Democracy will be once again compelled to venture into the red-hot atmosphere of the soviets in order to try to repeat the manoeuvre of Ebert, Scheidemann, Haase, etc, in 1918-1919: here the outcome will depend not so much on the bad faith of these gentlemen as upon the degree and manner in which history will seize them in its vice.

The formation of the first important local soviet in which the Communist and Social Democratic workers would represent not individuals but organisations, would have an enormous effect upon the entire German working class. Not only Social Democratic and non-party workers but also the Catholic and liberal workers would be unable long to resist the pull of the centripetal force. All the sections of the German proletariat most adapted to and capable of organisation would be drawn to the soviets, as are iron filings to the poles of a magnet. Within the soviets, the Communist Party would obtain a new and exceptionally favourable arena for fighting for the leading role in the proletarian revolution. One may hold absolutely incontrovertible the statement that even today the overwhelming majority of the Social Democratic apparatus would be participating within the framework of soviets, had not the leadership of the Communist Party so zealously aided the Social Democratic leaders in paralysing the pressure of the masses.

If the Communist Party holds inadmissible any agreement

on a programme of definite practical tasks with Social Democratic, trade-union and other organisations, then this means nothing else but that it holds inadmissible the joint creation of the soviets together with the Social Democracy. And since there cannot be purely Communist soviets, and since, indeed, there wouldn't be any need of them in that case, then *the refusal by the Communist Party to make agreements and take joint action with other parties within the working class means nothing else but the refusal to create soviets.*

Die Rote Fahne will doubtless answer this deduction with a volley of curses, and proceed to prove that just as two times two are four, so am I surely Brüning's campaign agent, Wels' secret ally, etc. I am ready to stand indicted under all these charges, but under one condition: that *Die Rote Fahne* on its part undertakes to explain to the German workers when and in what manner the soviets may be organised in Germany without accepting the policies of the united front in relation to other workers' organisations.

Just to clarify the question of the soviets as the organs of the united front, the opinions expressed on this subject by one of the provincial communist papers, *Der Klassenkampf* of Halle-Merseburg, are extremely instructive. 'All workers' organisations,' says this paper ironically,

> in their present form, with all their faults and weaknesses, must be combined into great anti-fascist defensive unions. What does this mean? We may dispense with lengthy theoretic explanations; history itself proved a severe teacher in these questions to the German working class: the formless hodge-podge united front of all workers' organisations was paid for by the German working class at the price of the lost revolution in 1918-1919.

In truth, an unsurpassable sample of superficial verbiage!

In 1918-1919, the united front was realised primarily through the soviets. Should the Spartacists have entered the soviets or shouldn't they? According to the exact meaning of the passage cited, they should have remained apart from the soviets. But since the Spartacists represented only a small minority of the working class, and since they could in no way substitute for the

Social Democratic soviets their own, then their isolation from the soviets would have meant simply their isolation from the revolution. If the united front was 'formless' and a 'hodge-podge', the fault lay not with the soviets, as the organs of the united front, but with the political condition of the working class itself; with the weakness of the Spartakusbund; and with the extreme power of the Social Democracy. The united front, in general, is never a substitute for a strong revolutionary party; it can only aid the latter to become stronger. This applies fully to the soviets. The weak Spartakusbund, by its fear to let slip the extraordinary occasion, was pushed into taking ultra-left courses and premature demonstrations. Had the Sparticists kept apart from the united front, that is, the soviets, these negative traits would undoubtedly have been yet more sharply pronounced.

Can it be possible that these people have gathered nothing at all from the experience of the German revolution in 1918-1919? Have they at least read **Left-Wing Communism**? Truly, the Stalinist regime has caused a mental havoc that is horrifying! After bureaucratising the soviets in the USSR, the epigones look upon them as a technical weapon in the hands of the party apparatus. Forgotten is the fact that the soviets were founded as workers' parliaments and that they drew the masses because they offered the possibility of welding together all sections of the proletariat, independently of party distinctions; forgotten is the fact that therein precisely lay the great educational and revolutionary power of the soviets. Everything is forgotten; everything is jumbled and distorted. O, thrice-cursed epigonism!

The question of the interrelationship between the party and the soviets is of decisive importance for revolutionary policy. While the present course of the party is in fact directed towards supplanting the soviets by the party, Hugo Urbahns, loath to miss the opportunity to add to the confusion, is preparing to supplant the party by the soviets. According to a **Sozialistische Arbeiter Zeitung** dispatch, Urbahns, in refuting the pretension of the Communist Party to the leadership of the working class, said at a meeting in Berlin, in January: 'The leadership will be kept in the hands of the soviets, elected by the masses themselves and not in accordance with the desires or at the discretion of the one and only party. (Violent applause.)'

One can easily understand that by its ultimatism the Communist Party irritates the workers, who are ready to applaud every protest against bureaucratic presumption. But this does not alter the fact that Urbahns in this question as well has nothing in common with Marxism. No one will gainsay that the workers will elect the soviets 'themselves'. But the whole question lies in *whom* they will elect. We must enter the soviets together with all other organisations such as they are, 'with all their faults and weaknesses.' But to avow that the soviets 'by themselves' are capable of leading the struggle of the proletariat for power—is only to sow abroad vulgar soviet fetishism. Everything depends upon the party that leads the soviets. Therefore, in contradistinction to Urbahns, the Bolshevik-Leninists do not all deny the Communist Party the right to lead the soviets; on the contrary, they say: 'Only on the basis of the united front, only through the mass organisations, can the KPD *conquer* the leading position within the future soviets and lead the proletariat to the conquest of power.'

9. The SAP (Socialist Workers Party of Germany)

Only functionaries gone mad, who are sure they can do anything, or stupid parrots, who repeat epithets without understanding their meaning, can label the SAP as a 'social fascist' or 'counter-revolutionary' party. Yet it would be an act of inexcusable lightmindedness and cheap optimism to place one's faith, in advance, in an organisation which after breaking with the Social Democracy still finds itself midway between reformism and Communism, under a leadership which is closer to reformism than to Communism. In respect to this question as well, the Left Opposition does not assume the slightest responsibility for Urbahns's politics.

The SAP is without a programme. We are not discussing the matter of a formal document; the programme holds water only in the event that its text is tied up with the revolutionary experience of the party and with the lessons gained from battles which have entered into the flesh and blood of its cadres. The SAP has none of these. The Russian Revolution, its separate stages, the struggle of its factions; the German crises of 1923;

the civil war in Bulgaria; the events of the Chinese Revolutions; the battles of the British proletariat (1926); the revolutionary crisis in Spain—all these events, which must live in the consciousness of a revolutionist as luminous guideposts for the political road, are for the cadres of the SAP only murky recollections culled from newspapers and not revolutionary experiences lived through and assimilated.

That a workers' party is compelled to carry out the policy of the united front—that is not to be gainsaid. But the policy of the united front has its dangers. Only an experienced and a tested revolutionary party can carry on this policy successfully. In any case, the policy of the united front cannot serve as a programme for a revolutionary party. And in the meantime, the entire activity of the SAP is now being built on it. As a result, the policy of the united front is carried over into the party itself, that is, it serves to smear over the contradictions between the various tendencies. And that is precisely the fundamental function of centrism.

The daily paper of the SAP is steeped in the spirit of going fifty-fifty. Despite Ströbel's departure, the paper remains semi-pacifist and not Marxist. Isolated revolutionary articles do not change its physiognomy; on the contrary, they only accentuate it. The paper goes into raptures over Küster's letter to Brüning on militarism which is, in spirit, tasteless and petty-bourgeois through and through. It applauds a Danish 'socialist,' former minister to His Majesty, for refusing to accept a place in the government delegation upon terms too degrading. Centrism is content with trifles. But the revolution demands a great deal. The revolution demands everything—absolutely everything.

The SAP condemns the trade-union policy of the Communist Party: the splitting of the unions and the formation of the RGO (Revolutionary Trade Union Opposition). Undoubtedly the policy of the Communist Party in the sphere of the trade unions is extremely erroneous: Lozovsky's leadership is not being bought cheaply by the international proletarian vanguard. But the criticism of the SAP is not a bit less false. The fault of the Communist Party does not lie in that it 'splits' the ranks of the proletariat, and 'weakens' the Social Democratic unions. That is not a revolutionary criterion because, under the present leadership, the unions serve not the workers, but the capitalists. The Communist Party is guilty of a crime not because it 'weakens' Leipart's organisation but because it weakens itself. The participation of the Communists in reactionary unions is dictated not by the abstract principle of unity but by the concrete necessity to wage battle in order to purge the organisations of the agents of capital. With the SAP this active, revolutionary, attacking element in the policy is made subservient to the bald principle of the unity of unions that are led by agents of capital.

The SAP accuses the Communist Party of a leaning toward putschism. Such an accusation is also borne out by certain facts and methods; but before it has the right to fling this accusation, the SAP must formulate in detail and show in action its own attitude to the basic questions of the proletarian revolution. The Mensheviks were forever accusing the Bolsheviks of Blanquism and adventurism i.e., of putschism. On the contrary, the Leninist strategy was as far removed from putschism as heaven is from earth. But Lenin himself understood and taught others to understand the significance of 'the art of insurrection' in the proletarian struggle.

The criticism of the SAP in this respect becomes all the more suspicious in character the more it leans upon the authority of Paul Levi, who became frightened of the infantile diseases of the Communist Party and preferred to them the senile complications of the Social Democracy. During the intimate conferences on the events of March 1921 in Germany, Lenin said about Levi: 'The man has lost his head entirely.' True, Lenin immediately added slyly: 'He, at least, had something to lose; one can't even say that about the others.' The term 'others' denoted Bela Kun, Thalheimer, etc. No one can deny that Paul Levi had a head on his shoulders. But the man who lost his head and in that condition made a leap from the ranks of the Communists into the ranks of the reformists, is hardly qualified to be a teacher for a proletarian party. The tragic end of Levi, his leaping out of a window in an irresponsible state of mind, seems to symbolise his political orbit.

Although for the masses centrism is only a transition from one stage to the next, for individual politicians centrism can become a second nature. At the head of the SAP stands a group of desperate Social Democratic functionaries, lawyers, and journalists—all people of such an age that one must consider their political education as having been completed. A desperate Social Democrat still does not mean a revolutionist.

Representative of this type—its best representative—is Georg Ledebour. Not long ago I chanced to read the official report of his trial in 1919. And while reading, more than once I mentally applauded the old warrior, for his sincerity, his temperament, and his nobility of nature. But Ledebour just the same did not step over the boundaries of centrism. Wherever the matter touches mass actions, the highest forms of class struggle, their preparation, and the assumption by the party of the outright responsibility of leadership in mass battles, there Ledebour remains only the best representative of centrism. This separates him from Liebknecht and Rosa Luxemburg. It separates him from us now.

Indignant over Stalin's accusation that the radical wing of the old German Social Democracy is passive in its attitude to the struggle of oppressed nations, Ledebour in response refers to the fact that he always had evinced great initiative on precisely national questions. Ledebour personally never failed to respond with great passion to the notes of chauvinism in the old German Social Democracy, not at all hiding thereby his own powerfully developed national feeling. Ledebour was always the best friend of Russian, Polish, and other revolutionary emigrants; and many of them preserve a cherished memory of the old revolutionist, who in the ranks of the Social Democratic bureaucracy was referred to with patronising irony either as 'Ledebourov' or 'Ledeboursky.'

Nevertheless Stalin, who is acquainted with neither the facts nor the literature of that period, is correct on this point, at least insofar as he repeats Lenin's general appraisal. In his attempt to refute, Ledebour only corroborates this appraisal. He advances the fact that in his articles he gave vent to his indignation more than once over the complacency with which the parties of the Second International observed the handiwork of their fellow members; Ramsay MacDonald, for instance, while he was solving India's national problems with the aid of bombing planes. This indignation and protest provides an undebatable and honourable distinction between Ledebour and an Otto Bauer, not to mention the Hilferdings and the Welses; those gentlemen lack only an India for proceeding with democratic bombings.

Nevertheless, Ledebour's position even on this question does not leave the precincts of centrism. Ledebour demands that a battle be waged against colonial oppression; he is ready to vote in parliament against colonial credits; he is ready to take upon himself a fearless defence of the victims of a crushed colonial insurrection. But Ledebour will not participate in preparing a colonial insurrection. Such work he considers putschism, adventurism, Bolshevism. And therein is the whole gist of the matter.

What characterises Bolshevism on the national question is that in its attitude toward oppressed nations, even the most backward, it considers them not only the object but also the subject of politics. Bolshevism does not confine itself to recognising their 'right' to self-determination and to parliamentary protests against the trampling upon of this right. Bolshevism penetrates into the midst of the oppressed nations; it raises them up against their oppressors; it ties up their struggle with the struggle of the proletariat in capitalist countries; it instructs the oppressed Chinese, Hindus, or Arabs in the art of insurrection and it assumes full responsibility for this work in the face of civilised executioners. Here only does Bolshevism begin, that is revolutionary Marxism in action. Everything that does not step over this boundary remains centrism.

The policy of a proletarian party can never be appraised solely on the basis of national criteria. The Marxist holds this as an axiom. What then are the international connections and sympathies of the SAP? Norwegian, Swedish and Dutch centrists, organisations, groups, or individuals, whose passive and provincial character enables them to straddle between reformism and Communism—such are its closest friends. Angelica Balabanoff is the symbolic figure for the international affiliations of the SAP; she is even now busy trying to merge the new party with the shreds of the Two-and-a-half International!

Leon Blum, the defender of reparations, the socialist godfather of the banker Oustric, is termed 'comrade' in the pages of Seydewitz's paper. What is this, politeness? No, lack of principle, lack of character, lack of backbone! 'Petty quibbling,' some office wiseacre will reply. No, these trifles reveal the political under-current much more correctly and honestly than does the abstract recognition of the soviets, which is not attested by revolutionary experience. There is no sense in making oneself ridiculous by calling Blum a fascist. But he who does not feel hatred and disgust toward this political breed—is no revolutionist.

The SAP divorces itself from 'comrade' Otto Bauer within the same limits as does Max Adler. To Rosenfeld and Seydewitz, Bauer is only an ideological antagonist, perhaps even a temporary one, whereas to us he is an irreconcilable foe who has led the proletariat of Austria into a fearful quagmire.

Max Adler — there one has quite a sensitive centrist barometer. One cannot deny the usefulness of such an instrument, but one must know definitely that while it is capable of registering changes in the weather, it is incapable of acting on them. Under the pressure of the capitalist *impasse*, Max Adler is ready once again, not without philosophic grief, to accept the inevitability of revolution. But what an acceptance! What reservations! What sighs! The best thing possible would be for the Second and Third Internationals to merge. The most would be gained if socialism were installed in a democratic manner. But, alas, this method is apparently impossible. It seems that even in civilised countries, not only among barbarians, the workers will have to—O me, O my—make a revolution. But even this melancholy acceptance of the revolution is—only a literary fact. Such conditions as would enable Max Adler to say 'The hour has struck' never obtained in history and never will.

People like Adler are capable of justifying the revolution in the past, and of accepting its inevitability in the future, but they can never issue a call to it in the present. One must accept as hopeless this entire group of old left Social Democrats who were changed neither by the imperialist war nor by the Russian Revolution. As barometric instruments—if you please. As revolutionary leaders— never.

Towards the end of September, the SAP issued an appeal to all workers' organisations that meetings be organised during which orators of every tendency would be allotted equal times. It is plain enough that nothing can be achieved in that fashion. Indeed, what sense can there be in the Communist Party or the

Social Democratic Party sharing the platform on equal terms with Brandler and Urbahns and the spokesmen of other organisations and groups too insignificant to pretend to a special place in the movement? The united front is to unite the Communist and Social Democratic working masses and not to patch up an agreement with political groups that are without the masses.

We shall be told that the bloc between Rosenfeld-Brandler-Urbahns is only a propaganda bloc for the united front. But it is precisely in the sphere of propaganda that a bloc is out of the question. Propaganda must lean upon clear-cut principles and on a definite programme. March separately, strike together. A bloc is solely for practical mass actions. Deals arranged from above which lack a basis in principle will bring nothing except confusion.

The idea of nominating a candidate for president on the part of the united workers' front is at its root a false one. A candidate can be nominated only on the grounds of a definite programme. The party has no right to sacrifice during elections the mobilisation of its supporters and the census of its strength. The party candidacy, in opposition to all other candidates, can in no instance conflict with any agreement made with other organisations for immediate aims of struggle. Communists, whether official members of the party or not, will support Thälmann's candidacy to their utmost. What we are concerned with is not Thälmann but the banner of Communism. We shall defend it against all other parties. Breaking down the prejudices with which the rank and file of the Communists have been inoculated by the Stalinist bureaucracy, the Left Opposition will clear the road into their consciousness for itself.*

What were the policies of the Bolsheviks in relation to those workers' organisations that developed from the left of reformism or centrism toward Communism?

In Petrograd, in 1917, there existed an intermediate inter-district organisation, embracing about 4,000 workers. The Bolshevik organisation in Petrograd counted tens of thousands

* Unfortunately, an article was printed in **Die Permanente Revolution**, not an editorial one, true enough, but in defence of a single workers' candidate. There cannot be any doubt that the German Bolshevik-Leninists will condemn such a position.

of workers. Nevertheless, the Petrograd Committee of the Bolsheviks entered into agreements on every question with the inter-district organisation and advised it of all plans and in this way facilitated the complete merger.

It might be argued that the inter-district workers were politically close to the Bolsheviks. But the matter was not confined solely to the inter-district workers. When the Menshevik-Internationalists (Martov's group) aligned themselves against the social patriots, the Bolsheviks left nothing undone in order to achieve joint action with the Martovists, and if in the majority of instances this was not achieved, it was not the Bolsheviks who were to blame. Incidentally, one must add the fact that the Menshevik-internationalists formally remained within the framework of their party in common with Tseretelli and Dan.

The same tactic, but in an immeasurably wider scope, was likewise applied in relation to the Left Social Revolutionaries. The Bolsheviks even drew a section of the Left Social Revolutionaries into the Revolutionary War Committee, i.e., the organ of the overturn, although at the time the Left Social Revolutionaries still belonged to the same party with Kerensky against whom the overturn was directly aimed. Of course, this was not very logical procedure on the part of the Left Social Revolutionariess and it showed that not everything was in order in their heads. But if one waited until everything was in order in everybody's head, there would never have been victorious revolutions on this earth. Subsequently, the Bolsheviks concluded a governmental bloc with the party of the Left Social Revolutionaries (left 'Kornilovists,' or left 'fascists' according to the new terminology), which lasted a few months, and broke up only after the insurrection of the Left Social Revolutionaries.

Here is how Lenin summarised the experience of the Bolsheviks in relation to the left-leaning centrists:

The correct tactic of the Communists must consist of exploiting these vacillations, and not at all of ignoring them: to exploit them, *concessions* must necessarily be made to those elements which turn to the proletariat and join ranks with it when and wherever and insofar as they do so in the struggle against those elements which turn to the bourgeoisie... By making a rapid-fire decision 'to dispense with all compromises whatsoever and not to tack or veer on our course', one can only do harm to the further strengthening of the revolutionary proletariat...

In this question as well, the tactic of the Bolsheviks had nothing in common with bureaucratic ultimatism.

It is not so long since Thälmann and Remmele were themselves in an independent party. If they strain their memories they will succeed perhaps in recalling their political sensibilities during those years when, after breaking with the Social Democrats, they joined an independent party and pushed it to the left. Suppose somebody had then said to them that they only represented 'the left wing of the monarchist counter-revolution'? In all probability they would have concluded that their accuser was either drunk or crazy. And yet this is just their manner at present of defining the SAP!

Let us recall the manner in which Lenin reasoned upon the inception of an independent party:

> Why is it that in Germany the same, entirely identical [with that in Russia 1917] gravitation of the workers from the right to the left has brought not the immediate strengthening of the Communists but of the intermediate party of the 'Independents' at first?... Obviously one of the causes for this lies in the erroneous tactic of the German Communists, who should admit their mistake fearlessly and honestly and who must learn how to correct it... Their mistake originated in the numerous manifestations of that 'left' infantile disease, which has now broken out openly, and which will be cured all the better and sooner and to the greatest advantage of the organism.

Yes, this was indeed written just for the present moment!

The present German Communist Party is much stronger than the then Spartakusbund. But if today there appears the second edition of the independent party, under the same leadership in part, then the blame for it that falls upon the Communist Party is so much the greater.

The SAP is a contradictory fact. Of course, it would have been best had the workers joined the Communist Party directly. But for this, the Communist Party must have another policy and another leadership. In appraising the SAP, one must take one's point of departure not from an ideal Communist Party, but from the one that actually exists. To the extent to which the Communist Party, remaining on the positions of bureaucratic ultimatism, counteracts the centrifugal forces within the Social Democracy, to that extent, the inception of the SAP is an inevitable and a progressive fact.

The progressive character of this fact is, however, extremely weakened by the centrist leadership. Should the latter entrench itself, it will wreck the SAP. To reconcile oneself with the centrism of the SAP for the sake of its general progressive role would mean that one would thereby liquidate its progressive role.

The conciliationist, compromising elements that stand at the head of the party are experienced manoeuvrers, and they will smear over the contradictions and put off the crisis. But these means will suffice only until the first serious onset of events. The crisis within the party may develop at the very moment that the revolutionary crisis flares up, and it may paralyse its proletarian elements.

The task of the Communists consists in giving timely aid to the workers of the SAP to purge their ranks of centrism and to rid themselves of the leadership of their centrist leaders. To achieve this, it is imperative that nothing be hushed, that good intentions be not accepted for deeds, and that all things be called by their names. But only criticise, not vilify. One must seek ways for coming together and not hold one's fist ready to slam away.

Regarding the left wing of the independent party, Lenin wrote:

> To fear compromise with this wing of the party—that is simply comical. On the contrary, it is obligatory that the Communists seek and find a suitable form for a compromise with them; i.e., such a compromise as would on the one hand facilitate and hasten the inevitable final fusion with this wing; and on the other in no way hamper the Commun-

ists in their ideological political battle against the right wing of the Independents.

There is nothing to add even today to this tactical course.

To the left elements of the SAP we say: 'Revolutionists are tempered not only during struggles for the correct policies of their own party. Take the "twenty-one conditions" worked out, in their own time, for the admission of new parties into the Comintern. Take the works of the Left Opposition where the "twenty-one conditions" are applied to the political developments of the last eight years. In the light of these "conditions" open a planned attack against centrism within your own ranks and lead the matter to its conclusion. Otherwise nothing will remain for you except the hardly respectable role of serving as a left cover for centrism.'

And then what? And then—face in the direction of the Communist Party. Revolutionists do not ever straddle fences between the Social Democracy and the Communist Party, as Rosenfeld and Seydewitz would like to. No, the Social Democratic leaders represent the agencies of the class enemy within the proletariat. The Communist leaders, though confused, poor, and incapable, are revolutionists or semi-revolutionists that have been led from the right track. That is not one and the same thing. The Social Democracy must be destroyed. The Communist Party must be corrected. You say that this is impossible? But have you seriously tried working at it?

Just now, at this very moment, when events are pressing down on the Communist Party, we must help the events with the onset of our criticism. The Communist workers will all the more attentively listen to us the sooner they are convinced in action that we do not seek a 'third' party but are sincerely straining to help them turn the present Communist Party into an authentic leader of the working class.

And what if we don't succeed?

Should we not succeed, that would almost certainly signify in the given historical environment the victory of fascism. But on the eve of great battles the revolutionist does not ask what will be if he fails but how to perform that which means success. It is possible, it can be done—therefore it must be done.

10. Centrism 'in general' and centrism of the Stalinist Bureaucracy

The errors of the leadership of the Comintern and consequently the errors of the German Communist Party pertain, in the familiar terminology of Lenin, to the category of 'ultra-left stupidities'. Even wise men are capable of stupidities, especially when young. But, as Heine counselled, this privilege should not be abused. When, however, political stupidities of a given type are repeated systematically in the course of a lengthy period, and moreover in the sphere of the most important questions, then they cease being simply stupidities and become tendencies. What sort of a tendency is this? What historical necessities does it meet? What are its social roots?

Ultra-leftism has a different social foundation in different countries and at different periods. The most thoroughgoing expressions of ultra-leftism were to be found in anarchism and Blanquism, and in their different combinations, among them the latest one, anarcho-syndicalism.

The social soil for these trends which have spread primarily through Latin countries was to be found in the old and classic small industries of Paris. Their stability added an indubitable significance to the French varieties of ultra-radicalism and allowed them to a certain degree to influence ideologically the workers' movements in other countries. The development of large-scale industries in France, the war, and the Russian Revolution broke the spine of anarcho-syndicalism. Having been thrown back, it has become transformed into a debased opportunism. At both of its stages French syndicalism is headed by one and the same Jouhaux; the times change and we change with them.

Spanish anarcho-syndicalism preserved its seeming revolutionary character only in the environment of political stagnation. By posing all the questions point-blank, the revolution has compelled the anarcho-syndicalist leaders to cast off their ultra-radicalism and to reveal their opportunist nature. We can rest definitely assured that the Spanish revolution will drive out the prejudice of syndicalism from its last Latin hide-out.

The anarchist and Blanquist elements join all kinds of other ultra-left trends and groups. On the periphery of a great revolutionary movement there are always to be observed the manifestations of putschism and adventurism, the standard-bearers of which are recruited either from backward and quite often semi-artisan strata of the workers, or from the intellectual fellow travellers. But such a type of ultra-leftism does not attain ordinarily to independent historical significance, retaining, in most instances, its episodic character.

In historically backward countries, which are compelled to go through their bourgeois revolutions within the environment of a full-fledged and worldwide workers' movement, the left intelligentsia often introduces the most extreme slogans and methods into the semi-elementary movements of the predominantly petty-bourgeois masses. Such is the nature of petty-bourgeois parties of the type of the Russian Social Revolutionaries, with their tendencies toward putschism, individual terrorism, etc. Thanks to the effectiveness of the Communist parties in the West, the independent adventuristic groups will hardly attain there to the importance of the Russian Social Revolutionaries. But on this account the young Communist parties of the West may include within themselves the elements of adventurism. As regards the Russian Social Revolutionaries, under the influence of the evolution of bourgeois society they have become transformed into the party of the imperialist petty bourgeoisie and have taken a counter-revolutionary position in relation to the October Revolution.

It is entirely self-evident that the ultra-leftism of the present Comintern does not fall under any one of the above specified historic types. The chief party of the Comintern, the CPSU, as is well known, leans upon the industrial proletariat, and operates for better or for worse from the revolutionary traditions of Bolshevism. The majority of other sections of the Comintern are proletarian organisations. Are not the very differences in conditions in the various countries in which the ultra-left policies of official Communism are raging simultaneously and to the same degree, tokens of the fact that there are no common roots underlying this trend? Indeed, an ultra-left course is being taken in China and in Great Britain, moreover one having the same 'principled' character. But if so, where are we then to seek for the key to the new ultra-leftism?

The question is complicated, but at the same time is also clarified by one other extremely important circumstance: ultra-leftism is not at all an unvarying or a fundamental trait of the present leadership of the Comintern. The same apparatus, in its basic composition, held to an openly opportunistic policy until 1928, and in many of the most important questions switched over completely onto the tracks of Menshevism. During 1924-27, agreements with reformists were not only considered obligatory but were permitted even if thereby the party renounced its independence, its freedom of criticism, and even its proletarian foundation.* Therefore the discussion concerns not at all a particular ultra-left trend, but a prolonged ultra-left zigzag of such a trend as has demonstrated in the past its capacity for launching into profound ultra-right zigzags. Even these outward symptoms suggest that what we are dealing with is centrism.

Speaking formally and descriptively, centrism is composed of all those trends within the proletariat and on its periphery which are distributed between reformism and Marxism, and which most often represent various stages of evolution from reformism to Marxism—and vice versa. Both Marxism and reformism have a solid social support underlying them. Marxism expresses the historical interests of the proletariat. Reformism speaks for the privileged position of proletarian bureaucracy and aristocracy within the capitalist state. Centrism, as we have known it in the past, did not have and could not have an independent social foundation. Different layers of the proletariat develop in the revolutionary direction in different ways and at different times. In periods of prolonged industrial uplift or in the periods of political ebb tide, after defeats, different layers of the proletariat shift politically from left to right, clashing with other layers who are just beginning to evolve to the left. Different groups are delayed on separate stages of their evolution; they find their temporary leaders and they create their programmes and organisations. Small wonder then that such a diversity of trends is embraced in the concept of 'centrism'! Depending upon

* A detailed analysis of this opportunistic chapter of the Comintern that lasted a few years is given in our works **The Third International after Lenin, The Permanent Revolution**, and **Who is leading the Comintern today?**

their origin, their social composition, and the direction of their evolution, different groupings may be engaged in the most savage warfare with one another, without losing thereby their character of being a variety of centrism.

While centrism *in general* fulfils ordinarily the function of serving as a left cover for reformism, the question as to which of the basic camps, reformist or Marxist, *a given* centrism may belong, cannot be solved once for all with a ready-made formula. Here, more than anywhere else, it is necessary to analyse each time the concrete composition of the process and the inner tendencies of its development. Thus, some of Rosa Luxemburg's political mistakes may be with sufficient theoretical justification characterised as left centrist. One could go still further and say that the majority of divergences between Rosa Luxemburg and Lenin represented a stronger or weaker leaning toward centrism. But only the idiots and ignoramuses and charlatans of the Comintern bureaucracy are capable of placing Luxemburgism, as an historical tendency, in the category of centrism. It goes without saying that the present 'leaders' of the Comintern, from Stalin down, politically, theoretically, and morally do not come up to the knees of the great woman and revolutionist.

Critics who have not pondered the gist of the matter have recently accused me more than once of abusing the word 'centrism' by including under this name too great a variety of tendencies and groups within the workers' movement. In reality, the diversity of the types of centrism originates, as has been said already, in the essence of the phenomenon itself and not at all in an abuse of terminology. We need only recall how often the Marxists have been accused of assigning to the petty bourgeoisie the most diverse and contradictory phenomena. And actually, under the category 'petty bourgeois', one is obliged to include facts, ideas, and tendencies that at first glance appear entirely incompatible. The petty-bourgeois character pertains to the peasant movement and to *the radical tendencies of urban reformism*; both French Jacobins and Russian Narodniks are petty bourgeois; Proudhonists are petty bourgeois, but so are Blanquists; contemporary Social Democracy is petty bourgeois, but so is fascism; also petty bourgeois are: the French anarcho-syndicalists, the 'Salvation Army', Gandhi's movement in India, etc. If we turn to the sphere of philosophy and art, a still more polychromatic picture obtains.

Does this mean that Marxism indulges in playing with terminology? Not at all; this only means that the petty bourgeoisie is *characterised by the extreme heterogeneity of its social nature*. At the bottom it fuses with the proletariat and extends into the lumpenproletariat; on top it passes over into the capitalist bourgeoisie. It may lean upon old forms of production but it may rapidly develop on the basis of most modern industry (the new 'middle class'). No wonder that ideologically it scintillates with all the colours of the rainbow.

Centrism within the workers' movement plays in a certain sense the same role as does petty-bourgeois ideology of all types in relation to bourgeois society as a whole. Centrism reflects the processes of the evolution of the proletariat, its political growth as well as its revolutionary setbacks conjoint with the pressure of all other classes of society upon the proletariat. No wonder that the palette of centrism is distinguished by such iridescence! From this it follows, however, not that one must give up trying to comprehend centrism but simply that one must discover the true nature of a given variety of centrism by means of a concrete and historical analysis in every individual instance.

The ruling faction of the Comintern does not represent centrism 'in general' but a quite definite historical form, which has its social roots, rather recent but powerful. First of all, the matter concerns the *Soviet bureaucracy*. In the writings of the Stalinist theoreticians this social stratum does not exist at all. We are only told of 'Leninism', of disembodied leadership, of the ideological tradition, of the spirit of Bolshevism, of the imponderable 'general line', but we never hear a word about the functionary, breathing and living, in flesh and bone, who manipulates the general line like a fireman his hose.

In the meantime this same functionary bears the least resemblance to an incorporeal spirit. He eats and guzzles and procreates and grows himself a respectable potbelly. He lays down the law with a sonorous voice, hand-picks from below people faithful to him, remains faithful to his superiors, prohibits others from criticising himself, and sees in all this the gist of the general line. Of such functionaries there are a few million. A few million! Their number is greater than the number of industrial workers in the period of the October Revolution.

The majority of these functionaries never participated in the class struggle, which is bound up with sacrifices, self-denials, and dangers. These people in their overwhelming mass began their political lives already in the category of a ruling layer. They are backed by the state power. It assures them their livelihood and raises them considerably above the surrounding masses. They know nothing of the dangers of unemployment, if they are gifted with the capacity to stand at attention. The grossest errors are forgiven them so long as they are ready to fulfil the role of the sacrificial scapegoat at the required moment, and thus remove the responsibility from the shoulders of their nearest superiors. Well, then, has this ruling stratum of many millions any social weight and political influence in the life of a country? Yes or no?

We know from older books that the labour bureaucracy and the labour aristocracy are the social foundation for opportunism. In Russia this phenomenon has taken on new forms. On the foundation of the dictatorship of the proletariat—in a backward country, surrounded by capitalism—for the first time a powerful bureaucratic apparatus has been created from among the upper layers of the workers, that is raised above the masses, that lays down the law to them, that has at its disposal colossal resources, that is bound together by an inner mutual responsibility, and that intrudes into the policies of a workers' government its own interests, methods, and regulations.

We are not anarchists. We understand the necessity of a workers' government and therefore the historical inevitability of a bureaucracy during a transitional period. But we likewise understand the dangers that are inherent in this fact, particularly for a backward and an isolated country. The idealisation of Soviet bureaucracy is the most shameful mistake than can be made by a Marxist. Lenin strove with all his might to raise the party as a self-acting vanguard of the working class above the governmental apparatus in order to control, check, direct, and purge it, placing the historical interests of the proletariat—international, not only national—above the interests of the ruling bureaucracy. As the first condition of the party control over the government Lenin prescribed control by the party masses over the party apparatus. Read over attentively his articles, speeches, and letters during the Soviet period, particularly for the last two years of his life—and you will remark with what alarm his mind turned time and again to this burning question.

But what has happened in the subsequent period? The entire leading stratum of the party and of the government that was at the helm during the revolution and the civil war has been replaced, removed, and crushed. Their place has been taken by the anonymous functionary. At the same time the struggle against bureaucratism which was so acute in character during Lenin's lifetime, when the bureaucracy was not yet out of its diapers, has ceased entirely now when the apparatus has grown sky-high.

And indeed, who is there capable of carrying on this struggle? The party as a self-controlling vanguard of the proletariat no longer exists now. The party apparatus has been fused with the administrative. The most important instrument of the general line within the party is the GPU. The bureaucracy not only prohibits the criticism of the top from below, but it also prohibits its theoreticians from even talking about it and noticing it. The mad hatred for the Left Opposition is aroused, first of all, by the fact that the Opposition talks openly about the bureaucracy, about its particular role and its interests, thus revealing the secret that the general line is inseparable from the flesh and blood of the new national ruling stratum, which is not at all identical with the proletariat.

From the proletarian character of the government, the bureaucracy deduces its birthright to infallibility: how can the bureaucracy of a *workers'* state degenerate? The state and the bureaucracy are thereby taken not as historical processes but as eternal categories: how can the holy church and its God-inspired priests sin? Yet, if a workers' bureaucracy which has raised itself over the proletariat, waging battle in a capitalist society, could degenerate into the party of Noske, Scheidemann, Ebert, and Wels, why can't it degenerate after raising itself over the victorious proletariat?

The ruling and uncontrolled position of the Soviet bureaucracy is conductive to a psychology which in many ways is directly contradictory to the psychology of a proletarian revolutionist. Its own aims and combinations in domestic as well as international politics are placed by the bureaucracy above the tasks of the revolutionary education of the masses and have no connection with the tasks of international revolution. In the course of a number of years the Stalinist faction demonstrated that the interests and the psychology of the prosperous peasant, engineer, administrator, Chinese bourgeois intellectual, and British trade-union functionary were much closer and more comprehensible to it than the psychology and the needs of the unskilled labourer, the peasant poor, the Chinese national masses in revolt, the British strikers, etc.

But why, in that case, didn't the Stalinist faction carry to the very end its line of national opportunism? Because it is the bureaucracy of a *workers'* state. While the international Social Democracy defends the foundations of the bourgeois sovereignty, the Soviet bureaucracy, not having achieved a governmental overturn, is compelled to adapt itself to the social foundations laid down by the October Revolution. From this is derived the dual psychology and politics of the Stalinist bureaucracy. *Centrism*, but centrism on the foundation of a *workers'* state, is the sole possible expression for this duality.

Whereas in capitalist countries, the centrist groupings are most often temporary or transitional in character, reflecting the evolution of certain workers' strata to the right or to the left, under the conditions of the Soviet republic centrism is equipped with a much more solid and organised base in the shape of a multi-millioned bureaucracy. Representing in itself a natural environment for opportunist and nationalist tendencies, it is compelled, however, to maintain the foundations of its hegemony in the struggle with the *kulak* [rich peasant] and also to bother about its 'Bolshevik' prestige in the worldwide movement. Following its attempted chase after the Kuomintang and the Amsterdam bureaucracy,[7] which in many ways is close to it spiritually, the Soviet bureaucracy each time entered into sharp conflict with the Social Democracy, which reflects the enmity of the world bourgeoisie to the Soviet state. Such are the sources of the present left zigzags.

The peculiarity of the situation arises not from the supposed special immunity of the Soviet bureaucracy to opportunism and nationalism but from the fact that, being unable to occupy a thoroughgoing national-reformist position, it is compelled to describe zigzags between Marxism and national reformism. The oscillations of this *bureaucratic centrism*, in conformity with its power, its resources, and the acute contradictions in its position, have attained an altogether unheard-of sweep: from ultra-left adventurism in Bulgaria and Estonia to the alliance with Chiang Kai-shek, Radich, and Purcell; and from the shameful fraternisation with British strikebreakers to a complete renunciation of the policy of the united front with mass organisations.

The Stalinist bureaucracy carries over its methods and zigzags to other countries, insofar as it not only leads the Comintern through the party apparatus but also lays down the law to it. Thälmann was for the Kuomintang when Stalin was for the Kuomintang. At the seventh plenum of the Executive Committee of the Comunnist International in the fall of 1926, the delegate of the Kuomintang, ambassador of Chiang Kai-shek, Shao Li-tsi by name, fraternally came forward together with Thälmann, Semard, and all the Remmeles against 'Trotskyism'. 'Comrade' Shao Li-tsi said: 'We are all convinced that under the leadership of the Comintern, the Kuomintang will fulfil its historic task.'[8] This is a historical fact!

If you take up *Die Rote Fahne* for 1926, you will find in it multitudinous articles all harping on one note, to wit, that by demanding a break with the British General Council of strikebreakers, Trotsky demonstrates his... Menshevism! And today 'Menshevism' consists already in defending the united front with mass organisations, that is, in applying that policy which was formulated by the Third and Fourth Congresses under the leadership of Lenin (against all the Thälmanns, Thalheimers, Bela Kuns, Frossards, etc).

These breakneck zigzags would have been impossible were it not for the fact that within all Communist sections a self-sufficient bureaucracy—i.e, independent of the party—had been formed. Here is the root of all evil!

The strength of a revolutionary party consists in the independence of its vanguard, which checks and selects its cadres and, while educating its leaders, gradually elevates them by its confidence. This creates an unbroken connection between the cadres and the mass, between the leaders and the cadres, and it induces in the entire leadership an inward confidence in themselves. There is nothing of the kind in the contemporary Communist parties! The leaders are appointed. They hand-pick their aides. The rank and file of the masses is forced to accept the appointed leaders, around whom there is built up the artificial atmosphere of publicity. The cadres depend upon the upper crust and not upon the underlying masses. Consequently, to a considerable degree they seek for the source of their influence as well as for the source of their livelihood outside of the masses. They draw their political slogans not from the experience in the struggle, but from the telegraph. And in the meantime Stalin's files secrete incriminating documents against possible emergency. Each leader knows that at any moment he can be blown away like a feather.

Thus, throughout the entire Comintern a closed bureaucratic stratum is being created which constitutes a culture broth for the bacilli of centrism. While organisationally it is very stable and solid, for it is backed by the bureaucracy of the Soviet state, the centrism of the Thälmanns, Remmeles & Co, is distinguished by extreme instability in political relations. Bereft of assurance, which can be derived only from an organic liaison with the masses, the infallible Central Executive Committee suffices only for monstrous zigzags. The less it is prepared for a serious ideological battle, the more proficient it is in profanity, insinuations, and calumnies. Stalin's image, 'coarse' and 'disloyal,' as described by Lenin, is the personification of this layer.

The characterisation of bureaucratic centrism given above determines the attitude of the Left Opposition to the Stalinist bureaucracy: a complete and unqualified support insofar as the bureaucracy defends the boundaries of the Soviet republic and the foundations of the October Revolution; an outspoken criticism insofar as the bureaucracy hinders by its administrative zigzags the defence of the revolution and of socialist construction; a merciless resistance insofar as it disorganises by its bureaucratic overlordship the struggle of the international proletariat.

11. The contradictions between the economic successes of the USSR and the bureaucratisation of the regime

One cannot work out the foundations of revolutionary policy 'in one country'. The problem of the German revolution is at present inextricably tied up with the question of political leadership in the USSR. This connection must be understood thoroughly.

The proletarian dictatorship is the reply to the resistance of the possessing classes. The restriction of liberties arises from the military regime of the revolution, i.e., from the conditions of the class war. From this point of view it is entirely self-evident that the inner stabilisation of the Soviet republic, its economic growth, and the weakening of the resistance of the bourgeoisie, especially the successes in 'liquidating' the last capitalist class, the *kulaks*, should result in the burgeoning of party, trade-union, and Soviet democracy.

The Stalinists never weary of repeating that 'we have already entered into socialism'; that the present collectivisation signifies by itself the liquidation of the *kulaks* as a class; and that the next five-year plan will carry these processes to their conclusion. That being so, why did this same process lead to the complete suppression of the party, the trade unions, and the soviets by the bureaucratic apparatus, while the latter in its turn has taken on the character of plebiscitarian Bonapartism? Why did the life of the party proceed in full swing in the days of famine and civil war? Why didn't it even enter into anyone's mind to question whether it was or wasn't permissible to criticise Lenin or the Central Executive Committee as a whole? And why does the slightest divergence with Stalin now lead to expulsion from the party and to administrative repressions?

The threat of war on the part of imperialist governments can in no case explain, much less justify, the growth of bureaucratic despotism. If within a national socialist society the classes have been liquidated more or less, then that should signify that the dissolution of the state is beginning. The socialist society may victoriously combat foes from without precisely as a socialist society and not as state of proletarian dictatorship, much less a bureaucratic one.

But we are not speaking of the dissolution of the dictatorship: it is too early for that, we have not as yet 'entered into socialism'. We speak of something else. We want to know: how to explain the bureaucratic degeneration of the dictatorship? What is the origin of the strident, monstrous and murderous contradiction between the successes of the socialist construction and the regime of personal dictatorship which leans upon an impersonal apparatus and which holds by the throat the ruling class of the nation? How explain the fact economics and politics are developing in directions directly opposite?

The economic successes are very great. Economically the October Revolution has justified itself fully even now. The high coefficients of economic growth are irrefutable demonstrations of the fact that socialist methods reveal themselves to be immeasurably superior even for the solving of those problems of production which were solved in the West by capitalist methods. How great then will be the superiority of socialist economy in the advanced countries!

Nevertheless, the question posed by the October overturn has not been answered as yet even in outline.

The Stalinist bureaucracy calls the economy 'socialist' on the strength of its postulates and tendencies. These are not enough. The economic successes of the Soviet Union are still taking shape on a low economic base. The nationalised industry is passing through stages which have been passed long since by the foremost capitalist nations. The working woman who stands in line has *her own* criterion of socialism, and this 'consumer's' criterion, as the functionary scornfully refers to it, is the decisive one in the given question. In the conflict between the views of the working woman and the bureaucrat, we, the Left Opposition, side with the working woman against the bureaucrat who exaggerates the achievements, glosses over the contradictions, and holds the working woman by the throat lest she dare criticise.

Last year, a sharp about-face was made from the equalised to the differential (piecework) working wage. It is absolutely undebatable that given a low level of productive forces and hence of general culture, equality in payment for labour cannot be realised. But this itself means that the problem of socialism is not solved by social forms of ownership only, but postulates a certain technical power of society. Meanwhile the growth of technical power automatically draws the productive forces beyond the national boundaries.

After returning to wages by piecework, which was abandoned too soon, the bureaucracy refers to the equalised wage as a 'kulak' principle. This is an out-and-out absurdity and shows into what blind alleys of hypocrisy and falsehood the Stalinists drive themselves. As a matter of fact they should have said: 'We have rushed too far ahead with methods of equalised wages for labour; we are still far from socialism; and since we are still poor, we must needs turn back to semi-capitalist or kulak methods of paying for labour.' We repeat, in this there is no contradiction woth the socialist goal. Here we only leave an irreconcilable contradiction with the bureaucratic falsification of reality.

The retreat to piecework wages was necessitated by the resistance of a backward economy. There will be many such retreats, especially in the sphere of rural economy, where too great an administrative leap forward has been executed.

Industrialisation and collectivisation are being put through by the one-sided and uncontrolled laying down of the law to the labouring masses by the bureaucracy. The trade unions are deprived entirely of any means of influencing the correlation between consumption and accumulation. The differentiation within the peasantry is still being liquidated not so much economically as administratively. The social measures of the bureaucracy as regards the liquidation of the classes run much too far ahead of the basic process, the development of productive forces.

This leads to the rise in basic industrial costs, to the lowering of the quality of products, to an increase in prices, and to a dearth in goods for consumption, and it offers as a perspective the threat of a return to unemployment.

The extreme tension in the national political atmosphere is the consequence of the contradictions between the growth of Soviet economy and the economic policies of the bureaucracy, which either straggles monstrously behind the economic needs (1923-28) or, taking fright at its own straggling, leaps forward and tries to make up for lost time by purely administrative measures (1928-32). Here, too, after the right zigzag, we get a zigzag to the left. During both zigzags, the bureaucracy finds itself in contradiction with the realities of economy and consequently with the mood of the workers. It cannot permit them to criticise—neither when it straggles behind, nor when it leaps ahead.

The bureaucracy cannot exercise its pressure upon workers and peasants except by depriving them of all possibility of participating in decisions upon questions that touch their own labour and their entire future. Herein lies the greatest danger! The constant dread of meeting opposition on the part of the masses leads in politics to the 'closed ranks in double time' of the bureaucratic and personal dictatorship.

Does this mean that the tempos of industrialisation and collectivisation should be lowered? For a given period—undoubtedly. But this period may not long endure. The participation of workers themselves in the leadership of the nation, of its politics and economy; an actual control over the bureaucracy; and the growth in the feeling of responsibility of those in charge to those under them—all these would doubtless react favourably on production itself: the friction within would be reduced, the costly economic zigzags would likewise be reduced to a minimum, a healthier distribution of forces and equipment would be assured, and ultimately the coefficients of growth would be raised. Soviet democracy is first of all the vital need of national economy itself. On the contrary, bureaucracy secretes within itself tragic economic surprises.

Surveying as a whole the history of the period of epigonism in the development of the USSR, it is not difficult to arrive at the conclusion that the basic political postulate for the bureaucratisation of the regime was the weariness of the masses after the shocks of the revolution and civil war. Famine and epidemics ruled the land. Political questions were relegated to the background. All thoughts centred on a piece of bread. Under War Communism, everybody received the same famine ration. The transition to the New Economic Policy brought the first economic successes. The rations became more ample but they were no longer allotted to everybody. The re-establishment of a commodity economy led to the calculation of basic costs, to rudimentary rationalisation, and to the elimination of surplus hands from the factories. For a long time economic successes went hand in hand with the growth of *unemployment*.

One must not forget for a single moment that the strengthening of the power of the apparatus arose from unemployment. After the years of famine, every proletarian at his bench stood in fear of the reserve army. Independent and critical workers were fired from factories, blacklists of oppositionists were kept. In the hands of the Stalinist bureaucracy this became one of the most important and effective weapons. Lacking this condition, it could have never succeeded in strangling the Leninist party.

Subsequent economic successes gradually led to the liquidation of the reserve army of industrial workers (the concealed rural overpopulation, masked by collectivisation, still remains in full force). The industrial worker already no longer fears that he will be thrown out of the factory. Through his daily experience, he knows that the lack of foresight and the self-will of the bureaucracy interfered enormously with the fulfilment of his tasks. The Soviet press exposes individual workshops and factories where insufficient freedom is allowed the initiative of workers, as if the initiative of the proletariat can be restricted to factories, as if factories can be oases of industrial democracy amidst the complete subjugation of the proletariat within the party, the soviets, and the trade unions!

The general state of mind of the proletariat now is no longer what it was in 1922-23. The proletariat has grown numerically and culturally. Having accomplished the gigantic labour of restoring and uplifting the national economy, the workers are now experiencing the restoration and uplift of their self-confidence. This growing inner confidence is beginning to change into dissatisfaction with the bureaucratic regime.

The strangling of the party and the overgrowth of the personal regime and the personal arbitrariness may at first glance evoke the idea that the Soviet system is weakening. But that is not so. The Soviet system has become very much stronger; but simultaneously the contradiction between this system and the iron rule of its bureaucracy has been sharpened extremely. With amazement the Stalinist apparatus observes that *economic successes, instead of strengthening, are undermining its sway*. In fighting for its positions, it is forced to turn the screws still tighter and to forbid all forms of 'self-criticism' other than the Byzantine flattery addressed to the leaders.

It is not the first time in history that economic development has come into contradiction with those political conditions within whose framework it is achieved. But one must clearly understand precisely which of these conditions engenders dissatisfaction. The oncoming opposition wave is not in the least degree directed against socialist tasks, Soviet forms, or the Communist Party. The dissatisfaction is directed against the apparatus and its personification, Stalin. Whence arises the new phase of the furious battle against the so-called 'Trotskyist contraband'.

The adversary threatens to become unconquerable; he is everywhere and nowhere. He bobs up in factories and in schools, he penetrates into historical journals and into all textbooks. This means that facts and documents convict the bureaucracy, exposing its vacillations and mistakes. One cannot calmly and objectively recall the bygone day, one must remodel the past, one must plaster up all the cracks, through which suspicions might leak out as regards the infallibility of the apparatus and its head. We have before us all the traits of a ruling caste that has lost its head. Yaroslavsky himself proves to be unreliable! These are not accidental episodes, not trifles, nor personal quarrels: the root of the matter lies in the fact that the economic successes, which in their first stages strengthened the bureaucracy, are now becoming, by the dialectic of their development, opposed to the bureaucracy. That is why during the last party conference, i.e., during the conference of the Stalinist apparatus, the thrice and four times annihilated and buried 'Trotskyism' was decreed to be 'the vanguard of bourgeois counter-revolution'.

This silly and politically quite unterrifying resolution lifts the veil from some very 'practical' plans of Stalin in the sphere of personal reprisals. Not for nothing did Lenin warn against the appointment of Stalin as general secretary, 'This cook will prepare only peppery dishes.' ...The cook has not yet completely exhausted his culinary prowess.

But despite the tightening of all theoretical and administrative screws, the personal dictatorship of Stalin is clearly nearing its eclipse. The apparatus is all in cracks. The crack called Yaroslavsky is only one of a hundred cracks who today still remain nameless. The fact that the new political crisis is being prepared on the basis of the self-evident and undebatable successes of Soviet economy and the numerical growth of the proletariat and the initial successes of collective farming—that is sufficient guarantee that the liquidation of bureaucratic absolutism will coincide not with the breakdown of the Soviet system, which was a danger some three or four years ago, but on the contrary, with its liberation, advance, and flowering.

But precisely in this, its final period, the Stalinist bureaucracy is capable of causing much evil. The question of prestige has now become for it the central question of politics. If non-political historians are expelled from the party only because they proved incapable of shedding lustre on Stalin's feats in 1917, can the plebiscitary regime permit the recognition of the mistakes it perpetrated in 1931-1932? Can it renounce its theory of social fascism? Can it whitewash Stalin, who formulated the gist of the German situation as follows: let the fascists come first, then we will follow?

By themselves the objective conditions in Germany are so imperative that, had the leadership of the German Communist Party at their command the necessary freedom of action, they would no doubt even now be orienting to our side. But they are not free. At the same time when the Left Opposition submits the ideas and slogans tested by the victory of 1917, the Stalinist clique, aiming to create a diversion, sends orders by telegraph to inaugurate an international campaign against 'Trotskyism'. The campaign is carried on not on the basis of the questions of the German revolution, that is, on the life-and-death questions of the world proletariat, but on the basis of a wretched and falsified article of Stalin on the questions of the history of Bolshevism. It is difficult to conceive of a greater disproportion between the tasks of the epoch on the one hand and the petty ideological resources of the official leadership on the other. So degrading and unworthy and at the same time profoundly tragic is the position of the Comintern.

The problem of the Stalinist regime and the problem of the German revolution are tied up with an absolutely indissoluble knot. The coming events will untie or cut this knot—in the interests of the Russian as well as of the German revolution.

12. The Brandlerites (KPO) and the Stalinist Bureaucracy

Between the interests of the Soviet state and those of the international proletariat there is and there can be no contradiction. But it is false at the root to transfer this law over to the Stalinist bureaucracy. Its regime is coming into an ever greater contradiction with the interests of the Soviet Union as well as the interests of the world revolution.

Hugo Urbahns cannot see the social foundations of the proletarian state for the Soviet bureaucracy. Together with Otto Bauer, Urbahns constructs the conception of a state resting above the classes, but in contradiction to Bauer he finds the example not in Austria but in the present Soviet republic.

On the other side, Thalheimer asserts that 'the Trotskyist position as regards the Soviet Union, which casts doubt [?] upon the proletarian character [?] of the Soviet state and the socialist character of the economic construction' bears a 'centrist' character.[9] Thereby Thalheimer only demonstrates the extent to which he identifies *the workers' government with the Soviet bureaucracy*. He demands the Soviet Union be regarded not through the eyes of the international proletariat, but exclusively through the spectacles of the Stalinist faction. In other words, he reasons not as a theoretician of the proletarian revolution but as a flunkey of the Stalinist bureaucracy. Insulted and disgraced, but a flunkey just the same, who awaits forgiveness. Wherefore even when in 'opposition' he does not dare so much as mention the bureaucracy out loud: it, like Jehovah, does not pardon this: 'Thou shalt not take my name in vain.'

Such are these two poles in the Communist groupings: the one cannot see the forest for the trees, the other is kept by the forest from distinguishing the trees. However there is absolutely nothing unexpected in the fact that Thalheimer and Urbahns find in each other kindred souls and actually make a bloc—against the Marxist appraisal of the Soviet state.

A perfunctory 'support,' which commits them to nothing, of the 'Russian experiment' from the sidelines has become, in recent years, a rather widespread and very cheap commodity. In all parts of the world there is no lack of radical and semi-radical, humanitarian and pacifist 'also-socialists,' journalists, tourists, and artistes who take toward the USSR and Stalin the same attitude of unconditional approval as do the Brandlerites. Bernard Shaw, who in his time savagely criticised Lenin and the author of these lines, is now wholeheartedly in favour of Stalin's policies. Maxim Gorky, who was in opposition to the Communist Party during Lenin's period, is now wholeheartedly for Stalin. Barbusse, who went hand in hand with the French Social Democrats, supports Stalin. The American monthly **New Masses**, a publication of second-rate petty-bourgeois radicals, defends Stalin against Rakovsky. In Germany, Ossietzky, who cites with sympathy my article on fascism, finds it imperative to remark that I am unjust in my criticism of Stalin. Old Ledebour says:

> as regards the chief question in dispute between Stalin and Trotsky, to wit: may socialisation be undertaken in one country and worked out happily to its conclusion, I am entirely on Stalin's side.

The number of such examples can be produced *ad infinitum*. All these 'friends' of the USSR approach the problems of the Soviet state from the sidelines, as observers, as sympathisers, and occasionally as *flaneurs*. Of course it accrues more to one's honour to be a friend of the Soviet five-year plan than a friend of the New York stock market. But just the same this passive, middle-class left sympathy is too far removed from Bolshevism. The first major failure of Moscow will suffice to scatter the majority of this public like dust before the wind.

By what is the position of the Brandlerites in relation to the Soviet state to be distinguished from the position of all these 'friends'? Perhaps only by a greater lack of sincerity. Such support is neither fish nor fowl to the Soviet republic. and when Thalheimer lectures *us*, the Left Opposition, the Russian Bolshevik-Leninists, on what our attitude should be to the Soviet Union, he cannot fail to evoke a feeling of aversion.

Rakovsky was in direct charge of the defence of the frontiers of the Soviet revolution; he participated in the first steps taken by the Soviet national economy and in the elaboration of the policies towards the peasantry; he was the initiator of the committees of landless villagers (the peasant poor) in the Ukraine; he was in charge of applying the policies of the New

Economic Policy to the singular Ukrainian conditions; he knows every twist and turn of this policy, he is following it even now, from Barnaul, with passionate interest and from day to day he warns against mistakes and suggests the correct ways. The old warrior Kote Tsintsadze who died in exile, Muralov, Carl Grünstein, Kasparova, Sosnovsky, Kossior, Aussem, the Elzins—father and son— Dingelstedt, Shumskaya, Solntzev, Stopalov, Poznansky, Sermux, Blumkin, shot down by Stalin, Butov, tortured to death in prison by Stalin, and tens, hundreds, thousands of others thrown into prisons and exile—yes, these are all warriors who fought in the October insurrection and in the civil war; these are all participants in the socialist construction who are abashed by no difficulties and who at the first signal are ready to take their post in the front line. Are they to go to school to Thalheimer to learn the correct attitude toward the workers' state?

Everything which is progressive in Stalin's policies was formulated by the Left Opposition and was hounded down on the part of the bureaucracy. For its initiative in inaugurating the planned economy, the higher tempos of development, the fight against the *kulaks* and for broader collectivisation, the Left Opposition has paid and is paying with years in prison and exile. What has been the contribution to the economic policies of the USSR by all these unconditional supporters and sympathetic friends, including the Brandlerites? All told—nothing! Behind their vague and uncritical support of everything that is being done in the USSR there lurks no international enthusiasm whatever but only a lukewarm sympathy; because, you see, the things are taking place beyond the frontiers of their own fatherland. Brandler and Thalheimer opine and declare openly on occasion: 'For us Germans, Stalin's regime would of course, hardly do; but for the Russians it's good enough!'

The reformist looks upon the international situation as a sum of the national situations; the Marxist observes the national policy as a function of the international. In this key question the group of the KPO (Brandlerites) takes a national-reformist position, i.e., it rejects in deeds, if not in words, international principles and the criteria of national policy.

The closest adherent and colleague of Thalheimer was Roy,

whose political programme for India as well as for China was entirely derived from the Stalinist idea of 'worker-peasant' parties for the East. For a number of years, Roy came forward as the propagandist of a national-democratic party for India; in other words, not as a proletarian revolutionist but as a petty-bourgeois national democrat. This did not interfere in any way with his active participation in the central staff of the Brandlerites.*

The national opportunism of the Brandlerites evinces itself most crudely in their attitude toward the Soviet Union. The Stalinist bureaucracy, if you take their word, operates in its own back yard absolutely without mistakes. But somehow or other the leadership of the identical Stalinist faction becomes fatal for Germany. How is that? For involved in the matter are not Stalin's personal mistakes, which are engendered by his not being acquainted with other countries, but a definite *course* of mistakes, an entire trend. Thälmann and Remmele know Germany as Stalin knows Russia, as Cachin, Semard, or Thorez know of France. Jointly they form an international faction and elaborate the policies for the different countries. But, it appears, this policy, irreproachable in Russia, is ruinous to the revolution in all other countries.

Brandler's position becomes particularly jinxed if it is transferred into the USSR, where a Brandlerite is bound to support Stalin unconditionally. Radek, who essentially was always closer to Brandler than to the Left Opposition, capitulated to Stalin. Brandler could not but approve this action. But Stalin immediately compelled Radek, after he had capitulated, to proclaim Brandler and Thalheimer as 'social fascists.' The platonic wooers of the Stalinist regime in Berlin do not even attempt to crawl out from under these degrading contradictions. Their practical goal is self-evident, however, even without commentaries. 'If you place me at the head of the party in Germany,' says Brandler to Stalin, 'I on my part shall bind myself to recognise your infall-

* Roy has just been sentenced to many years imprisonment by MacDonald's government. The papers of the Comintern do not feel themselves obligated even to protest against this: one may ally oneself intimately with Chiang Kai-shek, but one absolutely cannot defend the Indian Brandlerite Roy against the imperial butchers.

ibility in Russian matters, provided you permit me to put through my own policies in German matters.' Can one have any respect for such 'revolutionists'?

But the Brandlerites also criticise the Comintern policies of the Stalinist bureaucracy in a manner extremely one-sided and theoretically dishonest. Its sole vice appears to be 'ultra-leftism'. But can anyone accuse Stalin's four-year bloc with Chiang Kai-shek of being 'ultra-left'? Can one call the creation of the Peasant International ultra-left? Can one assign to putschism the bloc with the strikebreakers of the General Council? Or the creation of worker-peasant parties in Asia and the Farmer-Labour Party in the United States?

Furthermore, what is the social nature of Stalinist ultra-leftism? What is it? A temporary mood? A fit of sickness? One seeks in vain for an answer from theoretician Thalheimer.

Meanwhile the riddle has long been solved by the Left Opposition: the matter concerns the ultra-left zigzag of centrism. But precisely this definition, which has been verified by the developments of the last nine years, cannot be accepted by the Brandlerites because it finishes them off too. They perpetuated with the Stalinist faction all its *right* zigzags but rebelled against the *left*; thereby they demonstrated that they are the right wing of centrism. That they, like a dry branch, broke off from the main trunk of the tree—that is in the nature of things; during sharp evolutions of centrism, groups and layers are inevitably torn off from the right and from the left.

What has been said above does not imply that the Brandlerites were mistaken in *everything*. Not at all. Against Thälmann and Remmele they were and they remain right in many things. There is nothing extraordinary in this. Opportunists may occupy correct positions in their struggle against adventurism. And, on the contrary, an ultra-left trend may correctly seize the moment of the transition from the struggle for the masses to the struggle for power. In their criticism of Brandler, the ultra-lefts aired many correct ideas at the end of 1923, which did not hinder them from committing the grossest mistakes in 1924-25. The fact that in their criticism of the monkeyshines of the 'third period' the Brandlerites reiterated a number of old but correct concepts does not at all vouch for the correctness of their general position. The policies of each group must be analysed in several stages: during defensive battles as well as during offensives; during periods of high as well as ebb tide; under the conditions of the struggle to win the masses; and under the conditions of a direct struggle for power.

There can be no Marxist leadership specialising in questions of defence or offence, or the united front, or the general strike. The correct application of all these methods is possible only if there exists the capacity for synthetically appraising the environment as a whole; the ability to analyse its moving forces, to establish stages and turns, and to build upon this analysis a system of action which corresponds to the existing environment and which prepares for the next stage.

Brandler and Thalheimer consider themselves to be almost monopolistic specialists in 'the struggle for the masses'. Keeping their faces straight and serious, these gentlemen insist that the arguments of the Left Opposition for the policy of the united front are in themselves... a plagiarism of their—the Brandlerites'—views. One should deny no one the privileges of being ambitious! Just imagine, for example, that while you are explaining to Heinz Neumann his error in multiplication, some valiant teacher of arithmetic appears on the scene and informs you that you are committing a plagiarism because he, year in and year out, expounds in just this way the mysteries of the art of reckoning.

The pretensions of the Brandlerites have at any rate afforded me a merry moment in the present uncomical situation. The strategic wisdom of these gentlemen is no older than the Third Congress of the Comintern. I was then defending the ABC of the struggle for the masses against the then existing 'left' wing. In my book **The New Course**, which was devoted to a popular exposition of the policy of the united front, and which was in its time published by the Comintern in various languages, I stressed in every which way the elementary character of the ideas therein propounded. Thus, for instance, we read on page 70 of the German edition: 'All that has been said constitutes *ABC truths* from the point of view of the serious revolutionary experience. But certain 'left' elements of the congress have discovered in this tactic a shift to the right.' ...Among those certain elements, together with Zinoviev, Bukharin, Radek, Maslow, and Thälmann, was to be found Thalheimer himself.

The charge of plagiarism is not the only charge. After stealing Thalheimer's spiritual property, the Opposition, it appears, gives it an opportunistic interpretation. This oddity deserves notice insofar as it enables us in the course of our discussion to throw into sharper relief the question of the policies of fascism.

In an earlier pamphlet, I expressed the thought that Hitler cannot attain power through parliamentary procedure; even if we allow that he could muster his 51 per cent of the votes, the growth of the economic and the sharpening of the political contradictions would necessarily lead to an open outburst before that moment could be reached. In this connection the Brandlerites ascribe to me the idea that the National Socialists will leave the scene of action 'without the need of extra-parliamentary mass action on the part of the workers.' Wherein is this superior to the fabrications of *Die Rote Fahne*?

From the impossibility of the National Socialists coming 'peacefully' into power, I deduced the inevitability of other ways of attaining power: either by way of a direct overturn of the government or by way of a coalition stage with the subsequent inevitable governmental overturn. A painless self-liquidation of fascism would have been a possibility in one and only in one case: in the event that Hitler applied that policy in 1932 to which Brandler had resorted in 1923. Without overestimating the National Socialist strategies, I still am of the opinion that they are more farsighted and of sterner stuff than Brandler & Co.

Even more profound is the second refutation of Thalheimer: the question as to whether Hitler attains power in a parliamentary manner or otherwise has no significance whatever, because it does not change 'the essence' of fascism which in either case can entrench its rule only on the fragments of the workers' organisations.

> The workers may calmly leave to the editors of the Vorwärts the task of research as regards the contrasts between the constitutional and unconstitutional coming of Hitler to power.[10]

Should the most advanced workers listen to Thalheimer, Hitler will without fail cut their throats. To our sage schoolteacher only the 'essence' of fascism is important, and he leaves the editors of **Vorwärts** to judge how that 'essence' will be realised. But the whole matter lies in the fact that the pogrom 'essence' of fascism can become palpable only after it comes to power. And the task consists precisely in not permitting it to attain power. For this, one must understand the strategy of the foe and explain it to the workers.

Hitler is straining to his utmost to bring the movement outwardly into the constitutional channel. Only a pedant who deems himself a 'materialist' is capable of thinking that such behaviour leaves no effect on the political consciousness of the masses. Hitler's constitutionalism serves not only to keep the door open for a bloc with the centrists but also to fool the Social Democrats, or to put it more correctly, to make it easier for the leaders of the Social Democracy to fool the workers. If Hitler swears that he will attain to power only constitutionally then it is clear that the danger of fascism is not so great today. At any rate there will be time enough left to verify a few more times the correlation of forces during all sorts of elections. Under the cover of the constitutional perspective which lulls his adversaries, Hitler aims to reserve for himself the possibility of striking the blow at a convenient moment. The military cunning, no matter how simple in itself, secretes a tremendous force, for it leans upon not only the psychology of the intermediate parties, which would like to settle the question peacefully and legally, but, what is more dangerous, upon the gullibility of the national masses.

It is also necessary to add that Hitler's manoeuvre is two-edged: he fools not only his adversaries but his supporters. And meanwhile, a militant spirit is essential for a struggle, particularly an offensive one. It can be sustained only by instilling in one's army the understanding that an open battle is inescapable. This consideration bespeaks also the fact that Hitler cannot too long protract his tender romance with the Weimar Constitution without demoralising his ranks. He must in due time produce the knife from under his shirt.

It is not enough to understand only the 'essence' of fascism. One must be capable of appraising it as a living political phenomenon, as a conscious and wily foe. Our schoolteacher is too 'sociological' to be a revolutionist. Isn't it clear, in reality, that Thalheimer's profundity enters into Hitler's reckoning as a favourable circumstance; for when one lumps together into one pile the broadcasting of constitutional illusions by the **Vorwärts** and the exposure of the military cunning of the enemy that is built upon these illusions, then one aids the enemy.

An organisation may be significant either because of the mass it embraces or because of the content of those ideas that it is capable of bringing into the workers' movement. The Brandlerites have neither the one nor the other. But despite this, with what grandiloquent contempt do Brandler and Thalheimer hold forth on the centrist morass of the SAP! In reality, if one juxtaposes these two organisations—the SAP and the KPO—all the advantages are on the side of the former. The SAP is not a morass but a live stream. Its direction is from the right to the left, to the side of Communism. The stream has not been cleared, there is much rubbish and slime in it, but it is no swamp. The denomination 'morass' is much more applicable to the organisation of Brandler-Thalheimer, which is characterised by a complete ideological stagnation.

Within the KPO group there has long existed its own opposition which is chiefly dissatisfied with the fact that their leaders tried to adapt their policies not so much to the objective conditions as to the moods of the Stalinist general staff in Moscow.

That the opposition of Walcher-Frölich, etc, has tolerated for a number of years the policies of Brandler-Thalheimer, which, particularly in relation to the USSR, bore not simply an erroneous but a consciously hypocritical and politically dishonest character—that, of course, no one will enter to the credit of the group that has split off. But the fact remains that the group of Walcher-Frölich has finally recognised the utter hopelessness of the organisation, whose leaders orient themselves at the beck and call of their superiors. The minority deems it necessary that an independent and active policy be undertaken not against the hapless Remmele but against the course and the regime of the Stalinist bureaucracy in the USSR and in the Comintern. If we interpret correctly, on the basis of still rather extremely insufficient material, the position of Walcher-Frölich, then it represents a step forward in this question. But having split from an obviously dead group, the minority is only now faced with the question of a new orientation, national and, particularly, international.

The minority that split off, so far as one can judge, sees its chief task in the immediate future in concentrating upon the left wing of the SAP, and after winning over the new party for Communism, in subsequently breaking up with its aid the bureaucratic conservatism of the KPD. In regard to this plan in its general and undefined form, it is impossible to comment, because those basic principles upon which the minority stands are still unclear, as are the methods which it intends to apply in the struggle for these principles. A platform is essential! We have in mind not a document recapitulating the common-places of the Communist catechism, but clear and concrete answers to those questions of the proletarian revolution which have torn the ranks of Communism for the past nine years and which retain their burning significance even now. Lacking this, one can only become dissolved in the SAP and hinder, not facilitate, its development toward Communism.

The Left Opposition will follow the evolution of the minority attentively and without any preconceived opinions. More than once in history, the rift within a lifeless organisation has given an impulse to the progressive development of its viable section. We shall rejoice indeed should this law verify itself in this case also, in the fate of the minority. But only the future can supply the answer.

13. Strike Strategy

In the sphere of the trade unions the Communist leadership has entirely confused the party. The common course of the 'third period' was directed toward parallel trade unions. The presupposition was that the mass movement would surge over the old organisations and that the organs of the RGO (the Revolutionary Trade Union Opposition) would become the initiative committees of the economic struggle. A mere trifle was lacking for the realisation of this plan: the mass movement. During floods in springtime, the waters carry away many a fence. Let us try removing the fence, decided Lozovsky, perhaps the floods of spring will then rise!

The reformist trade unions have survived. The Communist Party succeeded in getting itself thrown out of the factories. Thereupon partial corrections began to be introduced into the trade-union policy. The Communist Party has refused to call upon the unorganised workers to join reformist unions. But it likewise has taken a stand against workers leaving the trade unions. While creating parallel organisations it has resurrected the slogans of a battle for influence within the reformist unions. The whole mechanism represents an ideal self-sabotage.

Die Rote Fahne complains that many Communists consider meaningless the participation in reformist unions. 'Why should we revive the old pushcart?' they declare. And as a matter of fact, why? If one intends seriously to fight for the control of the old unions, one should appeal to the unorganised that they enter them; it is precisely the new strata that can supply the backing for the left wing. But in that case one cannot build parallel unions, i.e., create a competitive agency to enrol the workers.

The policy that is recommended from above for work within the reformist unions is on a par with the rest of the hopeless mess. *Die Rote Fahne* on 28 January laced into the Communist members of the Metal Workers' Union of Düsseldorf because they issued the slogan 'War without mercy against the participation of trade-union leaders' in the support of the Brüning government. Such 'opportunistic' demands are disallowed because they presuppose (!) that the reformists are capable of refusing to support Brüning and his emergency decrees. Truly, this is like a bad joke! *Die Rote Fahne* deems it sufficient to call the leaders names but disallows their being subjected to a political test by the masses.

And all the while it is precisely within the trade unions that an exceptionally fruitful field is now open for action. While the Social Democratic Party still has the wherewithal to fool the workers by political hullabaloo, the trade unions are confronted by the *impasse* of capitalism as by a hopeless prison wall. The 200,000 to 300,000 workers who are now organised in independent RGO unions could serve as a priceless leaven within the reformist brotherhoods.

Towards the end of January there was held in Berlin a

Communist conference of the factory committees from the entire county. *Die Rote Fahne* carried the report, 'The factory committees are welding the Red Workers Front'.[11] But you would seek in vain for information regarding the composition of the conference, the number of industries and workers represented. In contradistinction to Bolshevism, which painstakingly and openly marked every change in the correlation of forces within the working class, the German Stalinists, following in the footsteps of the Russian, play hide and seek. They are loath to admit that less than 4 per cent of the factory committees are Communist, as against 84 per cent which are Social Democratic! In this correlation is summed up the balance of the 'third period'. Suppose one does call the isolation of Communists in industry the 'Red United Front'; will this really help advance matters?

The prolonged crisis of capitalism induces within the proletariat the most virulent and dangerous line of demarcation: between the employed and the unemployed. Through the circumstance that the reformists control the industrial centres while the Communists control the unemployed, both sections of the proletariat are being paralysed. The employed are in a position to bide a while longer. The unemployed are more impatient. At present their impatience bears a revolutionary character. But should the Communist Party fail to find such forms and slogans for the struggle as would unite the employed and the unemployed and thereby open the perspective of a revolutionary solution, the impatience of the unemployed will inevitably react against the Communist Party.

In 1917, despite the correct policy of the Bolshevik Party and the rapid development of the revolution, the more badly off and the more impatient strata of the proletariat, even in Petrograd, began between September and October to look away from the Bolsheviks towards the syndicalists and anarchists. Had not the October insurrection broken out in time, the disintegration within the proletariat would have become acute and would have led to the decay of the revolution. In Germany there is no need for anarchists; their place can be taken by the National Socialists who have wedded anarchist demagogy to conscious reactionary aims.

The workers are by no means immunised once for all

against the influence of fascism. The proletariat and the petty bourgeoisie interpenetrate, especially under the present conditions, when the reserve army of workers cannot but produce petty traders and hawkers, etc, while the bankrupt petty bourgeoisie effuses proletarians and lumpenproletarians.

Salaried employees, the technical and administrative personnel, and certain strata of the functionaries, composed in the past one of the most important supports of the Social Democracy. At present, these elements have gone or are going over to the National Socialists. They are capable of drawing in their wake, if they haven't already begun to do so, a stratum of the labour aristocracy. In this direction, National Socialism is penetrating into the proletariat from above.

Considerably more dangerous, however, is its possible penetration *from below*, through the unemployed. No class can long exist without prospects and hopes. The unemployed do not represent a class, but they already compose a very compact and substantial layer, which is vainly striving to tear itself away from intolerable conditions. If it is true in general that only the proletarian revolution can save Germany from disintegration and decay, this is especially true as regards the millions of unemployed.

Alongside of the impotence of the Communist Party in the factories and in trade unions, the numerical growth of the party resolves nothing. Within a tottering nation shot through with crisis and contradictions, an extreme left party can find new supporters in the tens of thousands, especially if its entire apparatus is directed to the sole purpose of capturing members, by way of 'competition'. Everything depends upon the interrelation between the party and the class. A single employed Communist who is elected to the factory committee or to the administration of a trade union has a greater significance than a thousand new members, picked up here and there, who enter the party today in order to leave it tomorrow.

But the individual influx of members into the party will not at all continue indefinitely. If the Communist Party continues any longer to delay the struggle until that moment when it shall have entirely pushed out the reformists, then it will learn for certain that after a given point the Social Democracy will cease losing its influence to the Communist Party, while the fascists will begin disintegrating the unemployed who are the chief support of the Communist Party. Failure to utilise its forces for the tasks that spring from the total situation never allows a political party to go scot-free.

In order to clear the road for the mass struggle, the Communist Party strives to stimulate isolated strikes. The successes in this sphere have not been great. As ever, the Stalinists devote themselves to self-criticism: 'We are as yet incapable of organising' ... 'We haven't yet learned how to attract' ... 'We haven't as yet learned how to capture' ... And when they say 'we', it unfailingly means 'you'. That theory of the March Days in 1921, of blessed memory, is being resurrected, which proposed to 'electrify' the proletariat by means of the offensive activities of the minority. But the workers are in no need whatever of being 'electrified'. What they want is to be given a clear perspective, and to be aided in creating the basis for a mass movement.

In its strike strategy the Communist Party is obviously motivated by isolated citations from Lenin as interpreted by Manuilsky or Lozovsky. As a matter of fact, there were periods when the Mensheviks fought against the 'strike frenzy', while the Bolsheviks, on the contrary, took their place at the head of every new strike, drawing into the movement ever-increasing masses. That corresponded to the period of the awakening of new working-class strata. Such was the tactic of the Bolsheviks in 1905; during the industrial upward trend in the years preceding the war; and during the first months of the February revolution.

But in the period directly preceding October, beginning with the July clash of 1917, the tactic of the Bolsheviks assumed another character: they held back strikes; they applied the brake to them, because every large strike had the tendency to turn into a decisive battle, while the political postulates for it had not as yet matured.

However, during those months the Bolsheviks continued to place themselves at the head of all strikes which flared up, despite their warnings, chiefly in the more backward branches of industry (among textile workers, leather workers, etc).

While under some conditions the Bolsheviks boldly stimulate strikes in the interests of the revolution, under other conditions, on the contrary, they restrained strikes in the interests of the revolution. In this sphere as well as in others, there is no ready-made formula. But in every given period, the strike tacticsof the Bolsheviks always formed part of their general tactics, and to the advanced workers the connection between the part and the whole was always clear.

How do matters stand now in Germany? The employed workers do not resist wage cuts because they are in fear of the unemployed. Small wonder; in the face of several million unemployed, the ordinary trade-union strike, so organised, is obviously futile. It is doubly futile in the face of political antagonism between the employed and the unemployed. This does not exclude the possibility of individual strikes, especially in the more backward and less centralised branches of industry. But it is just the workers of the more important branches of industry who, in such a situation, are inclined to heed the voices of the reformist leaders. The attempts of the Communist Party to unleash a strike struggle without changing the general situation within the proletariat lead only to minor guerrilla operations, which, even if successful, remain without a sequel.

According to the testimony of Communist workers (compare, say, **Der Rote Aufbau**), there is a great deal being said in factories to the effect that the strikes in different industries have no meaning at present, and that only a general strike could lead the workers out of their troubles. 'The general strike' here signifies the prospect of struggle. The workers are less apt to become inspired by isolated strikes because they have to deal directly with the state power; monopoly capital speaks to the workers in the language of Brüning's emergency decrees.*

---

* Some ultra-lefts (for instance the Italian Bordigist group) hold that the united front is permissible only in economic struggles. The attempt to separate the economic struggle from the political is less feasible in our epoch than ever before. The example of Germany, where wage agreements and workers' wages are cut by means of administrative decrees, should instil this truth even in small children.
We shall add in passing that in their present stage, the Stalinists are reviving many of the early crotchets of Bordigism. Small wonder that the 'Prometto group', which has learned nothing and which has not taken one step forward, stand today, in the period of the ultra-left zig-zag of the Comintern, much closer to the Stalinists than to us.

At the dawn of the workers' movement, in order to draw the workers into a strike, the agitator often refrained from launching into revolutionary and socialist perspectives, in order not to scare the workers away. At present the situation bears just the opposite character. The leading strata of the German workers can decide to begin a defensive economic struggle only in the event that they are clear about the general perspectives of subsequent struggles. They do not feel that these perspectives obtain among the Communist leadership.

In relation to the tactic of the March Days of 1921 in Germany (to 'electrify' the minority of the proletariat instead of capturing its majority), the writer spoke at the Third Congress as follows:

> When the overwhelming majority of the working class takes no account of the movement, does not sympathise with it, or is doubtful of its success, at the same time when the minority rushes ahead and by mechanical means strives to drive the workers into strikes—then this impatient minority in the guise of the party can fall foul of the working class and break its own head.

Does this mean that the strike struggle should be renounced? No, not renounced but sustained, by creating for it necessary political and organisational premises. One of these is the restoration of the unity of the *trade unions*. The reformist bureaucracy of course, is averse to this. The split has hitherto assured its position in the best manner possible. But the immediate threat of fascism is changing the situation within the trade unions to the detriment of the bureaucracy. The gravitation to unity is growing. Should Leipart's clique try under present conditions to prohibit the restoration of unity, this would immediately double or triple the Communist influence within the unions. Should the unification materialise, nothing could be better; a wide sphere of activity would be opened to the Communists. Not halfway measures are urgent, but a bold about-face!

Without a widespread campaign against the high cost of living, for a shorter work week, against wage cuts; without drawing the unemployed into this struggle hand in hand with the employed; without a successful application of the policy of the united front, the improvised small strikes will not lead the movement out onto the open road.

The left Social Democrats chat about the necessity of resorting to the general strike 'in the event that the fascists come into power.' Very likely, Leipart himself flaunts such threats within the four walls of his study. On this account **Die Rote Fahne** makes reference to Luxemburgism. This is vilifying the great revolutionist. Even though Rosa Luxemburg overestimated the independent importance of the general strike in the question of power she understood quite well that a general strike could not be declared arbitrarily, that it must be prepared for by the whole preceding course of the workers' movement, by the policies of the party and the trade unions. On the lips of the left Social Democrats, however, the mass strike is more of a consoling myth superimposed over sorry reality.

For many years , the French Social Democrats had promised that they would resort to the general strike in the event of war. The Basle Congress of 1912 even promised to resort to a revolutionary uprising. But the threat of general strikes as well as of uprisings assumed in these instances the nature of theatrical thunder. What is here involved is not the counterposition of the strike to the uprising, but the lifeless, formal, and merely verbal attitude to the strike as well as to the uprising. The reformist armed with the abstraction of the revolution—such in general was the Bebel type of Social Democrat prior to the war. Next to him the post-war reformist brandishing the threat of a general strike is an outright caricature.

The Communist leadership, of course, bears to the general strike an attitude that is much more conscientious. But it lacks clarity on this question also. And clarity is urgent. The general strike is a very important weapon of struggle, but it is not universal. There are conditions under which a general strike may weaken the workers more than their immediate enemy. The strike must be an important element in the calculation of strategy and not a panacea in which is submerged all other strategy.

Generally speaking, the general strike is the weapon of struggle of the weaker against the stronger; or, to put it more precisely, of the one who at the beginning of the struggle feels himself weaker against him whom one considers to be the stronger; seeing that I myself cannot make use of an important weapon, I shall try to prevent my opponents using it; if I cannot shoot from cannon, I shall at least remove the gun-locks. Such is the 'idea' of the general strike.

The general strike was always the weapon of struggle against an entrenched state power that had at its disposal rail-roads, telegraph, police and army, etc. By paralysing the government apparatus the general strike either 'scared' the government, or created the postulates for a revolutionary solution of the question of power.

The general strike is the most effective method of fighting under the conditions where the masses are united only by revolutionary indignation but are lacking military organisations and staffs, and cannot beforehand either estimate the correlation of forces, or work out a plan of action. Thus, one may suppose that the anti-fascist revolution in Italy, after beginning from one or another sectional clash, will inevitably go through the stage of the general strike. Only in this way will the present disjointed proletariat of Italy once again feel itself as a united class and match the strength of the enemy's resistance, whom it must overthrow.

One would have to fight in Germany against fascism by means of the general strike only in the event that fascism was already in power, and had firmly seized the state apparatus. But so long as the matter concerns the repelling of the fascist attempt to seize power, the slogan of the general strike turns out to be just so much space wasted.

At the time of Kornilov's march against Petrograd neither the Bolsheviks, nor the soviets as a whole, even thought of declaring a general strike. On the railroads the fight was waged to have the workers and the railroad personnel transport the revolutionary troops and retard the Kornilov detachments. The factories stopped functioning only in proportion as the workers had to leave for the front. The industries that served the revolutionary front worked with redoubled energy.

At the time of the October insurrection there was likewise no talk of a general strike. The factories and regiments in their overwhelming majority were already, on the eve of the overturn, following the leadership of the Bolshevik Soviet. Under these conditions, to call the factories to a strike meant to weaken oneself and not the enemy. At the railroads the workers strove to aid the uprising; the railway officials, under the guise of neutrality, aided the counter-revolution. A general strike of railroad workers would have lacked any significance: the question was decided by the preponderance of the workers over the officials.

Should the struggle flare up in Germany through sectional clashes initiated by fascist provocation, the call for a general strike would hardly meet the general situation. The general strike would first of all mean that city would be isolated from city, one section of the city from another, and even one factory from the next. It is more difficult to find and collect the unemployed. Under such conditions the fascists, who have no lack of staffs, can obtain a certain preponderance thanks to centralised leadership. True, their masses are so disjointed that even under these conditions the fascist attempt could be repelled. But that is already another side of the matter.

The question of railroad communications, for instance, must be taken up not from the point of view of 'prestige', which demands that everybody should strike, but from the point of view of military expediency: for whom and against whom would the ways of communication serve in the time of conflict?

It is necessary, therefore, to prepare not for a general strike but for the repulsion of fascists. This means that everywhere there should be created bases of operation, shock troops, reserves, local staffs and central authorities, smoothly working means of communication, and elementary plans of mobilisation.

That which was accomplished by the local organisations in a provincial corner, in Bruchsal and Klingenthal, where the Communists together with the SAP and the trade unions, although boycotted by the upper crust of the reformist bureaucracy, have created the organisation for defence—that, despite its modest scope, serves as a model for the whole country. O, supreme leaders!—would that one's voice could carry from here and one could shout—O, sevenfold sages of strategy, learn from the workers of Bruchsal and Klingenthal! Imitate them! Widen the scope of their experience and elaborate upon their forms!

Learn from the workers of Bruchsal and Klingenthal!

The German working class has at its command potent political, economic and sport organisations. Therein lies the difference between 'Brüning's regime' and 'Hitler's regime'. This is not Brüning's virtue; a weak bureaucracy is no virtue. But one must see what is. The chief, the fundamental and crowning fact is that the working class of Germany stands even today in the full panoply of its organisations. If it is weak, that is only because its organised force is incorrectly applied. But it is only necessary to spread throughout the country the experience of Bruchsal and Klingenthal and the entire outlook in Germany would be different. In relation to the fascists, the working class under these conditions would be able to apply much more effective and direct methods of struggle than the general strike. But if through a concatenation of circumstances, the need for resorting to the general strike should still arise (such a need could arise from definite interrelation between the fascists and government organs), then the system of the Committees of Defence on the basis of the united front could put through the mass strike with success assured beforehand.

The struggle would not stop on this stage. For what is the Bruchsal or Klingenthal organisation of defence in its essence? One must be able to observe the great in the little; it is the local soviet of workers' deputies. That is not what it calls itself; that is not how it feels, for the matter concerns a small provincial nook. Quantity here too determines quality. Transfer this experiment to Berlin and you will get the Berlin soviet of workers' deputies!

14. Workers' control and collaboration with the USSR

Whenever we speak of the slogans of the revolutionary period, the latter should not be constructed in too narrow a sense. The soviets should be created only in a revolutionary period. But when does that begin? One cannot consult the calendar and thus learn. One can only feel one's way through action. The soviets *must* be created at the time when they *can* be created*

* Let it be borne in mind that in China, the Stalinists worked against the

The slogan of workers' control over production relates, particularly and in general, to the same period as the creation of soviets. But neither should this be constructed mechanically. Special conditions may draw the masses toward control over production considerably prior to the time when they will show themselves ready to create soviets.

Brandler and his left shadow—Urbahns—have used the slogan of control over production independently of the political background. This has served no purpose other than to discredit the slogan. But it would be incorrect to reject the slogan now, under the conditions of the looming political crisis, only because on the face of it the mass offensive doesn't exist as yet. For the offensive itself, slogans are necessary which would define the perspectives of the movement. The period of propaganda must inevitably precede the penetration of the slogan into the masses.

The campaign for workers' control can develop, depending upon the circumstances, not from the angle of production but from that of consumption. The promise of the Brüning government to lower the price of commodities simultaneously with the decrease in wages has not materialised. This question cannot but absorb the most backward strata of the proletariat, who are today very far from the thought of seizing power.

Workers' control over the outlays of industry and the profits of trade is the only real form of the struggle for lower prices. Under the conditions of general dissatisfaction, workers' commissions with the participation of worker-housewives for the purpose of checking up on the increased cost of margarine can become very palpable beginnings of workers' control over industry. It is self-evident that this is only one of the possible manners of approach and it is given only as an example. Here the matter will not as yet concern the management of industry; the working woman will not go so far at once; such a thought is far removed from her mind. But it is easier for her to pass from consumer control to control over production and from the latter to direct management, depending upon the general development of the

---

creation of soviets during the period of revolutionary upsurge; whereas, when they decided upon an uprising in Canton during the wave of recession, they appealed to the masses to create soviets on the very day of the insurrection!

revolution.

In contemporary Germany, under the conditions of the present crisis, control over industry signifies control not only over the operating but also over the partly operating and shutdown industries. This presupposes participation in control by those workers who worked in those industries prior to their dismissal. The task must consist of setting the dead industries into motion, under the leadership of factory committees on the basis of an economic plan. This leads directly to the question of the governmental administration of industry, i.e., to the expropriation of the capitalists by the workers' government. Workers' control, then, is not a prolonged, 'normal' condition, like wage-scale agreements or social insurance. The control is a transitional measure, under the conditions of the highest tension of the class war, and conceivable only as a bridge to the revolutionary nationalisation of industry.

The Brandlerites accuse the Left Opposition of having snitched from them the slogan of control over production after having jeered at this slogan for a number of years. The accusation has quite an unexpected tone! The slogan of control over industry was first issued, on a wide scale, by the Bolshevik Party in 1917. In Petrograd, the charge over the entire campaign in this sphere, as well as in others, was placed in the hands of the Petrograd Soviet. As an individual who watched this work and participated in it, I bear witness that we were never obliged to turn to Thalheimer-Brandler for initiative, or to make use of their theoretical information. The accusation of 'plagiarism' is formulated with a certain imprudence.

But that is not the chief trouble. The second part of the accusation is much more serious—until now, the 'Trotskyists' have argued against a campaign under the slogan of control over production, but right now they come out for this slogan. The Brandlerites see herein our inconsistency! As a matter of fact they only reveal a complete ignorance of the revolutionary dialectic embodied in that slogan of workers' control, which they reduce to a technical prescription for 'mobilising the masses'. They condemn themselves when they cite the fact that they have been repeating for a number of years the slogan which is suitable only for a revolutionary period. The woodpecker who has drilled away at the bark of an oak tree, year in and year out, in all probability at the bottom of his heart also holds to the conviction that the woodsman who chops down the tree with the blows of his axe has criminally plagiarised from him, the woodpecker.

For us, therefore, the slogan of control is tied up with the period of dual power in industry, which corresponds to the transition from the bourgeois regime to the proletarian. Not at all, objects Thalheimer: dual power must signify 'equality [!] with the proprietors'; but the workers are fighting for total direction of industries. They, the Brandlerites, will not allow the revolutionary slogan to be 'castrated' (that is the way they put it!). To them, 'control over production signifies the management of the industries by the workers' (17 January 1932). But why then designate management as *control*? In the language of all mankind control is understood to mean the surveillance and checking of one institution over the work of another. Control may be active, dominant, and all-embracing. But it remains control. The very idea of this slogan was the outgrowth of the transitional regime in industry when the capitalist and his administrators could no longer take a step without the consent of the workers; but on the other hand, when the workers had not as yet provided the political prerequisites for nationalisation, nor yet seized the technical management, nor yet created the organs essential for this. Let us not forget that what is involved here concerns not only taking charge of factories, but also the sale of products and supplying of factories with raw materials and new equipment, as well as credit operations, etc.

The correlation of forces in the factory is determined by the strength of the overall drive of the proletariat against the bourgeoisie. Generally speaking, control is conceivable only during the indubitable preponderance of the political forces of the proletariat over the forces of capitalism. But it is wrong to think that in a revolution all questions need to be and are solved by force; the factories may be seized with the aid of the Red Guard, but their management requires new legal and administrative prerequisites and over and above that, knowledge, skills, and proper organisational forms. A certain period of apprenticeship is required. The proletariat is interested in leaving the management during that period in the hands of an experienced administration, but compelling it to keep all the books open and establishing an alert supervision over all its affiliations and actions.

Workers' control begins with the individual workshop. The organ of control is the factory committee. The factory organs of control join together with each other, according to the economic ties of the industries between themselves. At this stage, there is no general economic plan as yet. The practice of workers' control only prepares the elements of this plan.

On the contrary, the workers' management of industry, to a much greater degree even in its initial steps, proceeds from above, for it is inseparable from state power and the general economic plan. The organs of management are not factory *committees* but centralised *soviets*. The role of the factory committees remains important, of course. But in the sphere of management of industry it has no longer a leading but an auxiliary role.

In Russia where, like the bourgeoisie, the technical intelligentsia was convinced that the Bolshevik experiment would endure only a few weeks, and therefore had steered its course towards all sorts of sabotage and had refused to enter into any agreements, the stage of workers' control did not develop. Moreover, the war was destroying the economic structure by changing the workers into soldiers. Therefore there is comparatively little in the Russian experience to be found in relation to workers' control, as a special regime in industry. But this experience is all the more valuable for the opposite reason: it demonstrates that even in a backward country under the general sabotage of not only the proprietors but also of the administrative-technical personnel, the young and inexperienced proletariat, surrounded by a ring of enemies, was able nevertheless to organise the management of industry. What wouldn't the German working class then be able to accomplish!

The proletariat, as has been said above, is interested in seeing to it that the transitions from the private capitalist to the state capitalist and then to the socialist method of production be accomplished with the least economic convulsions and the least drain upon the national wealth. That is why, while nearing power and even after seizing power by way of the boldest and most decisive struggle, the proletariat will demonstrate complete readiness to establish a transitional regime in the factories, plants, and banks.

Will the relations in industry in Germany during the period of revolution differ from those in Russia? It is not easy to answer this question, particularly from the sidelines. The actual course of the class struggle may not leave room for workers' control as a special stage. Under the extreme tension of the developing struggle, under the increased pressure of the workers on the one side and the sabotage on the part of the proprietors and administrators on the other, there may be no room left for agreements, even though temporary. In such a case, the proletariat will have to assume, together with the power, the full management of industry. The present semi-paralysed state of industry and the presence of a great army of unemployed make such an abridgement quite possible.

But on the other hand the presence of mighty organisations within the working class, the education of the German workers in the spirit of systematic activities and not of improvisations, and the tardiness of the masses in swinging towards revolution can tip the scale in favour of the first way. Therefore it would be inexcusable to reject beforehand the slogan of control over production.

In any event, it is obvious that in Germany, even more than in Russia, the slogan of workers' control has a meaning apart from workers' management. Like many other transitional slogans, it retains an enormous significance independent of the degree to which it will be realised in reality, if realised at all.

By its readiness to establish transitional forms of workers' control, the proletarian vanguard wins over to its side the more conservative strata of the proletariat, and neutralises certain groups of the petty bourgeoisie, especially the technical, administrative, and banking staffs. Should the capitalists and the entire upper layer of the administration demonstrate an utter irreconcilability by resorting to methods of economic sabotage, the responsibility will fall, in the eyes of the nation, not upon the workers but upon the hostile classes. Such is the additional, political import of the slogan of workers' control, along with the above-mentioned economic and administrative meaning.

In any case, the extremes of political cynicism are attested by the fact that those people who have issued the slogan of control in a non-revolutionary situation, and have thereby given it a purely reformist character, accuse us of centrist duality, because of our refusal to identify control with management.

The workers who rise to comprehend the problems of the management of industry will not wish nor will they be able to become drunk with words. They have become used in factories to dealing with materials, less flexible than phrases, and they will comprehend our thoughts better than bureaucrats; genuine revolutionary thinking does not consist in applying force everywhere and at all times, and far less in choking with verbal enthusiasm over force. Where force is necessary, there it must be applied boldly, decisively, and completely. But one must know the limitations of force, one must know when to blend force with a manoeuvre, a blow with an agreement. On anniversaries of Lenin's death, the Stalinist bureaucracy repeats memorised phrases about 'revolutionary realism' in order the more freely to jeer at it during the remaining 364 days.

The prostituted theoreticians of reformism attempt to discover the dawn of socialism in the emergency decrees against the workers. From the 'military socialism' of the Hohenzollerns to the police socialism of Brüning!

Left bourgeois ideologists dream of a planned capitalist economy. But capitalism has had time to demonstrate that in the line of plans it is capable only of draining the productive forces for the sake of war. Disregarding everything else, in what manner can the dependence of Germany—with its enormous figures of import and export—upon the world market be regulated?

We, on our side, propose to begin with the sector of German-Soviet relations, i.e., the elaboration of a broad plan of collaboration between the Soviet and German economy in connection with and supplementary to the second five-year plan. Tens and hundreds of the largest factories could go ahead full steam. The unemployment in Germany could be entirely liquidated—it would hardly take more than two or three years—on the basis of an all-embracing economic plan involving just these two countries.

The leaders of capitalist industry in Germany, obviously,

cannot make such a plan, because it means their social self-elimination. But the Soviet government, with the aid of German technology, can and must work out an entirely practical plan, capable of opening truly grandiose perspectives. How petty all these 'problems' of reparations and added *pfennigs* for customs will appear in comparison to those possibilities which will be opened by coupling the natural, technical, and organisational resources of the Soviet and German national economies.

The German Communists are spreading widescale propaganda concerning the successes of Soviet construction. This work is necessary. But they go off into sickly-sweet rhapsodies. That is entirely superfluous. But worse yet, they have been unable to link together both the successes and the difficulties of the Soviet economy with the immediate interests of the German proletariat; with unemployment, with the lowering of wages, and with the general economic *impasse* of Germany. They have been unable and unwilling to pose the question of Soviet-German collaboration on a strictly practical and at the same time deeply revolutionary basis.

During the first stage of the crisis—more than two years ago—we posed this question in print. And the Stalinists immediately set up a hue and cry that we believe in the peaceful coexistence of socialism and capitalism, that we want to save capitalism, etc. They failed to foresee and understand just one thing, to wit, what a potent factor in a socialist revolution a concrete economic plan of collaboration could become, if it were made the subject of discussion in trade unions and at factory meetings, among workers of operating as well as shut-down industries; and if it were linked with the slogan of workers' control over production and subsequently with the slogan of seizing power. For international planned collaboration can be realised only under monopoly of foreign trade in Germany and the nationalisation of the means of production, in other words, under the dictatorship of the proletariat. Along this road, one could pull new millions of workers, non-party, Social Democrat, and Catholic, into the struggle for power.

The Tarnows are scaring the German workers with the prospect that the industrial breakdown as a consequence of the revolution would result in frightful chaos, famine, etc. Let it be kept in mind that these same people supported the imperialist war, which could bring to the proletariat in its train nothing save tortures, hardships, and degradation. To burden the proletariat with the agonies of war under the banner of the Hohenzollerns? Yes! Revolutionary sacrifices under the banner of socialism? No, never!

Discussions concerning the topic that 'our German workers' would never agree to suffer 'such sacrifices' consist in simultaneously flattering the German workers and vilifying them. Unfortunately, the German workers are too patient. The socialist revolution will not exact from the German proletariat one hundredth of the sacrifices that were swallowed up in the war of Hohenzollern-Leipart-Wels.

15. Is the situation hopeless?

It is a difficult task to arouse all at once the majority of the German working class for an offensive. As a consequence of the adventures of the 'third period', the German workers, who on top of that are bound by powerful conservative organisations, have developed strong centres of inhibition. But, on the other hand, the organisational solidarity of the German workers, which has almost altogether prevented until now the penetration of fascism into their ranks, opens the very greatest possibilities of *defensive* struggle.

One must bear in mind that the policy of the united front is in general much more effective for the defensive than the offensive. The more conservative or backward strata of the proletariat are more easily drawn into a struggle to fight for what they have already than for new conquests.

Brüning's emergency decrees and the threat on the part of Hitler are, in this sense, an 'ideal' signal of alarm for the policy of the united front. It is a matter of defence in the most elementary and obvious meaning of that word. Under such conditions the united front can encompass the widest mass of the working class. And moreover, the goals of the struggle cannot but evoke the sympathy of the lowest layers of the petty bourgeoisie, right down to the street vendors in the workers' sections and districts.

With all its difficulties and dangers the present situation in Germany bears in itself also tremendous advantages for a revolutionary party; it imperiously dictates a clear strategic plan, beginning on the defensive, then assuming the offensive. Without for an instant renouncing its basic goal—the conquest of power—the Communist Party may occupy a defensive position for the sake of immediate and urgent actions. 'Class against class!' It is time to restore to this formula its real significance!

The repulsion by the workers of the offensive of capital and the government will inevitably call forth a redoubled offensive on the part of fascism. No matter how modest the first steps of the defence, the reaction from the enemy would immediately weld together the ranks of the united front, extend the tasks, compel the utilisation of more decisive measures, throw out the reactionary layers of the bureaucracy from the united front, extend the influence of Communism by weakening the barriers between the workers, and thus prepare for the transformation from the defensive to the offensive.

If the Communist Party conquers the leading position in defensive battles—and it is assured of this under a correct policy—then it will in no way require the assent of the reformist and centrist upper crust when the transition to the offensive is reached. The masses are the ones who decide; the moment that the masses are separated from the reformist leadership, any agreement with the latter loses all meaning. To perpetuate the united front would be to misunderstand the dialectic of revolutionary struggle, and to transform the united front from a springboard into a barrier.

The most difficult political situations are in a certain sense the easiest; they allow only of one solution. Once the task is lucidly stated then it is in principle already solved; from the united front in the name of defence to the conquest of power under the banner of Communism.

Can this be done? The situation is difficult. Reformism is backed by ultra-left ultimatism. The bureaucratic dictatorship of the bourgeoisie is supported by reformism. Brüning's bureaucratic dictatorship intensifies the economic agony of the nation and nourishes fascism.

The situation is very onerous, very dangerous, but far from hopeless. No matter how powerful the Stalinist apparatus may be, armed as it is with the usurped authority and the material resources of the October Revolution, it is not omnipotent. The dialectic of the class war is more powerful. One need only give it timely assistance.

At this moment many 'lefts' are making a display of pessimism as regards the fate of Germany. In 1923, they say, when fascism was yet very weak, while the Communist Party had a serious influence in the trade unions and factory committees, the proletariat failed of victory; how then may one expect victory now when the party has become weaker and fascism incomparably stronger?

Imposing as the argument may seem at first glance, it is nevertheless false. In 1923 matters did not reach the stage of battle; the party shunned battle before the phantom of fascism. Where there is no fight, there can be no victory. It is precisely the strength of fascism and its thrust that eliminate this time the possibility of avoiding battle. Battle will have to be given. And if the German working class begins to fight it may conquer. It must conquer.

Even yesterday the supreme leaders said: 'Let fascism assume power, we are not afraid, they will quickly shoot their bolt, etc.' This idea ruled the summits of the Communist Party several months at a stretch. Had it become absolutely entrenched, it would have signified that the Communist Party had undertaken to chloroform the proletariat prior to Hitler's lopping off its head. Herein lay the greatest danger. At this moment no one repeats it any longer. The first positions have been won by us. The working masses are becoming imbued with the idea that fascism must be crushed before they can come to power. That is a very valuable victory. One must lean upon it in all subsequent agitation.

The mood of the working class is deeply troubled. They are tormented by unemployment and need. But they are goaded even more by the confusion of their leadership and the general mess. The workers understand that Hitler must not be allowed to come to power. But how? No way is visible. From above there comes not assistance but interference. Yet the workers want to fight.

There is an astounding fact, insofar as one may judge from afar, which has been insufficiently appraised, to wit: the Hirsch-Duncker coal miners have resolved that the capitalist system must be supplanted by the socialist! Why, this means that tomorrow they will be ready to create soviets as the organs of the entire class. Perhaps they are ready for it even today; one must only know enough to ask them! This symptom alone is a thousand times more important and convincing than all the impressionistic appraisals of literary gentlemen and orators, who are haughtily displeased with the masses.

Within the ranks of the Communist Party there seems to be passivity, factually and demonstrably, despite the proddings of the apparatus. But why? The rank and file of the Communists attend more and more rarely the meetings of the cells, where they are fed dry chaff. The ideas, which are supplied to them from above, can be applied neither in the factory nor on the street. The worker feels the irreconcilable contradiction between that which he needs when he stands face to face with the mass and that which is dished out to him during the official meetings of the party. The false atmosphere that is created by the shrill and boastful apparatus that brooks no contradiction is becoming insufficient for the rank and file of the party. Hence we get emptiness and frigidity at party meetings. But this is not an unwillingness to fight, only political confusion as well as a dumb protest against the all-powerful but brainless leadership.

The perplexity in the ranks of the proletariat raises the spirits of the fascists. Their offensive is extended. The danger grows. But precisely the nearness of the fascist danger will sharpen extremely the sight nd hearing of the leading workers and will create an advantageous atmosphere for lucid and simple propositions that lead to action.

Citing Brunswick as an example, Münzenberg wrote in November of last year: 'As regards the fact that this united front will spring up all at once, elementally, under the pressure of the increased fascist terror and fascist attacks—as regards this fact, there can be no doubt even today.' Münzenberg does not explain to us why the Central Executive Committee, of which he is a member, has not made the Brunswick events a point of departure for a bold policy of the united front. But just the same, without ceasing thereby to be an admission of his own insufficiency, Münzenberg's prognosis is correct.

The imminence of the fascist danger cannot but lead to the

radicalisation of the Social Democratic workers and even of considerable sections of the reformist apparatus. The revolutionary wing of the SAP will indubitably take a step forward. So much the more inevitable, under these conditions, does the about-face of the Communist apparatus become, even at the cost of inner rifts and splits. One must orient oneself precisely towards this direction of developments.

A turn by the Stalinists is inevitable. Symptoms here and there, measuring the force of pressure from below, are to be observed already; some arguments are supplanted by others, the phraseology becomes more and more obscure, the slogans more equivocal; at the same time all those are being excluded from the party who were careless enough to comprehend the task before the Central Executive Committee. All these are unmistakable symptoms of the approaching about-face; but they are only symptoms.

More than once in the past it has happened that the Stalinist bureaucracy, having spoiled paper in hundreds of tons in polemics against counter-revolutionary 'Trotskyism', thereafter made an abrupt turnabout and tried to fulfil the program of the Left Opposition—in truth, sometimes after hopeless delays.

In China the turnabout came too late and in such form as to finish off the revolution (the Canton insurrection!). In Britain the 'turnabout' was made by the adversaries, i.e., the General Council, which broke off with the Stalinists when it no longer needed them. But in the USSR the 1928 turnabout came in time to save the dictatorship from the impending catastrophe. It is not hard to find the reasons for the differences in these three important examples. In China, the young and inexperienced Communist Party believed blindly in the Moscow leadership; the voice of the Russian Opposition did not, generally, succeed even in getting there. Approximately the same thing happened in Britain. In the USSR, the Left Opposition was on the spot and ceaselessly continued its campaign against the *kulak* policies. In China and Russia, Stalin and Co took risks at a distance; in the USSR the matter concerned their own heads directly.

The political advantages of the German working class consist in the fact that all questions are posed openly and in good time; that the authority of the leadership of the Comintern has been greatly weakened; that the Marxist Opposition operates on the scene, in Germany itself; and that in the composition of the proletarian vanguard there are to be found thousands of experienced and critical individuals, who are capable of making themselves heard, and who are beginning to make themselves heard.

Numerically, the Left Opposition in Germany is weak. But its political influence may prove decisive on the given, sharp, historical turn. As the switchman, by the timely turn of the switch, shifts a heavily laden train onto different tracks, so the small Opposition, by a strong and sure turn of the ideological switch, can compel the train of the German Communist Party, and the still heavier train of the German proletariat, to go on in a different direction.

The correctness of our position will become apparent in action with each passing day. When the ceiling overhead bursts into flame, the most stubborn bureaucrats must forget about prestige. Even genuine privy councillors, in such situations, jump out of windows in their underwear. The pedagogy of facts will come to the assistance of our criticism.

Will the German Communist Party succeed in making the turn in time? At present one may speak of timeliness only conventionally. Had it not been for the frenzy of the 'third period', the German proletariat would today be in power. Had the Communist Party, after the last elections to the Reichstag, taken the programme of action proposed by the Left Opposition, victory would have been assured. One cannot now speak of an assured victory. It is necessary now to call that turn timely which will enable the German workers to give battle before fascism takes over the state apparatus.

To accomplish such a turn, it is necessary to exert every effort. It is necessary for the leading elements of Communism, within the party and without, not to shy away from action. It is necessary to fight openly against the dumb ultimatism of the bureaucracy both within the party and in the face of the working masses.

'But that is a breach of discipline,' the wavering Communist will say. Of course, it is a breach of Stalinist discipline. No serious revolutionary will commit a breach of discipline, even formally, if there are no imperative reasons for it. Yet they are no revolutionists but rags and irresolute riff-raff who under the cover of discipline tolerate policies the balefulness of which is quite obvious to them.

It would be a criminal act on the part of the Opposition Communists to take, like Urbahns and Co, to the road of creating a new Communist Party, before making some serious efforts to change the course of the old party. It is not difficult to create a small independent organisation. To create a new Communist Party is a gigantic task. Are there cadres for such a task? If there are, what have they done to influence tens of thousands of workers that are enrolled in the official party? If these cadres consider themselves capable of explaining to the workers the need for a new party, they should first of all test themselves in the work of reviving the existing party.

To pose now the question of a third party is to counterpose oneself on the eve of a great historical solution to the millions of Communist workers who are dissatisfied with the leadership but who, from a feeling of self-preservation, hold on to the party. One must find a common tongue with these millions of Communist workers. One must find access to the consciousness of these workers, ignoring curses, calumny, and the persecutions of functionaries; one must show them that we want the same things as they do, that we have no interests other than the interests of Communism, that the road we point out is the only correct road.

We must mercilessly expose ultra-radical capitulators and demand from the 'leaders' clear answers to the question *what to do*; and we must offer our answer, for the entire country, for every section, every city, every district, every factory.

Within the party, nuclei of Bolshevik-Leninists must be created. On their banner they must inscribe: change the course and reform the party regime. Wherever they can assure themselves of serious support, they must proceed to the actual application of the policy of the united front, even within a small local scope. The party bureaucracy will resort to expulsions? Certainly. But under the present conditions its omnipotence will not long endure.

Within the ranks of Communism and the entire proletariat there must be free discussion, without breaking up meetings, without falsified citations, without venomous vilification—but an honest interchange of opinions on the basis of proletarian democracy. It was thus that we conducted debates with all parties and within our own party throughout the entire year of 1917. Through a widespread discussion the extraordinary session of the party must be prepared for, with the sole question on the order of the day: 'What next?'

Left Oppositionists are not intermediaries between the Communist Party and the Social Democracy. They are the soldiers of Communism, its agitators, its propagandists and its organisers. All eyes to the Communist Party! We must explain to it, we must convince it!

Should the Communist Party be compelled to apply the policy of the united front, this will almost certainly make it possible to beat off the fascist attack. In its own turn, a serious victory over fascism will clear the road for the dictatorship of the proletariat.

But even at the helm of revolution, the Communist Party will still bear within itself many contradictions. The mission of the Left Opposition will not at all be completed. In a certain sense it will only begin. In the first place, the victory of proletarian revolution in Germany would signify the liquidation of the bureaucratic dependence of the Communist Party upon the Stalinist apparatus.

On the very next day after the victory of the German proletariat, even before, while yet in the process of its struggle for power, the hoops that bind the Comintern will burst. The barrenness of the ideas of bureaucratic centrism, the national limitations of its outlook, the anti-proletarian character of its regime—all these will at once be revealed in the light of the German Revolution, which will be immeasurably more brilliant than the light of the October Revolution. The ideas of Marx and Lenin will gain their inevitable hegemony within the German proletariat.

Conclusions

A cattle dealer once drove some bulls to the slaughter-house. And the butcher came nigh with his sharp knife. 'Let us close ranks and jack up this executioner on our horns,' suggested one of the bulls.

'If you please, in what way is the butcher any worse than the dealer who drove us hither with his cudgel?' replied the bulls, who had received their political education in Manuilsky's institute.

'But we shall be able to attend to the dealer as well afterwards!'

'Nothing doing,' replied the bulls, firm in their principles, to the counsellor. 'You are trying to shield our enemies from the left; you are a social-butcher yourself.'

And they refused to close ranks.

—from **Aesop's Fables**.

To put the liberation from the Peace of Versailles necessarily, absolutely, and immediately first in precedence to the liberation of other nations downtrodden by imperialism, from the yoke of imperialism—that is middle-class nationalism (worthy of Kautskys, Hilferdings, Otto Bauer & Co) but not revolutionary internationalism.

—Lenin, **Left-Wing Communism: An Infantile Disorder**.

What we need is the complete rejection of national Communism; an open and decisive liquidation of such slogans as 'People's Revolution' and 'National Liberation'. Not 'Down with the Versailles Treaty!' but 'Long live the Soviet United States of Europe!'

Socialism can be realised only on the basis of the highest achievements of contemporary technology and on the basis of the international division of labour.

The socialist construction of the USSR is not a self-sufficient national process, but an integral part of the international revolution.

The conquest of power by the German and European proletariat is a task infinitely more real and immediate than the building of a closed and self-sufficient society within the boundaries of the USSR.

Unconditional defence of the USSR, the first workers' state, against the inside and outside foes of the proletarian dictatorship!

But the defence of the USSR cannot be carried on with the

eyes blindfolded. International proletarian control over the Soviet bureaucracy. Merciless exposure of its national-reformist and Thermidorean tendencies that find their generalisation in the theory of socialism in one country.

What does the Communist Party require?

The return to the strategical school of the first four congresses of the Comintern.

The rejection of ultimatism in relations with mass workers' organisations; Communist leadership cannot be imposed; it can only be won.

The rejection of the theory of social fascism which aids both Social Democracy and fascism.

Persistent exploitation of the antagonism between Social Democracy and fascism: (a) for the sake of more effective struggle against fascism; (b) for the sake of counterposing the Social Democratic workers to the reformist leadership.

To us the criteria for appraising changes in political regimes of bourgeois rule are not the principles of formal democracy but the vital interests of proletarian democracy.

No direct or indirect support of Brüning's regime!

Bold, self-sacrificing defence of proletarian organisations against fascism.

'Class against class!' This means all organisations of the proletariat must take their place in the united front against the bourgeoisie.

The practical programme of the united front is determined by agreements with organisations made in full view of the masses. Every organisation remains under its own banner and its own leadership. Every organisation obeys in action the discipline of the united front.

'Class against class!' Indefatigable agitation must be conducted in order that the Social Democratic organisations and the reformist trade unions shall break with the perfidious bourgeois allies in the 'Iron Front' and that they join in common with the Communists and all other organisations of the proletariat.

'Class against class!' Propaganda and organisational preparation for workers' soviets, as the highest forms of the proletarian united front.

Full organisational and political independence of the Communist Party at all times and under all conditions.

No combining whatever of programmes or banners. No unprincipled deals. Complete freedom of criticism of temporary allies.

The candidacy of Thälmann for the presidency is, self-evidently, the candidacy supported by the Left Opposition. In the struggle for the mobilisation of workers under the banner of the official Communist candidacy, the Bolshevik-Leninists must be in the front line.

The German Communists must take their inspiration not from the present regime in the CPSU, which reflects the domination of the apparatus on the foundation of a victorious revolution, but from that party regime which led to the victory of the revolution.

The liquidation of bossing by the apparatus within the German Communist Party is a life-and-death question.

There must be a return to party democracy.

Worker-Communists must attempt first of all to initiate an honest and serious discussion in the party on questions of strategy and tactics. The voice of the Left Opposition (Bolshevik-Leninists)must be heard by the party.

After a thorough discussion, the decisions must be passed by a freely elected special congress of the party.

A correct policy of the Communist Party in relation to the SAP should consist of an irreconcilable criticism (but conscientious, that is, corresponding to the facts) of the dual nature of its leadership; an attentive, comradely, and sensitive relation to the left wing—with a complete readiness for practical agreements with the SAP and for more intimate political ties with the revolutionary wing.

A sharp turn of the helm in the trade-union policy; a struggle against the reformist leadership on the basis of trade-union unity.

A systematically applied policy of the united front in industry. Agreements with reformist factory committees on the basis of a definite programme of demands.

Fight for lower prices. Fight against lower wages. Switch this fight onto the tracks of a campaign for workers' control over production.

Campaign for collaboration with the USSR on the basis of a single economic plan.

A draft plan must be worked out by the respective organs of the USSR with the participation of interested organisations of the German proletariat.

Campaign for the change of Germany to socialism on the basis of such a plan.

They lie who say that the situation seems hopeless. Pessimists and sceptics must be driven out of the proletarian ranks, as carriers of a deadly infection. The inner forces of the German proletariat are inexhaustible. They will clear the road for themselves.

Part Three | **1932**

Chris Harman

1932: Background

IN 1932 the economic situation worsened. There were eight million unemployed. A third of the urban population depended on the dole. The real wages of those with jobs had fallen by a third since 1928. All sections of German society were discontented with the government. The Nazi vote seemed to be growing at an irresistible pace. Furthermore, willing industrialists seemed only too prepared to finance the fascists. The number of members of the SA had risen to 400,000.

Yet Hitler was far from having the majority of the German people behind him. Brüning persuaded the ageing reactionary Field Marshal Hindenburg to stand for re-election as president. Despite Hindenburg's opposition to everything they purported to stand for, the SPD and the free trade unions supported him as the 'lesser evil' against Hitler. The Nazis obtained their biggest vote yet—36.8 per cent of the total—but were far behind Hindenburg's 53 per cent (Thälmann got 10.2 per cent).

The Social Democrats continued to wait and hope. They continued to argue that the only sort of force they could employ was defensive force. They formed all the Social Democrat-influenced organisations, the free trade unions, the sports clubs, the Reichsbanner, into an 'Iron Front' to defend the republic—but not to fight the misery produced by capitalism in crisis under the republican Brüning. And the lynch-pin in their defensive system continued to be the Prussian police force.

The Brüning government fell at the end of May, basically because the only positive supporters it had—the Reichswehr—turned against it. During the presidential elections of April information was discovered that the Nazis were preparing a coup. Worried by this, Brüning, who had let the stormtroopers behave very much as they liked previously, now banned the SA and the SS. But the most politically influential member of the General Staff, Schleicher, took objection to this. He wanted to use control of the streets by the SA and SS for his own ends. He made it clear that the army was now against the government. When at the same time Brüning made one of his few positive proposals for dealing with the economic crisis—that the estates of bankrupt *Junkers* in East Prussia be bought up by the state and given to landless peasants—the agrarian interests close to Hindenberg turned against him as well. Brüning was replaced by an appointee of Schleicher, von Papen, who had virtually no parliamentary support and depended on Nazi votes, the ban on the SA and SS was lifted, and now elections were called.

The return of the SA to the streets led to street fighting everywhere. Eighty-two people were killed and 400 seriously injured. At the height of this violence von Papen dismissed the Prussian Social-Democratic government. Such an action was completely unconstitutional. Furthermore it was carried out by a government with no pretence of a parliamentary majority. It was precisely this sort of eventuality that the 'Iron Front' of the Social Democrats existed to fight. If they did not, their whole defensive strategy would have collapsed. The Social Democratic Minister of the Interior, Severing, and his police chief, Grzesinski, refused to resign.

> In the city [Berlin], that was in the throes of a violent election campaign, these proclamations...fell like a thunderbolt. Holding their breath people looked now to the Ministry of the Interior where Severing resided, now to the Wilhelmstrasse, where Papen resided. Everywhere discussions were to be heard on whether the Prussian police or the Reichswehr were superior in fighting... In the large works, workers waited all night for the order for a general strike.[1]

The massed forces of the 'Iron Front' had been prepared over the years for precisely such a moment. Yet the Social Democratic leaders did nothing. Force had to be used to arrest Severing and his police chief: four soldiers took them from buildings that were full of armed police who would have obeyed any order. There was no resistance whatsoever. After only two hours in prison Severing and Grzesinski resigned. The 'Social Democratic fortress' had fallen without a shot being fired.

The Communists were prepared to fight. It was they that had been resisting the SA in the street battles. Thirty of their members had been among those killed. They did issue a leaflet calling for a general strike. But they could not organise one alone. They had very few members in the factories: the majority of their members were unemployed (in the Trades Council elections of March 1933 they only received 5 per cent of the votes, compared with 73 per cent for the Social democrats and 12 per cent for the Nazis.[2] This perhaps would not have mattered at such a crucial juncture were it not for the inconsistency of the KPD. It was now calling upon workers to defend a government it had all along called 'social fascist' and, even worse, had worked alongside the Nazis to overthrow. No one took the belated call to action seriously.

In the elections that followed a week later the Nazis received their highest vote ever in a free election, nearly 14 million, twice that of the last election in 1930. The SPD lost 600,000 votes and the KPD gained the same number. The combined vote of the working-class parties was still only a few hundred thousand behind that of the Nazis. But the Prussian coup had made it clear that no combined resistance was likely.

The Communist leaders were still unable to see the danger before their very eyes. The Comintern executive at its September meeting still argued that the 'main attack' should be directed at the Social Democrats.[3] At the October Conference of the KPD, the call for a united front was referred to as a 'demagogic United Front manoeuvre in which the left allies of the social fascists and the counter-revolutionary Trotskyist group are especially active.'[4] Trotsky was called by Thälmann 'an utterly bankrupt fascist and counter-revolutionary.'

The Only Road was written in the weeks after the July election of 1932. Here Trotsky analyses the overall forces at work in the German situation. On the one hand he is concerned to show that Hitler can still be checked by united working-class action; on the other that the illusions of the Social Democrats, that the 'lesser evil' will prevent the greater one, and of the

Communists, that their electoral gains at the expense of the SPD will somehow stop Hitler or ensure that they follow him, are false.

What appears here is not the whole work. The chapters omitted (4, 5 and 6), however, merely repeat many of the arguments given in **What Next?** This translation, by Max Shachtman and B J Field, first appeared in the United States in 1933.

Leon Trotsky

The Only Road

THE DECLINE of capitalism promises to be still more stormy, dramatic, and bloody than its rise. German capitalism will surely prove no exception. If its agony is being stretched out too long, the fault lies—we must speak the truth—with the parties of the proletariat.

German capitalism appeared late on the scene, and was deprived of the privileges of the first-born. Russia's development placed it somewhere between England and India; Germany, in such a scheme, would have to occupy the place between England and Russia, but without the enormous overseas colonies of Great Britain and without the 'internal colonies' of Tsarist Russia. Germany, squeezed into the heart of Europe, was faced—at a time when the whole world had already been divided up—with the necessity of conquering foreign markets and redividing colonies which had already been divided.

German capitalism was not destined to swim with the stream, to give itself up to the free play of forces. Only Great Britain could afford this luxury, and then only for a limited historical period, which has recently ended before our eyes. German capitalism could not even afford the 'sense of moderation' of French capitalism, which is entrenched within its limitations and in addition is equipped with the rich colonial possessions as a reserve.

The German bourgeoisie, opportunist through and through in the domain of internal politics, had to rise to heights of audacity and rapidity in that of economy and of world politics; it had to expand its production immeasurably, to catch up with the older nations, to rattle the sword and hurl itself into the war.

The extreme rationalisation of German industry after the war likewise resulted from the necessity of overcoming the unfavourable conditions of historical delay, the geographical situation, and military defeat.

If the economic evils of our epoch, in the last analysis, result from the fact that the productive forces of humanity are incompatible with private ownership of the means of production as well as with national boundaries, German capitalism is going through the severest convulsions just because it is the most modern, most advanced, and most dynamic capitalism on the continent of Europe.

The physicians of German capitalism are divided into three schools: liberalism, planned economy, and autarchy.

Liberalism would like to restore the *'natural' laws of the market*. But the wretched political fate of liberalism only reflects the fact that German capitalism could never base itself on Manchesterism,[1] but went through protectionism to trusts and monopolies. German economy cannot be brought back to a 'healthy' past which never existed.

'National Socialism' promises to revise the work of Versailles in its own manner, i.e., to carry further the offensive of Hohenzollern imperialism. At the same time it wants to bring Germany to *autarchy*, i.e., onto the road of provincialism and voluntary restriction. The lion's roar in this case hides the psychology of the whipped dog. To adapt German capitalism to its national boundaries is about the same as to cure a sick man by cutting off his right hand, his left foot, and part of his skull.

To cure capitalism by means of *planned economy* would mean to eliminate competition. In such a case we must begin with the abolition of private ownership of the means of production. The bureaucratic-professorial reformers do not even dare to think of it. German economy is, least of all, purely German: it is an integral constituent of world economy. A German plan is conceivable only in the perspective of an international economic plan. A planned system within closed national boundaries would mean the abnegation of world economy, i.e., the attempt to retreat to the system of autarchy.

These three systems, with their mutual feuds, in reality resemble each other in the respect that they are all shut in within the magic circle of reactionary utopianism. What must be saved is not German capitalism, but Germany—from capitalism.

In the years of the crisis, the German bourgeoisie, or its theoreticians at least, have uttered speeches of repentance— yes, they had carried out much too risky policies, they had too lightly resorted to the help of foreign credits, had pushed forward too fast the modernisation of factory equipment, etc. In the future one must be more careful! In reality, however, as the Papen programme and the attitude of finance-capital toward it have shown, the leaders of the German bourgeoisie incline today more than ever to economic adventurism.

At first signs of an industrial revival, German capitalism will show itself to be what its historical past has made it, and not what the liberal moralists would like to make it. The entrepreneurs, hungry for profits, will again raise the steam pressure without looking at the pressure gauge. The chase for foreign credits will again take on a feverish character. Are the possibilities of expansion slight? All the more necessary to monopolise them for oneself. The terrified world will again see the picture of the preceding period, but in the form of still more violent convulsions. At the same time, the restoration of German militarism will proceed. As if the years 1914-1918 had never existed. The German bourgeoisie is again placing East Elbe barons at the head of the nation. Under Bonapartist auspices they are even more inclined to risk the head of the nation than under those of the legitimate monarchy.

In their lucid moments the leaders of the German Social Democracy must ask themselves: 'By what miracle does the party, after all the damage that it has done, still lead millions of workers?' Certainly, great importance must be given to the conservatism innate in every mass organisation. Several generations of the proletariat have gone through Social Democracy as a political school; this has created a great tradition. Yet that is not the main reason for the vitality of reformism. The workers cannot simply leave the Social Democracy, in spite of all the crimes of that party; they must be able to replace it by another party. Meanwhile the German Communist Party, in the person of its leaders, has for the past nine years done decidedly everything in its power to repel the masses, or at least prevent them from rallying around the Communist Party.

The policy of capitulation of Stalin-Brandler in the year 1923; the ultra-left zigzag of Maslow-Ruth Fischer-Thälmann in 1924-25; the opportunistic crawling before the Social Democracy in 1926-28; the adventurism of the 'third period' in 1928-1930; the theory and practice of 'social fascism' and of 'national liberation' in 1930-32—those are the items of the bill. The total reads: Hindenburg-Papen-Schleicher & Co.

On the capitalist road, there is no issue for the German people. Therein lies the important source of strength for the Communist Party. The example of the Soviet Union shows through experience that there is a way out on the socialist road. Therein lies the second source of strength for the Communist Party.

Only—thanks to the condition of development of the isolated proletarian state, there arrived at the leadership of the Soviet Union a national-opportunistic bureaucracy, which does not believe in the world revolution, which defends its independence of the world revolution and at the same time maintains an unlimited domination over the Communist International. Therein consists at the present time the greater misfortune for the German and the international proletariat.

The situation in Germany is as if purposely created to make it possible for the Communist Party to win the majority of the workers in a short time. Only, the Communist Party must understand that as yet, today, it represents the minority of the proletariat, and must firmly tread the road of united front tactics. Instead of this, the Communist Party has made its own a tactic which can be expressed in the following words: not to give the German workers the possibility of carrying on economic struggles, or offering resistance to fascism, or of seizing the weapon of the general strike, or of creating soviets—before the entire proletariat recognises in advance the leadership of the Communist Party. The political task is converted into an ultimatum.

From where could this destructive method have come? The answer to this is the policy of the Stalinist fraction in the Soviet Union. There the apparatus has converted political leadership into administrative command. In refusing to permit the workers to discuss, or criticise, or vote, the Stalinist bureaucracy speaks to them in no other language than that of the ultimatum. The policy of Thälmann is an attempt to translate Stalinism into bad German. But the difference consists in the fact that the bureaucracy of the USSR has at the disposal of its policy of command the state power, which it received at the hands of the October revolution. Thälmann, on the other hand, has, for the reinforcement of his ultimatum, only the formal authority of the Soviet Union. This is a great source of moral assistance, but under the given conditions it suffices only to close the mouths of the Communist workers, but not to win over the Social Democratic workers. But this latter task constitutes in fact the problem of the German revolution.

Continuing the former works of the author, devoted to the policy of the German proletariat, the present brochure attempts to investigate the questions of German revolutionary policy in a new stage.

Bonapartism and Fascism

Let us endeavour to realise briefly what has occurred and where we stand.

Thanks to the Social Democracy, the Brüning government had at its disposal the support of parliament for ruling with the aid of emergency decrees. The Social Democratic leaders said: 'In this manner we shall block the road of fascism to power.' The Stalinist bureaucracy said: 'No, fascism has already triumphed; it is the Brüning regime which is fascism.' Both were false. The Social Democrats palmed off a passive retreat before fascism as the struggle against fascism. The Stalinists presented the matter as if the victory of fascism was already behind them. The fighting power of the proletariat was sapped by both sides and the triumph of the enemy facilitated and brought closer.

In its time, we designated the Brüning government as *Bonapartism* ('a caricature of Bonapartism'), that is, as a regime of military-police dictatorship. As soon as the struggle of two social strata—the haves and the have-nots, the exploiters and the exploited—reaches its highest tension, the conditions are established for the domination of bureaucracy, police, soldiery. The government becomes 'independent' of society. Let us once more recall: if two forks are struck symmetrically into a cork, the latter can stand even on the head of a pin. That is precisely the schema of Bonapartism. To be sure, such a government does not cease being the clerk of the property owners. Yet the clerk sits on the back of the boss, rubs his neck raw and does not hesitate at times to dig his boots into his face.

It might have been assumed that Brüning would hold on until the final solution. Yet, in the course of events, another link inserted itself: the Papen government. Were we to be exact, we should have to make a rectification of our old designation: the Brüning government was a pre-Bonapartist government. Brüning was only a precursor. In a perfected form, Bonapartism came upon the scene in the Papen-Schleicher government.

Wherein lies the difference? Brüning asserted that he knew no greater happiness than to 'serve' Hindenburg and Paragraph 48. Hitler 'supported' Brüning's right flank with his fist. But with the left elbow Brüning rested on Wels' shoulder. In the Reichstag, Brüning found a majority which relieved him of the necessity of reckoning with the Reichstag.

The more Brüning's independence from the parliament grew, the more independent did the summits of the bureaucracy feel themselves from Brüning and the political groupings standing behind him. There only remained finally to break the bonds with the Reichstag. The Von Papen government emerged from an immaculate bureaucratic conception. With the right elbow it rests upon Hitler's shoulder. With the police fist it wards off the proletariat on the left. Therein lies the secret of its 'stability', that is, of the fact that it did not collapse at the moment of its birth.

The Brüning government bore a clerical-bureaucratic-police character. The Reichswehr still remained in reserve. Next to the police, the 'Iron Front' served as a direct prop of Order. It is precisely in wiping out the dependence on the 'Iron Front' that lay the essence of the Hindenburg-Papen *coup d'état*. The generals moved up automatically to first place.

The Social Democratic leaders turned out to be completely duped. And it is no more than proper for them in periods of social crisis. These petty bourgeois intriguers appear to be clever only under those conditions where cleverness is not necessary. Now they pull the covers over their heads at night, sweat and hope for a miracle: perhaps in the end we may yet be able to save not only our necks but also the over-stuffed furniture and the little, innocent savings. But there will be no more miracles...

Unfortunately, however, the Communist Party has also been taken completely by surprise by the events. The Stalinist bureaucracy was unable to foresee a thing. Today Thälmann, Remmele and others speak on every occasion of 'the *coup d'état* of July 20'. How is that? At first they contended that fascism had already arrived and that only 'counter-revolutionary Trotskyists' could speak of it as something in the future. Now it turns out that to pass over from Brüning to Papen—for the present not to Hitler but only to Papen—a whole '*coup d'état*' was necessary. Yet the class content of Severing, Brüning and Hitler, these sages taught us, is 'one and the same thing'. Then whence and wherefore the *coup d'état*?

But the confusion doesn't come to an end with this. Even though the difference between Bonapartism and fascism has now been revealed plainly enough, Thälmann, Remmele and others speak of the *fascist coup d'état* of 20 July. At the same time, they warn the workers against the approaching danger of the Hitlerist, that is, of the equally fascist, overturn. Finally the Social Democracy is designated just as before as social fascist. The unfolding events are in this way reduced to this: the species of Fascism take the power from each other with the aid of 'fascist' *coups d'état*. Isn't it clear that the whole Stalinist theory was created only for the purpose of gumming up the human brain?

The less prepared the workers were, the more the appearance of the Papen government on the scene had to arouse the impression of strength: complete ignoring of the parties, new emergency decrees, dissolution of the Reichstag, reprisals, state of siege in the capital, the abolition of the Prussian 'democracy'. And with what ease! A lion you kill with a shot; the flea you squash between the finger nails; Social Democratic ministers are finished off with a fillip.

Only, in spite of the appearance of concentrated forces, the Papen government 'as such' is weaker yet than its predecessor. The Bonapartist regime can attain a comparatively stable and durable character only in the event that it brings a revolutionary epoch to a close; when the relationship of forces has already been tested in battles; when the revolutionary classes are already spent; while the possessing classes have not yet freed themselves from the fear: will not the morrow bring new convulsions? Without this basic condition, that is, without a preceding exhaustion of the mass energies in battles, the Bonapartist regime is in no position to develop.

Through the Papen government, the barons, the magnates of capital and the bankers have undertaken to attempt to secure their weal by means of the police and the regular army. The idea of giving up all power to Hitler, who supports himself upon the avid and unleashed bands of the petty bourgeoisie, is far from a pleasant one to them. They do not, of course, doubt that in the long run Hitler will be a submissive instrument of their domination. Yet this is bound up with concessions, with the risk of a long and a weary civil war and great expense. To be sure, fascism, as the Italian example shows, leads in the end to a militarist-bureaucratic dictatorship of the Bonapartist type. But for that it requires a number of years even in the event of a complete victory: a longer span of years in Germany than in Italy. It is clear that the possessing classes would prefer a more economical path, that is, the path of Schleicher and not of Hitler, not to speak of the fact that Schleicher himself prefers it that way.

The fact that the source of existence of the Papen government consists in the neutralisation of the irreconcilable camps in no way signifies, of course, that the forces of the revolutionary proletariat and of the reactionary petty bourgeoisie weigh equally on the scale of history. The whole question shifts here on to the field of politics. Through the mechanics of the 'Iron Front' the Social Democracy paralyses the proletariat. With the policy of brainless ultimatism the Stalinist bureaucracy blocks the revolutionary way out for the workers. With a correct leadership of the proletariat, fascism would be exterminated without difficulty and not a chink could remain open for Bonapartism. Unfortunately that is not the situation. The paralysed strength of the proletariat has assumed the deceptive form of a 'strength' of the Bonapartist clique. Therein lies the political formula of the present day.

The Papen government represents the impersonal intersection of great historical forces. Its independent weight is next to nil. Therefore it could do nothing but take fright at its own gesticulations and grow dizzy from the voids arising on all sides of it. By this and only by this is to be explained that in the deeds of the government up to now there have been two parts of cowardice to each part of audacity. With Prussia, that is, the Social Democracy, the government played a sure game: it knew that these gentlemen would offer no resistance. But after it had dissolved the Reichstag, it summoned new elections and did not dare to postpone them. After proclaiming the state of martial law, it hastened to explain: it is only in order to facilitate the capitulation without a struggle of the Social Democratic leaders.

However, isn't there a Reichswehr? We are not inclined to forget it. Engels designated the state as armed detachments of people with material auxiliaries in the form of prisons, etc. With respect to the present governmental power, it can even be said that the Reichswehr alone really exists. But the Reichswehr in no way represents a submissive and guaranteed instrument in the hands of that group of people at whose head stands Papen. In reality, the government is rather a sort of political commission of the Reichswehr.

But with all its preponderance over the government, the Reichswehr can nevertheless lay no claim to any independent political role. A hundred thousand soldiers, no matter how fused and steeled they may be (which still requires testing), are incapable of commanding a nation of sixty-five millions, torn by the profoundest social antagonisms. The Reichswehr represents only one element in the interplay of forces, and not the decisive one.

In its fashion, the new Reichswehr does not reflect badly the political situation in the country which has led to the Bonapartist experiment. The parliament without a majority, with irreconcilable wings, offers an obvious and irrefutable argument in favour of dictatorship. Once more the limits of democracy emerge in all their obviousness. Where it is a question of the foundations of society itself, it is not parliamentary arithmetic; it is the struggle that decides.

We shall not try to guess from afar just what road the attempts at reshuffling the government will take in the immediate period ahead. Our hypotheses would come tardily in any case, and besides, it is not the possible transitional forms and combinations which decide the question. A bloc of the right wing with the centre would signify the 'legalisation' of the assumption of power by the Nazis, that is, would create the most suitable cloak for the fascist *coup d'état*. What relationships would develop in the early days between Hitler, Schleicher and the centre leaders, is more important for them than it is for the German people. Politically, all the conceivable combinations with Hitler signify the dissolution of bureaucracy, courts, police and army into fascism.

If it is assumed that the centre will not agree to a coalition, in which it would have to pay with a rupture with its own workers for the role of a brake in Hitler's locomotive—then in this case only the unconcealed extra-parliamentary road remains. A combination without the centre would more easily and speedily insure the predominance of the Nazis. If the latter do not immediately unite with Papen and at the same time do not pass over to the immediate assault, then the Bonapartist character of the government will have to emerge more sharply: von Schleicher would have his 'hundred days'... without the preceding Napoleonic years.

Hundred days—no, we are allotting far too generous a space of time. The Reichswehr does not decide. Schleicher does not suffice. The extra-parliamentary dictatorship of the *Junkers* and the magnates of finance capital can be stood firmly on its feet only by the method of a wearisome and relentless civil war. Will Hitler be able to fulfil this task? That depends not only upon the evil will of fascism, but also upon the revolutionary will of the proletariat.

Bourgeoisie, Petty Bourgeoisie and Proletariat

Any serious analysis of the political situation must take as its point of departure the mutual relations among the three classes: the bourgeoisie, the petty bourgeoisie (including the peasantry) and the proletariat.

The economically powerful big bourgeoisie, in itself, represents an infinitesimal minority of the nation. To enforce its domination, it must ensure a definite mutual relationship with the petty bourgeoisie and, through its mediation, with the proletariat.

To understand the dialectic of the relationship between the three classes, we must differentiate three historical stages: at the dawn of capitalist development, when the bourgeoisie required revolutionary methods to solve its tasks; the period of bloom and maturity of the capitalist regime, when the bourgeoisie endowed its domination with orderly, pacific, conservative, democratic forms; finally, at the decline of capitalism, when the bourgeoisie is forced to resort to methods of civil war against the proletariat to protect its right of exploitation.

The political programmes characteristic of these stages, *Jacobinism*, reformist *democracy*, (social democracy included) and *fascism* are basically programmes of petty-bourgeois currents. This fact alone, more than anything else, shows of what tremendous—rather, of what decisive—importance the self-determination of the petty bourgeois masses of the people is for the whole fate of bourgeois society. Nevertheless, the relationship between the bourgeoisie and its basic social support, the petty bourgeoisie, does not at all rest upon reciprocal confidence and pacific collaboration. In its mass, the petty bourgeoisie is an exploited and oppressed class. It regards the bourgeoisie with envy and often with hatred. The bourgeoisie, on the other hand, while utilising the support of the petty bourgeoisie, distrusts the latter, for it very correctly fears its tendency to break down the barriers set up for it from above.

While they were laying out and clearing the road for bourgeois development, the Jacobins engaged, at every step, in sharp clashes with the bourgeoisie. They served it in intransigent struggle against it. After they had culminated their limited historical role the Jacobins fell, for the domination of capital was predetermined.

For a whole series of stages, the bourgeoisie entrenched its power under the form of parliamentary democracy. Even then, not peacefully and not voluntarily. The bourgeoisie was mortally afraid of universal suffrage. But in the last instance, it succeeded, with the aid of a combination of violent measures and concessions, of privations and reforms, in subordinating within the framework of formal democracy, not only the petty bourgeoisie, but in considerable measure also the proletariat, by means of the new petty bourgeoisie—the labour bureaucracy. In August 1914 the imperialist bourgeoisie was able, with the means of parliamentary democracy, to lead millions of workers and peasants into the war.

But precisely with the war there begins the distinct decline of capitalism and above all of its democratic form of domination. It is now no longer a matter of new reforms and alms, but of cutting down and abolishing the old ones. Therewith the bourgeoisie comes into conflict not only with the institutions of proletarian democracy (trade unions and political parties) but also with parliamentary democracy, within the framework of which arose the labour organisations. Therefore, the campaign against 'Marxism' on the one hand and against democratic parliamentarism on the other.

But just as the summits of the liberal bourgeoisie in its time were unable, by their own force alone, to get rid of feudalism, monarchy and the church, so the magnates of finance capital are unable, by *their* force alone, to cope with the proletariat. They need the support of the petty bourgeoisie. For this purpose, it must be whipped up, put on its feet, mobilised, armed. But this method has its dangers. While it makes use of fascism, the bourgeoisie nevertheless fears it. Pilsudski was forced, in May 1926, to save bourgeois society by a *coup d'état* directed against the traditional parties of the Polish bourgeoisie. The matter went so far that the official leader of the Polish Communist Party, Warski, who came over from Rosa Luxemburg not to Lenin, but to Stalin, took the *coup d'état* of Pilsudski to be the rod of the revolutionary democratic dictatorship and called upon the workers to support Pilsudski.

At the session of the Polish Commission of the Executive Committee of the Communist International on 2 July 1926, the author of these lines said on the subject of the events in Poland:

> ...Taken as a whole, the Pilsudski overthrow is the petty bourgeois, 'plebeian' manner of solving the burning problems of bourgeois society in its state of decomposition and decline. We have here already a direct resemblance to Italian fascism.

These two currents indubitably possess common features:

they recruit their shock troops first of all from the petty bourgeoisie; Pilsudski and Mussolini work with extra-parliamentary means, with open violence, with the methods of civil war; both were concerned, not with the destruction, but with the preservation of bourgeois society. While they raise the petty bourgeois on its feet, they openly align themselves after the seizure of power with the big bourgeoisie. Involuntarily, a historical generalisation comes up here, recalling the evaluation given by Marx of Jacobinism as the plebeian method of settling accounts with the feudal enemies of the bourgeoisie... That was in the period of the rise of the bourgeoisie. Now we must say, in the period of the decline of bourgeois society, the bourgeoisie again needs the 'plebian' method of resolving its no longer progressive, but entirely reactionary tasks. In this sense, fascism is a caricature of Jacobinism.

The bourgeoisie is incapable of maintaining itself in power by the means and methods of the parliamentary state created by itself; it needs fascism as a weapon of self-defence, at least in critical instances. Nevertheless, the bourgeoisie does not like the 'plebian' method of resolving its tasks. It was always hostile to Jacobinism, which cleared the road for the development of bourgeois society with its blood. The fascists are immeasurably closer to the decadent bourgeoisie than the Jacobins were to the rising bourgeoisie. Nevertheless, the sober bourgeoisie does not look very favourably even upon the fascist mode of resolving its tasks, for the concessions, although they are brought forth in the interests of bourgeois society, are linked up with dangers to it. Therefore the opposition between fascism and the bourgeois parties.

The big bourgeoisie likes fascism as little as any man with aching molars likes to have his teeth pulled. The sober circles of bourgeois society have followed with misgivings the work of the dentist Pilsudski, but in the last analysis they have become reconciled to the inevitable, though with threats, with horse- deals and all sorts of trading. Thus the petty bourgeoisie's ideal of yesterday becomes transformed into the gendarme of capital.

To this attempt at marking out the historical place of fascism as the political reliever of the Social Democracy, there was counterposed the theory of social fascism. At first it could appear as a pretentious, blustering but harmless stupidity. Subsequent events have shown what a pernicious influence the Stalinist theory actually exercised on the entire development of the Communist International.*

Does it follow from the historical role of Jacobinism, of democracy and of fascism that the petty bourgeoisie is condemned to remain a tool in the hands of capital to the end of its days? If things were so, then the dictatorship of the proletariat would be impossible in a number of countries in which the petty bourgeoisie constitutes the majority of the nation and, more than that, it would be rendered extremely difficult in other countries in which the petty bourgeoisie represents an important minority. Fortunately, things are not so. The experience of the Paris Commune first showed, at least within the limits of one city, just as the experience of the October Revolution has shown after it on a much larger scale and over an incomparably longer period, that the alliance of the petty bourgeoisie and the big bourgeoisie is not indissoluble. Since the petty bourgeoisie is incapable of an *independent* policy (that is also why the petty bourgeois 'democratic dictatorship' is unrealisable) no other choice is left for it than that between the bourgeoisie and the proletariat.

In the epoch of the rise, the growth and the bloom of capitalism, the petty bourgeoisie, despite acute outbreaks of discontent, generally marched obediently in the capitalist harness. Nor could it do anything else. But under the conditions of capitalist disintegration and of the *impasse* in the economic situation, the petty bourgeoisie strives, seeks, attempts to tear itself loose from the fetters of the old masters and rulers of

* While concealing the speech quoted above from the party and the Comintern, the Stalinist press undertook one of its customary campaigns against it. Manuilsky wrote that I had dared to 'put on the same plane' fascists and Jacobins, who were, after all, our revolutionary ancestors. The latter remark is more or less correct. Unfortunately these ancestors can show more than a few descendants who are unable to exercise their minds. An echo of the old dispute can be found even in the latest productions of Münzenburg against 'Trotskyism'. But let us leave this subject.

society. It is quite capable of linking up its fate with that of the proletariat. For that, only one thing is needed: the petty bourgeoisie must acquire faith in the ability of the proletariat to lead society onto a new road. The proletariat can inspire this faith only by its strength, by the firmness of its actions, by a skilful offensive against the enemy, by the success of its revolutionary policy.

But, woe if the revolutionary party does not measure up to the height of the situation! The daily struggle of the proletariat sharpens the instability of bourgeois society. The strikes and the political disturbances aggravate the economic situation of the country. The petty bourgeoisie could reconcile itself temporarily to the growing privations, if it arrived by experience at the conviction that the proletariat is in a position to lead it onto a new road. But if the revolutionary party, in spite of the class struggle becoming incessantly more accentuated, proves time and again to be incapable of uniting the working class about it, if it vacillates, becomes confused, contradicts itself, then the petty bourgeoisie loses patience and begins to look upon the revolutionary workers as those responsible for its own misery. All the bourgeois parties, including the Social Democracy, turn its thoughts in this very direction. When the social crisis takes on an intolerable acuteness, a particular party appears on the scene with the direct aim of agitating the petty bourgeoisie to a white heat and of directing its hatred and its despair against the proletariat. In Germany, this historical function is fulfilled by Nazism, a broad current whose ideology is composed of all the putrid vapours of disintegrating bourgeois society.

The principal political responsibility for the growth of fascism rests, of course, on the shoulders of the Social Democracy. Ever since the imperialist war, the labours of this party have been reduced to uprooting from the consciousness of the proletariat the idea of an independent policy, to implanting within it the belief in the eternity of capitalism and forcing it to its knees time and again before the decadent bourgeoisie. The petty bourgeoisie can follow the worker only when it sees in him the new master. The Social Democracy teaches the worker to be a lackey. The petty bourgeoisie will not follow a lackey. The policy of reformism deprives the proletariat of the possibility of leading the plebeian masses of the petty bourgeoisie and thereby alone converts the latter into cannon fodder for fascism.

Politically, however, the question is not settled for us with the responsibility of the Social Democracy. Ever since the beginning of the war we have denounced this party as the agency of the imperialist bourgeoisie within the ranks of the proletariat. Out of this new orientation of the revolutionary Marxists arose the Third International. Its task consisted in uniting the proletariat under the banner of the revolution and thereby securing for it the directing influence over the oppressed masses of the petty bourgeoisie in the towns and in the countryside.

The post-war period, in Germany more than anywhere else, was an epoch of economic *impasse* and of civil war. The international conditions as well as the domestic ones pushed the country imperiously on the road to socialism. Every step of the Social Democracy revealed its decadence and its impotence, the reactionary import of its politics, the venality of its leaders. What other conditions are needed for the development of the Communist Party? And yet, after the first few years of significant successes, German Communism entered into an era of vacillations, zigzags, alternating turns to opportunism and adventurism. The centrist bureaucracy has systematically weakened the proletarian vanguard and prevented it from bringing the class under its leadership. Therewith, it has robbed the proletariat as a whole of the possibility of drawing under its direction the oppressed masses of the petty bourgeoisie. The Stalinist bureaucracy bears the direct and immediate responsibility for the growth of fascism before the proletarian vanguard.

Alliance or struggle between Social Democracy and fascism?

To understand the inter-relationship of the classes in the form of a scheme, fixed once and for all, is comparatively simple. The evaluation of the concrete relations between the classes in every given situation is immeasurably more difficult.

The German big bourgeoisie is at present vacillating—a condition which the big bourgeoisie, in general, very rarely experiences. One part has definitely come to be convinced of the inevitability of the fascist path and would like to accelerate the operation. The other part hopes to become master of the situation with the aid of a Bonapartist military-police dictatorship. No one in this camp desires a return to the Weimar 'democracy'.

The petty bourgeoisie is split up. Nazism, which has united the overwhelming majority of the intermediate classes under its banner, wants to take the whole power into its own hands. The democratic wing of the petty bourgeoisie, which still has millions of workers behind it, wants a return to democracy according to the Ebertian model. In the meantime, it is prepared to support the Bonapartist dictatorship at least passively. The Social Democracy figures as follows: under the pressure of the Nazis, the Papen-Schleicher government will be forced to establish a balance by strengthening its left wing; meanwhile, an alleviation of the crisis will perhaps ensue; the petty bourgeoisie will 'sober up'; capitalism will perhaps decrease its frantic pressure upon the working class—and with the aid of God everything will once again be in order.

The Bonapartist clique actually does not desire the complete victory of fascism. It would not by any means be disinclined to utilise the support of the Social Democracy within certain bounds. But for this purpose, it would have to 'tolerate' the workers' organisations, which is conceivable only if, at least to a certain extent, the legal existence of the Communist Party is to be allowed. Moreover, support of the military dictatorship by the Social Democracy would push the workers irresistibly into the ranks of Communism. By seeking a means of support against the brown devil, the government would very soon become subject to the blows of the red Beelzebub.

The official Communist press declares that the toleration of Brüning by the Social Democracy paved the road for Papen and that the half-toleration of Papen will accelerate the arrival of Hitler. That is entirely correct. Within these boundaries, there are no differences of opinion between ourselves and the Stalinists. But this precisely signified that in times of social crisis the politics of reformism no longer turn against the masses alone but against itself. In this process the critical moment has at present come into play.

Hitler tolerates Schleicher; the Social Democracy does not oppose Papen. If this situation could really be assured for a long period of time, then the Social Democracy would become transformed into the left wing of Bonapartism and leave to fascism the role of the right wing. Theoretically, it is not, of course, excluded that the present, unprecedented crisis of German capitalism will not lead to any conclusive solution, i.e., either end with the victory of the proletariat or with the triumph of the fascist counter-revolution. *If* the Communist Party continues its policy of stupid ultimatism and thereby saves the Social Democracy from inevitable collapse; *if* Hitler does not within the near future decide upon a *coup d'état* and thereby provokes disintegration within his own ranks; *if* the economic conjuncture takes an upward trend before Schleicher falls—then the Bonapartist combination of Paragraph 48 of the Weimar Constitution, of the Reichswehr, the semi-oppositional Social Democracy, and semi-oppositional fascism could perhaps maintain itself (up to a new social impetus, which is to be expected in any case).

But offhand, we are still far from such a happy fulfilment of the conditions which form the subject of Social Democratic daydreams. It is by no means guaranteed. Even the Stalinists hardly believe in the power of resistance or the durability of the Papen-Schleicher regime. All indications point to the decomposition of the Wels-Schleicher-Hitler triangle even before it has begun to take shape.

But perhaps it will be replaced by a Hitler-Wels combination? According to Stalin they are 'twins, not antipodes'. Let us assume that the Social Democracy would, without fearing its own workers, want to sell its toleration to Hitler. But Hitler does not need this commodity: he needs not the toleration, but the abolition of the Social Democracy. The Hitler government can only accomplish its task by breaking the resistance of the proletariat and by removing all the possible organs of its resistance. Therein lies the historical role of fascism

The Stalinists confine themselves to a purely psychological, or more exactly, to a purely moral evaluation of those cowardly and avaricious petty bourgeois who lead the Social Democracy. Can we actually assume that these inveterate traitors would separate themselves from the bourgeoisie and oppose it? Such an idealistic method has very little in common with Marxism, which proceeds not from what people think about themselves and what they desire, but from the conditions in which they are placed and from the changes which these conditions will undergo.

The Social Democracy supports the bourgeois regime, not for the gains of the coal, the steel and the other magnates, but for the sake of those gains which it itself can obtain as a party, in the person of its numerically great and powerful apparatus. To be sure, fascism in no way threatens the bourgeois regime, for the defence of which the Social Democracy exists. But fascism endangers that role which the Social Democracy fulfils in the bourgeois regime and the income which the Social Democracy derives from this role it plays. Even though the Stalinists forget this side of the matter, the Social Democracy itself does not for one moment lose from its sight the mortal danger with which a victory of fascism threatens it—the Social Democracy.

About three years ago, when we pointed out that the point of departure in the coming political crisis in Austria and in Germany would in all probability be fixed by the incompatibility of Social Democracy and fascism; when, based upon this, we rejected the theory of social fascism which was not disclosing but concealing the approaching conflict; when we called attention to the possibility that the Social Democracy, a significant part of its apparatus along with it, would be forced by the march of events into a struggle against fascism and that this would be a favourable point of departure for the Communist Party for a further attack, very many Communists—not only hired functionaries, but even quite honest revolutionists—accused us of... 'idealising' the Social Democracy. Nothing remained but to shrug our shoulders. It is hard to dispute with people whose thought stops where the question first begins for the Marxist.

In conversations, I often cited the following example: the Jewish bourgeoisie in Tsarist Russia represented an extremely frightened and demoralised part of the entire Russian bourgeoisie. And yet, insofar as the pogroms of the Black Hundreds, which were in the main directed against the Jewish poor, also hit the bourgeoisie, the latter was forced to take up its self-defence. To be sure, it did not show any remarkable bravery on this field either. But due to the danger hanging over their heads, the liberal Jewish bourgeoisie, for example, collected considerable sums for the arming of revolutionary workers and students. In this manner, a temporary practical agreement was arrived at between the most revolutionary workers, who were prepared to fight with guns in hand, and the most frightened group of the bourgeoisie, which had got into a scrape.

Last year I wrote that in the struggle against fascism the Communists were duty-bound to come to a practical agreement not only with the devil and his grandam, but even with Grzesinsky. This sentence made its way through the entire Stalinist world press. Was better proof needed of the 'social fascism' of the Left Opposition? Many comrades had warned me in advance: 'They are going to seize on this phrase'. I answered them: 'It has been written so that they seize on it. Just let them seize upon this hot iron and burn their fingers. The blockheads must get their lesson.'

The course of the struggle has led to von Papen making Grzesinsky acquainted with the inside of a jail. Did this episode follow from the theory of social fascism and from the prognoses of the Stalinist bureaucracy? No, it occurred in complete contradiction of the latter. Our evaluation of the situation, however, had such an eventuality in view and had assigned a definite place for it.

But the Social Democracy this time, too, avoided the struggle, some Stalinists will object. Yes, it did avoid it. Whoever expected the Social Democracy to go beyond the urging of its leaders and independently to take up the struggle, and at that, under conditions in which even the Communist Party showed itself incapable of struggle, naturally had to experience disappointment. We did not expect such miracles. Therefore we could not lay ourselves open to any 'disappointments' about the Social Democracy.

Grzesinsky has not become transformed into a revolutionary tiger; that we will readily grant. But nevertheless, there is quite a difference between a situation in which Grzesinsky, sitting in his fortress, sends out police detachments for the safeguarding of 'democracy' against revolutionary workers, and a situation in which the Bonapartist saviour of capitalism puts Grzesinsky himself in jail, is there not? And are we not to take this difference into account politically; are we not to take advantage of it?

Let us turn back to the example cited above: it is not hard to grasp the difference between a Jewish manufacturer who tips the Tsarist policeman for beating down the strikers and the same manufacturer who turns out money to the strikers of yesterday to obtain arms against the pogromists. The bourgeois remains the same. But from the change in the situation there results a change in relations. The Bolsheviks conducted the strike against the manufacturer. Later on, they took money from the same manufacturer for the struggle against the pogroms. That did not, naturally, prevent the workers, when their hour had come, from turning their arms against the bourgeoisie.

Does all that has been said mean that the Social Democracy as a whole will fight against fascism? To this we reply: part of the Social Democratic functionaries will undoubtedly go over to the fascists; a considerable section will creep under their beds in the hour of danger. The working masses also will not fight in their entirety. To guess in advance what part of the Social Democratic workers will be drawn into the struggle, and when, and what part of the apparatus they will tear along with them, is altogether impossible. That depends upon many circumstances, among them, also, upon the position of the Communist Party. The policy of the united front has at its task to separate those who want to fight from those who do not; to push forward those who vacillate; finally to compromise the capitulationist leaders in the eyes of the workers in order to consolidate the fighting capacity of the latter.

How much time has been lost—aimlessly, senselessly, shamefully! How much could have been achieved, even in the last two years alone! Was it not clear in advance that monopolistic capital and its fascist army would drive the Social Democracy with fists and blackjacks toward the road of opposition and of self-defence? This prognosis should have been unfolded before the eyes of the entire working class, the initiative should have been taken for the united front and this initiative should have been retained firmly in our hands at every new stage. It was not necessary to shout, nor to scream. An open game could have been played quietly. It would have sufficed to formulate, in a clear-cut manner, the inevitability of every next step of the enemy and to set up a practical programme for a united front, without exaggerations and without haggling, but also without weakness and without concessions. How high the Communist Party would stand today if it had assimilated the ABC of Leninist policy and applied it with the necessary perseverance!

The class struggle in the light of the economic cycle

If we have insistently demanded that a distinction be made between fascism and Bonapartism, it has been in no wise out of theoretical pedantry. Names are used to distinguish between concepts; concepts in politics, in turn serve to distinguish among real forces. The smashing of fascism would leave no room for Bonapartism, and, it is to be hoped, would mean the direct introduction to the social revolution.

Only—the proletariat is not armed for the revolution. The reciprocal relations between Social Democracy and the Bonapartist government on the one hand, and between Bonapartism and fascism on the other—while they do not decide the fundamental questions—distinguish by what roads and in what tempo the struggle between the proletariat and the fascist counter-revolution will be prepared. The contradictions between Schleicher, Hitler and Wels, in the given situation, render more difficult the victory of Fascism, and open for the Communist party a new credit, the most valuable of all—a credit in time.

'Fascism will come to power by the cold method,' we have heard more than once from Stalinist theoreticians. This formula means that the fascists will come to power legally, peacefully, through a coalition—without needing an open upheaval. Events have already refuted this prognosis. The Papen government came to power through a *coup d'état*, and it complemented it with a *coup d'état* in Prussia.

Even if we assume that a coalition between Nazis and the centre would overthrow the Bonapartist Papen government with 'constitutional' methods, in and of itself this still decides nothing. Between the 'peaceful' assumption of power by Hitler and the establishment of the fascist regime there still lies a long way. A coalition would only mean the facilitation of the *coup d'état*, but not replace it. Along with the final abolition of the Weimar constitution there would still remain the most important task— the abolition of the organs of proletarian democracy. From this point of view, what does the 'cold method' mean? Nothing else than the lack of resistance on the part of the workers. Papen's Bonapartist *coup d'état* remained in fact unpunished. Will not Hitler's fascist upheaval remain unpunished? It is precisely around this question that, consciously or unconsciously, the guessing about the 'cold method' turns.

If the Communist Party represented an overwhelming force, and if the proletariat were to march forward towards an immediate seizure of power, all the contradictions in the camp of the ruling class would temporarily be wiped out. Fascists, Bonapartists and democrats would stand in one front against the proletarian revolution. But this is not the case. The weaknesses of the Communist Party and the splitting up of the proletariat permit the possessing classes and the parties which serve them to carry their contradictions out into the open. Only by supporting itself on these contradictions will the Communist Party be able to strengthen itself.

But perhaps fascism in highly industrialised Germany will altogether decide not to validate its claims for full power? Undoubtedly, the German proletariat is incomparably more numerous and potentially stronger than the Italian. Although fascism in Germany represents a more numerous and better organised camp than Italy at the corresponding period, still the task of liquidating 'Marxism' must appear both difficult and risky to the German fascists. In addition, it is not excluded that Hitler's political peak has already been passed. The all-too-long period of waiting and the new barrier on its road in the shape of Bonapartism, undoubtedly weaken fascism, intensify its internal frictions and might materially weaken its pressure. But here we enter a domain of tendencies which at the present moment cannot be calculated in advance. Only the living struggle can answer these questions. To build in advance on the assumption that Nazism will inevitably stop half way would be most frivolous.

The theory of the 'cold method', carried to its conclusion, is not in the least better than the theory of 'social fascism'; more accurately, it only represents the obverse of that theory. The contradictions among the constituents of the enemy's camp are in both cases completely neglected, the successive stages of the process blurred. The Communist Party is left completely on the side. Not for nothing was the theoretician of the 'cold method', Hirsch, at the same time the theoretician of 'social fascism'.

The political crisis of the country develops on the foundation of the economic crisis. But economy too is not immovable. If yesterday we were obliged to say that the cyclical crisis only sharpens the fundamental, organic crisis of the capitalist system, so today we must recall that the general decline of capitalism does not exclude cyclical fluctuations. The present crisis will not last forever. The question of the struggle of political forces must be incorporated into the economic perspectives. Papen's programme makes it all the more impossible to postpone this, since it itself starts from the assumption of an approaching economic improvement.

The industrial revival steps on the scene for everyone to see as soon as it expresses itself in the form of growing turnover of goods, rising production, increased number of employed workers. But it does not begin in that way. The revival is preceded by preparatory processes in the field of money circulation and of credit. The capital invested in unprofitable undertakings and branches of industry must be released and receive the form of liquid money which seeks investment. The market, freed of its fatty deposits, growths and swellings, must show a real demand. The entrepreneurs must gain 'confidence' in the market and in each other. On the other hand, the 'confidence' of which the world press speaks so much must be spurred on, not only by economic, but also by political factors (reparations, war debts, disarmament-rearmament, etc.).

A rise in the turnover of goods, in production, in the number of employed workers, is nowhere to be seen as yet; on the contrary, the decline continues. As to the processes preparatory to a turn in the crisis, they have obviously fulfilled the greater part of the tasks assigned to them. Many signs really permit us to assume that the moment of turn in the economic circle has approached, if it is not immediately before us. That is the estimation, seen on a world scale.

But we must draw a distinction between the creditor countries (the United States, England, France) and the debtor countries, or more accurately the bankrupt countries; the first place in the latter group is occupied by Germany. Germany has no liquid capital. Its economy can receive an impetus only through an influx of capital from outside. But a country which is not in condition to pay its old debts receives no loans. In any case, before the creditors open their money-bags they must be convinced that Germany is again in condition to export a greater amount than it needs to import; the difference has to serve to cover the debts. The demand for German goods is to be expected primarily from the agrarian countries, in the first instance from South Europe. The agrarian countries, for their part, depend on the demand of the industrial countries for raw materials and foodstuffs. Germany will therefore be forced to wait; the stream of life will first have to flow through the series of its capitalist competitors and its agrarian counterparts before it affects Germany's own economic performance.

But the German bourgeoisie cannot wait. Still less can the Bonapartist clique wait. While it promises not to touch the stability of the currency, the Papen government is introducing a material inflation. Together with speeches on the rebirth of economic liberalism, it assumes the administrative disposition over the economic cycle; in the name of the freedom of private initiative it subordinates the taxpayers immediately to the capitalist private entrepreneurs.

The axis around which the government turns is the hope of a nearby turn in the crisis. If this does not take place soon, the two billions[2] will evaporate like two drops of water on a red-hot stove. Papen's plan has immeasurably more of a gambling, speculative character than the bullish movement which is currently taking place on the New York Stock Exchange. In any case, the consequences of a collapse of the Bonapartist gamble will be far more catastrophic.

The most immediate and tangible result of the gap between the plans of the government and the actual movement of the market will consist in the slipping of the mark. The social evils, increased by inflation, will assume an intolerable character. The bankruptcy of the Papen economic programme will demand its replacement by another and more effective programme. Which one? Obviously by the programme of fascism. Once the attempt has failed to force the recovery through Bonapartist therapy, it must be tried with fascist surgery. Social Democracy in the meantime will make 'left' gestures and fall to pieces. The Communist Party, if it does not put obstacles in its own way, will grow. All in all, this will mean a revolutionary situation. The question of the prospects of victory under these circumstances consists to the extent of three-quarters of the question of Communist strategy.

But the revolutionary party must also be prepared for another perspective, for that of a quicker appearance of a turn in the crisis. Let us assume that the Schleicher-Papen government were to succeed in maintaining itself until the beginning of a revival in commerce and industry. Would it be saved thereby? No, the beginning of the upward movement in business would mean the certain end of Bonapartism and might even mean more.

The forces of the German proletariat are not exhausted. But they have been undermined—by sacrifices, defeats, disappointments beginning with 1914; by the systematic betrayals of the Social Democracy, by the discredit which the Communist Party has thrown upon itself. Six or seven million unemployed hang like a heavy load on the feet of the proletariat. The emergency decrees of Brüning and Papen have found no resistance. The *coup d'état* of 20 July has remained unpunished.

We can predict with full assurance that an upward turn in the cycle would give a powerful impetus to the activity of the proletariat, at present in decline. At the moment when the factory stops discharging workers and takes on new ones, the self-confidence of the workers is strengthened; they are once again necessary. The compressed spirals begin to strengthen out again. Workers always enter into the struggle for the reconquest of lost positions more easily than for the conquest of new ones. Neither emergency decrees nor the use of the Reichswehr will be able to liquidate mass strikes which develop on the wave of the upturn. The Bonapartist regime, which is able to maintain itself only through the 'social truce', will be the first victim of the upturn in the cycle.

A growth of strike struggles is already to be observed in various countries (Belgium, England, Poland, in part in the United States, but not Germany). An evaluation of the mass strikes now developing, in the light of the worldwide economic cycle, is not an easy task. The statistics disclose fluctuations in the business cycle with unavoidable delay. The revival must become a fact before it can be registered. The workers usually sense the revival of economic life earlier than the statisticians. New orders or even the expectation of new orders, reorganisation of enterprises for expansion of production, or at least the interruption of the discharge of workers, immediately increase the powers of resistance and the demands of the workers. The defensive strike of the textile workers in Lancashire was unquestionably called forth by a certain upturn in the textile industry. As to the Belgium strike, it is obviously taking place on the basis of the still deepening crisis of the coal mining industry.

The transitional and pivotal character of the present section of the world economic cycle corresponds to the variety of the economic impulses which are the basis of the most recent strikes. But in general the growth of the mass movement rather tends to indicate an upward turn which is about to become perceptible. In any case, a real revival of economic activity, even in its first stages, will call forth a broad upswing in the mass struggle.

The ruling classes of all countries expect miracles from the industrial upswing; the speculation in stocks which has already broken out is a proof of this. If capitalism were really to enter upon the phase of a new prosperity or even of a gradual but persistent rise, this would naturally involve the stabilisation of capitalism and at the same time a strengthening of reformism. But there is not the least ground for the hope or fear that the economic revival, which in and of itself is inevitable, will be able to overcome the general tendencies of decay in world economy and in European economy in particular. If pre-war capitalism developed under the formula of expanded production of goods, present-day capitalism, with all its cyclical fluctuations, represents an expanded production of misery and of catastrophes. The new economic cycle will execute the inevitable readjustment of forces within the individual countries as well as within the capitalist camp as a whole, predominantly toward America and away from Europe. But within a very short time it will place the capitalist world before insoluble contradictions and condemn it to new and still more frightful convulsions.

Without the risk of error, we can set up the following

prediction—the economic revival will suffice to strengthen the self-confidence of the workers and give a new impetus to their struggle, but it will no way suffice to give capitalism, and particularly European capitalism, the possibility of rebirth.

The practical conquests which the new cyclical upturn in declining capitalism will open to the workers' movement will necessarily bear a most limited character. Will German capitalism, at the height of the new revival in economic activity, be able to restore those conditions for the working class which existed before the present crisis? Everything compels us to answer this question in advance with 'No'. All the more quickly will the awakened mass movement have to strike out along the road of politics.

Even the very first step of the industrial revival will be most dangerous for Social Democracy. The workers will throw themselves into struggle to win back what they have lost. The leaders of Social Democracy will again base their hopes on the restoration of the 'normal' order. Their main consideration will be the restoration of their fitness to join a coalition government. Leaders and masses will pull in opposite directions. In order to exploit to the limit the new crisis of reformism, the Communists need a correct orientation in the cyclical changes and the preparation sufficiently ahead of time of a practical programme of action, beginning first of all with the losses suffered by the workers during the years of crisis. The transition from economic struggles to political ones will constitute an especially suitable moment for the strengthening of the power and influence of the revolutionary proletarian party.

But success in this field as in others can be achieved only under one condition—the correct application of the policy of the united front. For the Communist Party of Germany this means, above all, an end of the present policy of sitting between two stools in the trade union field, a firm course toward the free trade unions, the drawing of the present cadres of the RTUO into the composition of the free trade unions, the opening of a systematic struggle for influence on the shop councils by means of trade unions, and the preparation of a broad campaign under the slogan of workers' control of production.

The Road to Socialism

Kautsky and Hilferding, among others, have declared more than once in recent years that they never shared the theory of the collapse of capitalism which the revisionists once ascribed to the Marxists and which the Kautskyans themselves now frequently attribute to the Communists.

The Bernsteinians outline two perspectives: one, unreal, allegedly orthodox 'Marxian', according to which, in the long run, under the influence of the internal antagonisms of capitalism, its mechanical collapse was supposed to take place; and a second, 'realistic', according to which a gradual evolution from capitalism to socialism was to be accomplished. Antithetical as these two schemas may be at first glance, they are nevertheless united by common trait: the absence of the revolutionary factor. While they disavowed the caricature of the automatic collapse of capitalism attributed to them, the Marxists demonstrated that under the influence of the sharpening class struggle, the proletariat would carry through the revolution much sooner than the objective contradictions of capitalism could lead to its automatic collapse.

This dispute was carried on as long ago as the end of the past century. It must, however, be acknowledged that the capitalist reality since the war approached, in a certain respect, much closer to the Bernsteinian caricature of Marxism than anyone might ever have assumed, above all—the revisionists themselves: for they had only portrayed the spectre of the collapse in order to bring out its unreality. Nevertheless, capitalism proves in actuality to be closer to automatic decay the more delayed is the revolutionary intervention of the proletariat in the destiny of society.

The most important component part of the theory of collapse was the theory of pauperisation. The Marxists contended with certain caution that the sharpening of the social antagonisms need not necessarily be equivalent to an absolute sinking of the standard of living of the masses. In reality, it is this latter process which is experiencing its unfolding. Wherein could the collapse of capitalism express itself more acutely than in chronic unemployment and the destruction of social insurance, that is in the refusal of the social order to feed its own slaves?

The opportunistic brakes in the working class have proved to be powerful enough to grant the elementary forces of outlived capitalism additional decades of life. As a result, it was not the idyll of the peaceful transformation of capitalism into socialism which took place, but a state of affairs infinitely closer to social decay.

The reformists sought for a long time to shift the responsibility for the present state of society upon the shoulders of the war. But in the first place, the war did not create the destructive tendencies of capitalism, but only brought them to the surface and accelerated them; secondly, the war would have been unable to accomplish its work of destruction without the political support of reformism; thirdly, the hopeless contradictions of capitalism are preparing new wars from various sides. Reformism will be unable to shift the historical responsibility from itself. By paralysing and curbing the revolutionary energy of the proletariat, the international Social Democracy invests the process of the capitalist collapse with the blindest, unruliest, most catastrophic and bloodiest forms.

Of course, one may speak only conditionally of a realisation of the revisionist caricature of Marxism, applicable to a definite historical period. The way out of decaying capitalism, however, will be found, even if after a great delay, not upon the road of the automatic collapse but upon the revolutionary road.

The present crisis has swept aside with a final flourish of the broom the remnants of the reformist utopias. Opportunist practice at the present time possesses no theoretical covering whatsoever. For in the long run it is pretty much a matter of indifference to Wels, Hilferding, Grzesinski and Noske as to the number of catastrophes that will still hurtle down upon the heads of the masses of the people, if only their own interests remain immune. Only the point is that the crisis of the bourgeois regime strikes at the reformist leaders too.

'Act, state, act!' the Social Democracy still cried a short while ago, as it fell back before fascism. And the state acted; Otto Braun and Severing were kicked into the street. Now, wrote the **Vorwärts**, everybody must recognise the advantages of democracy over the regime of dictatorship.—Yes, democracy has substantial advantages, reflected Grzesinsky while he made the acquaintance of prison from the inside.

From this experience resulted the conclusion: 'It is time to proceed to socialisation'! Tarnow, yesterday still a doctor of capitalism, suddenly decided to become its grave-digger. Now, when capitalism has turned the reformist ministers, police chiefs and lord lieutenants into unemployed, it has manifestly exhausted itself. Wels writes a programmatic article, 'The hour of socialism has struck!' There only remains for Schleicher to rob the deputies of their salary and the former ministers of their pension—and Hilferding will write a study on the historic role of the general strike.

The 'left' turn of the Social Democratic leaders startles one with its stupidity and deceitfulness. This by no means signifies, however, that the manoeuvre is condemned in advance to failure. This party, laden with crimes, still stands at the head of millions. It will not fall of its own accord. One must know how to overthrow it.

The Communist Party will declare that the Wels-Tarnow course towards socialism is a new form of mass deception, and that will be correct. It will relate the history of the last fourteen years. That will be useful. But it is insufficient: history, even the most recent, cannot take the place of active politics.

Tarnow seeks to reduce the question of the revolutionary or the reformist road to socialism to the simple question of the 'tempo' of the transformations. Lower a theoretician cannot sink. The tempo of the socialist transformation depends in reality upon the state of the productive forces of the country, its culture, the extent of the overhead imposed upon it for defence, etc. But socialist transformations, the speedy as well as the slow, are possible only if at the summits of society stands a class interested in socialism, and at the head of this class a party which does not dupe the exploited, and which is always ready to suppress the resistance of the exploiters. We must explain to the workers that precisely in that consists the regime of the *dictatorship of the proletariat*.

Only, even this does not suffice. Once it is a question of the burning problems of the world proletariat, one should not—as the Comintern does—forget the fact of the existence of the Soviet Union. With regard to Germany, the task today does not lie in commencing a socialist construction for the first time, but in tying together Germany's productive forces, its culture, its technical and organisational genius with the socialist construction already in process in the Soviet Union.

The German Communist Party confines itself to the mere eulogising of the Soviet successes, and in this connection commits gross and dangerous exaggerations. But it is completely incapable of linking together the socialist construction in the USSR, its enormous experiences and valuable achievements, with the tasks of the proletarian revolution in Germany. The Stalinist bureaucracy, on its part, is least of all in a position to render the German Communist Party any assistance in this highly important question: its perspectives are limited to one single country.

The incoherent and cowardly state capitalist projects of the Social Democracy must be countered with *a general plan for the joint socialist construction of the USSR and Germany*. Nobody demands that a detailed plan should be worked out instantly. A preliminary rough draft suffices. Foundation pillars are necessary. This plan must as speedily as possible be made the object of action by every organisation of the German working class, primarily of its trade unions.

Into this action must be drawn the progressive forces among the German technicians, statisticians and economists. The discussions about planned economy so widespread in Germany, reflecting the hopelessness of German capitalism, remains purely academic, bureaucratic, lifeless, pedantic. The Communist vanguard alone is capable of drawing the treatment of the question out of the charmed circle.

The socialist construction is already in progress—to this work a bridge must be thrown over the state frontiers. Here is the first plan: study it, improve it, make it concrete! Workers, elect special planning commissions, charge them with entering into contact with the trade unions and economic organs of the Soviets. On the basis of the German trade unions, the factory councils and other labour organisations, create a central planning commission which has the job of entering into contact with the Gosplan of the USSR. Draw into this work German engineers, organisers, economists!

This is the only correct preliminary to the question of planned economy, today, in the year 1932, after fourteen years of convulsions of the German capitalist republic.

Nothing is easier than to ridicule the Social Democratic bureaucracy, beginning with Wels, who has struck up a Song of Solomon to socialism. Yet it must not be forgotten that the reformist workers have a thoroughly serious attitude to the question of socialism. One must have a serious attitude to the reformist workers. Here the problem of the united front rises up once again in its full scope.

If the Social Democracy sets itself the task (in words: we know that!), not to save capitalism but to build up socialism, then it must seek an agreement not with the centre but with the Communists. Will the Communist Party reject such an agreement? By no means. On the contrary, it will itself propose such an agreement, demand it before the masses as a redemption of the just-signed socialist promissory note.

The attack of the Communist Party upon the Social Democracy must proceed at the present time along three lines. The task of demolishing fascism retains all its acuteness. The decisive battle of the proletariat against Fascism will signify simultaneously the collision with the Bonapartist state apparatus. This makes the *general strike* an indispensable fighting weapon. It must be prepared. A special general strike plan must be worked out, that is, a plan for the mobilisation of the forces to carry it out. Proceeding from this plan, to unfold a mass campaign. On the basis of this campaign, to propose to the Social Democracy an agreement for the carrying out of the general strike under definite political conditions. Repeated and made concrete at every new stage, this proposal will lead in the process of its development to the creation of the *soviets as the highest organs of the united front*.

That Papen's economic plan, which has now become law, brings the German proletariat unprecedented poverty, is recognised in words also by the leaders of the Social Democracy and the trade unions. In the press, they express themselves with a vehemence they have not voiced for a long time. Between their words and their deeds lie an abyss, we know that well—but we must understand how to pin them down to their word. *A system of joint measures of struggle against the regime of emergency decrees and Bonapartism must be elaborated.* This struggle imposed upon the proletariat by the whole situation cannot, by its very nature, be conducted within the framework of democracy. A situation where Hitler possesses an army of 400,000 men, Papen-Schleicher, besides the Reichswehr, the semi-private Stahlhelm army of 200,000 men, the bourgeois democracy the half-tolerated Reichsbanner army, the Communist Party the proscribed Red Front army—such a situation by itself lays bare the problem of the state as a problem of power. A better revolutionary school cannot be imagined!

The Communist Party must say to the working class: Schleicher is not to be overthrown by any parliamentary game. If the Social Democracy wants to set to work to overthrow the Bonapartist government with other means, the Communist Party is ready to aid the Social Democracy with all its strength. At the same time, the Communists obligate themselves in advance to use no violent methods against a Social Democratic government insofar as the latter bases itself upon the majority of the working class and insofar as it guarantees the Communist Party the freedom of agitation and organisation. Such a way of putting the question will be comprehensible to every Social Democratic and non-party worker.

The third line, finally, is the fight for socialism. Here too the iron must be forged while it is hot and the Social Democracy pressed to the wall with a concrete plan of collaboration with the USSR. What is necessary on this point has already been said above.

Naturally, these sectors of struggle, which are of varying significance in the complete strategical perspective, are not separated from each other, but rather overlap and merge. The political crisis of society demands the combining of the partial questions with the general questions: precisely therein lies the essence of the revolutionary situation.

The Only Road

Can it be expected that the Central Committee of the Communist Party will independently accomplish a turn to the right road? Its whole past demonstrates that it is incapable of doing this. Hardly had it begun to rectify itself than the apparatus saw before it the perspective of 'Trotskyism'. If Thälmann himself did not grasp it immediately, then he was told from Moscow that the 'part' must be sacrificed for the sake of the 'whole', that is, the interests of the German revolution for the sake of the interests of the Stalinist apparatus. The abashed attempts to revise the policy were once more withdrawn. The bureaucratic reaction triumphed again all along the line.

It is not, of course, a matter of Thälmann. Were the present day Comintern to give its sections the possibility of living, of thinking and of developing themselves they would long ago, in the last fifteen years, have been able to select their own leading cadres. But the bureaucracy erected instead a system of appointed leaders and their support by means of artificial bally-hoo. Thälmann is a product of this system and at the same time its victim.

The cadres, paralysed in their development, weaken the party. They supplement their inadequacy with repressions. The vacillations and uncertainty of the party are inexorably trans-mitted to the class as a whole. The masses cannot be summoned to bold actions when the party itself is robbed of revolutionary determination.

Even if Thälmann were to receive tomorrow a telegram from Manuilsky on the necessity of a turn to the path of the united front policy, the new zig-zag at the top would bring little good. The leadership is too compromised. A correct policy demands a healthy regime. Party democracy, at present a plaything of the bureaucracy, must rise again as a reality. The party must become a party, then the masses will believe it. Practically, this means to put on the order of the day: *an extraordinary party convention* and *an extraordinary congress of the Comintern*.

The party convention must naturally be preceded by an all-sided discussion. All apparatus barriers must be razed. Every party organisation, every nucleus has the right to call to its meetings and listen to every Communist, member of the party or expelled from it, if it considers this necessary for the working out of its opinion. The press must be put at the service of the discussion; adequate space must be allotted daily for critical articles in every party paper. Special press commissions, elected at mass meetings of the party members, must see to it that the papers serve the party and not the bureaucracy.

The discussion, it is true, will require no little time and energy. The apparatus will argue: how can the party permit itself the 'luxury of discussion' at such a critical period? The bureaucratic saviours believe that under difficult conditions the party must shut up. The Marxists, on the contrary, believe that the more difficult the situation, the more important the independent role of the party.

The leadership of the Bolshevik Party enjoyed, in 1917, a very great esteem. And notwithstanding this, a series of deep-going party discussions took place throughout the year 1917. On the eve of the October overturn the whole party debated passionately which of the two sections of the Central Committee was right: the majority which was for the uprising, or the minority, which was against the uprising. Expulsions, and repressions in general were nowhere to be seen, in spite of the differences of opinion. Into these discussions were drawn the non-party masses. In Petrograd, a meeting of non-party working women dispatched a delegation to the Central Committee in order to support the majority in it. To be sure, the discussion required time. But in return for that, there grew out of the open discussion, without threats, lies and falsifications, the general, indomitable certainty of the correctness of the policy, that is, that which alone makes possible the victory.

What course will things take in Germany? Will the small wheel of the Opposition succeed in turning the large party wheel in time? That is how the question stands now. Pessimistic voices are often raised. In the various Communist groupings, in the party itself, as well as in the periphery, there are not a few elements who say to themselves: in every important question the Left Opposition has a correct stand. But it is weak. Its cadres are small in number and politically inexperienced. Can such an organisation, with a small weekly paper (*Die Permanente Revolution*) successfully counterpose itself to the mighty Comintern machine?

The lessons of events are stronger than the Stalinist bureaucracy. We want to be the interpreters of these lessons to the Communist masses. Therein lies our historic role as a faction. We do not demand, as do Seydewitz and Co, that the revolutionary proletariat should believe us on credit. We allot ourselves a more modest role: we propose our assistance to the Communist vanguard in the elaboration of the correct line. For this work we are gathering and training our own cadres. This stage of preparation may not be jumped over. Every new stage of struggle will push to our side those in the proletariat who reflect the most and are most critical.

The revolutionary party begins with an idea, a programme, which is aimed against the most powerful apparatus of class society. It is not the cadre that creates the idea, but the idea that creates the cadre. Fear of the power of the apparatus is one of the most conspicuous features of that specific opportunism which the Stalinist bureaucracy cultivates. Marxian criticism is stronger than any and every apparatus.

The organisational forms, which the further evolution of the Left Opposition will assume, depend upon many circumstances: the momentum of the historical blows, the degree of the power of resistance of the Stalin bureaucracy, the activity of the rank and file Communists, the energy of the Opposition itself. But the principles and methods we fight for have been tested by the greatest events in world history, by the victories as well as by the defeats. They will make their way.

The successes of the Opposition in every country, Germany included, are indisputable and manifest. But they are developing slower than many of us expected. We may regret this, but we do not need be surprised at it. Every Communist who begins to listen to the Left Opposition is cynically given the choice by the bureaucracy: either go along with the baiting of 'Trotskyism' or else be kicked out of the ranks of the Comintern. For the party official, it is a question of position and wages: the Stalinist apparatus plays this key to perfection. But immeasurably more important are the thousands of rank and file Communists who are torn between their devotion to the ideas of Communism and the threatened expulsion from the ranks of the Comintern. That is why there are in the ranks of the official Communist Party a great number of partial, intimidated or concealed oppositionists.

This extraordinary combination of historical conditions sufficiently explains the slow organisational growth of the Left

Opposition. At the same time, in spite of this slowness, the spiritual life of the Comintern revolves, today more than ever before, around the struggle against 'Trotskyism'. The theoretical periodicals and theoretical newspaper articles of the CPSU, as well as the other sections of the Comintern, are chiefly devoted to the struggle against the Left Opposition, now openly, now maskedly. Still more symptomatic in significance is that mad organisational baiting which the apparatus pursues against the Opposition: disruption of its meetings by blackjack methods; employment of all sorts of other physical violence; behind-the-scenes agreements with bourgeois pacifists, French Radicals and Freemasons against the 'Trotskyites'; the dissemination of en-venomed calumnies from the Stalinist centre, etc.

The Stalinists perceive much more directly and know better than the Oppositionists to what extent our ideas are undermining the pillars of their apparatus. The methods of self-defence of the Stalinist faction, however, have a double-edged character. Up to a certain moment, they have an intimidating effect. But at the same time they prepare a mass reaction against the system of falsity and violence.

When, in July 1917, the government of the Mensheviks and the Social Revolutionaries branded the Bolsheviks as agents of the German General Staff, this despicable measure succeeded at first in exercising a strong influence upon the soldiers, the peasants and the backward strata of workers. But when all the further events clearly confirmed how right the Bolsheviks had been, the masses began to say to themselves: so they deliberately slandered the Leninists, they basely incited against them, only because they were right? And the feeling of suspicion against the Bolsheviks was converted into a feeling of warm devotion and love for them.

Although under different conditions, this very complex process is taking place now too. By means of a monstrous accumulation of calumnies and repressions, the Stalinist bureau-cracy has undeniably succeeded for a period of time in intimid-ating the rank and file party members; at the same time, it is preparing for the Bolshevik-Leninists an enormous rehabilitation in the eyes of the revolutionary masses. At the present time, there can no longer be the slightest doubt on this score.

Yes, today we are still weak. The Communist Party still has masses, but already it has neither doctrine nor strategic orientation. The Left Opposition has already worked out its Marxist orientation, but as yet it has no masses. The remaining groups of the 'left' camp possess neither the one nor the other. Hopelessly the Leninbund pines away, thinking to substitute the individual fantasies and whims of Urbahns for a serious principled policy. The Brandlerites, in spite of their apparatus cadre, are descending step by step; small tactical recipes cannot replace a revolutionary-strategical position. The SAP has put up its candidacy for the revolutionary leadership of the proletariat. Baseless pretension! Even the most serious representatives of this 'party' do not overstep, as Fritz Sternberg's latest book shows, the barriers of left centrism. The more assiduously they seek to create an 'independent' doctrine the more they reveal themselves to be disciples of Thalheimer. But this school is as hopeless as a corpse.

A new historical party cannot arise simply because a number of old Social Democrats have convinced themselves, very belatedly, of the counter-revolutionary character of the Ebert-Wels policy. A new party can just as little be improvised by a group of Communists who have as yet done nothing to warrant their claim to proletarian leadership. For a new party to rise, it is on the one hand necessary to have great historical events, which would break the backbone of the old parties, and on the other hand, a position in principle worked out, and cadres tested, in the experience of events.

While we are fighting with all our strength for the rebirth of the Comintern and the continuity of its further development, we are least of all inclined to any fetishism of form. The fate of the proletarian world revolution stands, for us, above the organisational fate of the Comintern. Should the worst variant materialise; should the present official parties, despite all our efforts, be led to a collapse by the Stalinist bureaucracy; should it mean in a certain sense to begin all over again, then the New International will trace its genealogy from the ideas and cadres of the Communist Left Opposition.

And that it why the short-term 'pessimism' and 'optimism' are not applicable to the work which we are carrying through.

It stands above the separate stages, the partial defeats and victories. Our policy is a policy of long range.

Afterword

The present brochure, whose different parts were written at different times, had already been finished when a telegram from Berlin brought the news of the conflict of the overwhelming majority of the Reichstag with the Papen government and consequently with the Reich President. We expect to follow the concrete development of subsequent events in the columns of **Die Permanente Revolution**. Here we wish only to emphasise some general conclusions, which seemed to be open to criticism when we began the brochure and which, thanks to the testimony of facts, have since become incontestable.

1. The Bonapartist character of the Schleicher-Papen government has been completely disclosed by its isolated position in the Reichstag. The agrarian-capitalist circles which stand directly behind the presidential government constitute an incomparably smaller percentage of the German nation than the percentage of votes given for Papen in the Reichstag.

2. The antagonism between Papen and Hitler is the antagonism between the agrarian-capitalist leadership and the reactionary petty bourgeoisie. Just as once the liberal bourgeoisie used the revolutionary movement of the petty bourgeoisie, but employed every means to keep it from seizing the power, so the monopolistic bourgeoisie is prepared to reward Hitler as its lackey but not as its master. Without compelling necessity it will not turn over the full power to fascism.

3. The fact that the various fractions of the grand, middle and petty bourgeoisie are carrying on an open struggle for power, without avoiding a most dangerous conflict, proves that the bourgeoisie does not see itself as being immediately threatened by the proletariat. Not only the Nazis and the centre, but also the leaders of the Social Democracy have dared enter on a struggle *for the constitution* only in the firm confidence that it will not change into a *revolutionary* struggle.

4. The only party whose vote against Papen was dictated by revolutionary purpose is the *Communist Party*. But it is a long way from revolutionary purposes to revolutionary achievements.

5. The logic of events is such that the struggle for 'parliament' and for 'democracy' becomes for every Social Democratic worker a question of *power*. Therein lies the main content of the whole conflict from the standpoint of the revolution. The question of power is the question of the revolutionary unity in action of the proletariat. The policy of the united front toward the Social Democracy must be prepared in the very near future to render possible, on the basis of proletarian democratic representation, the creation of class organs of struggle, i.e. of *workers' soviets*.

6. In view of the gifts to capitalists and the monstrous attack on the standard of living of the proletariat, the Communist Party must set up the slogan of *workers' control of production*.

7. The fractions of the possessing classes can afford to quarrel among themselves only because the revolutionary party is weak. The revolutionary party could become immeasurably stronger if it would correctly exploit the quarrels among the possessing classes. For this it is necessary to know how to distinguish the various fractions according to their social composition, but not to throw them all into one heap. The theory of 'social fascism', which has completely and finally been bankrupted, must at last be thrown out as worthless junk.

Part Four | 1933

Chris Harman

1933: Background

THE ELECTIONS of July 1932 had put the Nazis in a very strong position, but had not put them into power. The army and big business were prepared to use the Nazis, but not as yet to hand the state over to them. Their prospects seemed to be dimming in the last months of 1932. Stormtroopers who had mobilised to take power began to become disillusioned as it continued to elude them. The hesitancy of big business was drying up the flow of money needed by the fascist machine. In the elections of November the Nazi vote fell to a figure below the combined total of the working-class parties, while the KPD continued to gain votes at the expense of the Social Democrats. When von Papen fell from office in December, Schleicher, not Hitler, replaced him.

At this point two factors enabled the Nazis to reassert their control over the situation. The first was the continued ineffectiveness of the left; the Social Democrats refusing to fight back, the Communist leaders refusing to follow a united front policy that would force the Social Democrats to fight, even against the desires of their leaders. The second was the decision of the leaders of big business in January of 1933 to throw their weight behind Hitler.

On 30 January, Hitler was made Chancellor. This:

> brought out what were in fact the most impressive demonstrations of the German workers' will to resist. On the afternoon and evening of 30 January spontaneous and violent mass demonstrations of workers took place in German cities. Delegates from factories...from all parts of the country arrived on the same day in Berlin in expectation of battle orders...[1].

Yet the Social Democratic leaders decided that as Hitler had come to power 'legally' they would not strike yet. **Vorwärts** boasted:

> In the face of the government and its threats of a *coup d'état* the Social Democrats and the whole Iron Front stands foursquare on the ground of the constitution and of legality'.

The party devoted its energies to preventing premature resistance to the new regime.

Within a few days the paramilitary forces of the Nazis were being integrated into the state machine. SA, SS, Reichswehr and police were working together to harness the working class parties. After the Reichstag fire of 27 February this gave way to a policy of wholesale arrests, suppression of the Social Democratic press, banning of the Communist Party. All forms of personal freedom were suppressed by presidential decree.

Yet in the 'terror elections' of a week later, the working class *en masse* once again revealed its hostility to the government. The Social Democrats received more than seven million votes (dropping only 70,000), the Communists, four and three-quarter millions (a drop of 1,200,000).

Still the SPD leadership did nothing. Despite continual threats, their leaders made brave speeches in the Reichstag—and then vowed that their opposition to the Nazi government would be 'constitutional'. The trade union leaders appealed to their members to celebrate May Day in common with the Nazis as a 'National day of Labour'. This did not prevent the Nazis taking over trade union offices and putting these same leaders into concentration camps on 2 May.

Faced with Hitler's accession to power the Communist Party did attempt to mount resistance. Once again it issued a call for a general strike. Workers who had been told for three years that Hitler was not the major danger, and that anyway the previous governments were also fascist, did not respond. The party and Comintern leaders were themselves still blinded by their own theories. After Hitler's election victory the Comintern Praesidium said the 'current calm after the victory of fascism is temporary. Inevitably, despite the fascist terror, the revolutionary tide will grow...'[2] **Pravda** spoke of the 'rousing success of the German

Communist Party,' while Radek wrote in *Izvestia* (7 March 1933) of a 'defeat like the defeat on the Marne' for the Nazis.[3] Meanwhile thousands of Communists were being thrown into concentration camps and the last elements of working-class organisation being destroyed.

What is National Socialism? was written by Trotsky on the first anniversary of Hitler's victory. It first appeared in English in **Fourth International** in 1943.

Leon Trotsky

What is National Socialism?

NAIVE MINDS think that the office of kingship lodges in the king himself, in his ermine cloak and his crown, in his bones and veins. As a matter of fact, the office of kingship is an interrelation between people. The king is king only because the interests and prejudices of millions of people are refracted through his person. When the flood of development sweeps away these interrelations, then the king appears to be only a washed-out male with a flabby underlip. He who was once called Alfonso XIII [King of Spain, 1886-1931] could discourse upon this from fresh impressions.

The leader by will of the people differs from the leader by will of God in that the former is compelled to clear the road for himself or, at any rate, to assist the conjuncture of events in discovering him. Nevertheless, the leader is always a relation between people, the individualistic supply to meet the collective demand. The controversy over Hitler's personality becomes the sharper the more the secret of his success is sought in himself. In the meantime, another political figure would be difficult to find that is in the same measure the focus of anonymous historic forces. Not every exasperated petty bourgeois could have become Hitler, but an article of Hitler is lodged in every exasperated petty bourgeois.

The rapid growth of German capitalism prior to the First World War by no means signified a simple destruction of the intermediate classes. Although it ruined some layers of the petty bourgeoisie it created others anew: around the factories, artisans and shopkeepers; within the factories, technicians and executives. But while preserving themselves and even growing numerically—the old and the new petty bourgeois compose a little less than one-half of the German nation—the intermediate classes have lost the last shadow of independence. They live on the periphery of large-scale industry and the banking system, and they live off the crumbs from the table of monopolies and cartels, and off the ideological sops of their traditional theorists and politicians.

The defeat in 1918 raised a wall in the path of German imperialism. External dynamics changed to internal. The war passed over into revolution. Social Democracy, which aided the Hohenzollerns in bringing the war to its tragic conclusion, did not permit the proletariat to bring the revolution to its conclusion. It spent fourteen years in finding interminable excuses in its own existence for the Weimar democracy. The Communist Party called the workers to a new revolution but proved incapable of leading it. The German proletariat passed through the rise and collapse of war, revolution, parliamentarism, and pseudo-Bolshevism. At the time when the old ties of the bourgeois had drained themselves to the dregs, the dynamic power of the working class turned out to be impaired.

The post-war chaos hit the artisans, the pedlars, and the civil employees no less cruelly than the workers. The economic crisis in agriculture was ruining the peasantry. The decay of the middle strata did not mean that they were made into proletarians inasmuch as the proletariat itself was casting out a gigantic army of chronically unemployed. The pauperisation of the petty bourgeoisie, barely covered by ties and socks of artificial silk, eroded all official creeds and, first of all, the doctrine of democratic parliamentarism.

The multiplicity of parties, the icy fever of elections, the interminable changes of ministries aggravated the social crisis by creating a kaleidoscope of barren political combinations. In the atmosphere brought to white heat by war, defeat, reparations, inflation, occupation of the Ruhr, crisis, need, and despair, the petty bourgeoisie rose up against all the old parties that had bamboozled it. The sharp grievances of small proprietors, never far from bankruptcy, of their university sons without posts and clients, of their daughters without dowries and suitors, demanded order and an iron hand.

The banner of National Socialism was raised by upstarts from the lower and middle commanding ranks of the old army. Decorated with medals for distinguished service, commissioned and non-commissioned officers could not believe that their heroism and sufferings had not only come to nothing for the Fatherland but also gave them no special claims to gratitude. Hence their hatred of the revolution and the proletariat. At the same time, they did not want to reconcile themselves to being sent by the bankers, industrialists, and ministers back to the modest posts of book-keepers, engineers, postal clerks, and school teachers. Hence their 'socialism'. At the Iser and under Verdun they had learned to risk themselves and others, and to speak the language of command which powerfully overawed the petty bourgeois behind the lines. Thus these people become leaders.

At the start of his political career, Hitler stood out perhaps only because of his big temperament, a voice much louder than others, and a circumscribed mentality much more self-assured. He did not bring into the movement any ready-made programme, if one disregards the insulted soldier's thirst for vengeance. Hitler began with grievances and complaints about the Versailles terms, the high cost of living, the lack of respect for a meritorious non-commissioned officer, and the plots of bankers and journalists of the Mosaic persuasion. There were in the country plenty of ruined and drowning people with scars and fresh bruises. They all wanted to thump with their fists on the table. This Hitler could do better than others. True, he knew not how to cure the evil. But his harangues sounded now like commands and again like prayers addressed to inexorable fate. Doomed classes, like fatally ill people, never tire of making variations on their plaints or of listening to consolations. Hitler's speeches were all attuned to this pitch. Sentimental formlessness, absence of disciplined thought, ignorance along with gaudy erudition—all these minuses turned into pluses. They supplied him with the possibility of uniting all types of dissatisfaction around the beggar's sack of National Socialism, and of leading the mass in the direction in which it pushed him. In the mind of the agitator there was preserved his early personal improvisations, whatever had met with approbation. His political thoughts were the fruits of oratorical acoustics. That is how the selection of slogans went on. That is how the programme was consolidated. That is how the 'leader' took shape out of the raw material.

Mussolini, from the very beginning, reacted more consciously to social materials than Hitler, to whom the police mysticism of a Metternich is much closer than the political algebra of Machiavelli. Mussolini is mentally bolder and more cynical. It may be said that the Roman atheist only utilises religion as he does the police and the courts while his Berlin colleague really believes in the infallibility of the Church of Rome. During the time when the future Italian dictator considered Marx as 'our common immortal teacher', he defended not unskilfully the theory which sees in the life of contemporary society first of all the reciprocal action of two classes, the bourgeoisie and the proletariat. True, wrote Mussolini in 1914, there lie between them very numerous intermediate layers which seemingly form 'a joining web of the human collective', but 'during periods of crisis, the intermediate classes, gravitate, depending upon their interests and ideas, to one or the other of the basic classes.' A very important generalisation! Just as scientific medicine equips one with the possibility not only of curing the sick but of sending the healthy to meet their forefathers by the shortest route, so the scientific analysis of class relations, designed by its author for the mobilisation of the proletariat, enabled Mussolini, after he had jumped into the opposing camp, to mobilise the intermediate classes against the proletariat. Hitler accomplished the same feat, translating the methodology of fascism into the language of German mysticism.

The bonfires which burn the impious literature of Marxism light up brilliantly the class nature of National Socialism. While the Nazis acted as a party and not as a state power, they did not quite find an approach to the working class. On the other side, the big bourgeoisie, even those who supported Hitler with money, did not consider his party theirs. The national 'regeneration' leaned wholly upon the intermediate classes, the most backward part of the nation, the heavy ballast of history. Political art consisted in fusing the petty bourgeoisie into oneness through its solid hostility to the proletariat. What must be done in order to improve things? First of all, throttle those who are underneath. Impotent before large capital, the petty bourgeoisie hopes in the future to regain its social dignity by overwhelming the workers.

The Nazis call their overturn by the usurped title of revolution. As a matter of fact, in Germany as well as in Italy, fascism leaves the social system untouched. Taken by itself, Hitler's overturn has no right even to the name of counter-revolution. But it cannot be viewed as an isolated event; it is the conclusion of a cycle of shocks which began in Germany in 1918. The November revolution, which gave the power to the workers' and peasants' soviets, was proletarian in its fundamental tendencies. But the party that stood at the head of the proletariat returned the power to the bourgeoisie. In this sense the Social Democracy opened the era of counter-revolution, before the revolution could bring its work to completion. However, during the time when the bourgeoisie depended upon the Social Democracy, and consequently upon the workers, the regime retained elements of compromise. Concurrently, the international and the internal situation of German capitalism left no more room for concessions. The Social Democracy saved the bourgeoisie from the proletarian revolution; then came the turn of fascism to liberate the bourgeoisie from the Social Democracy. Hitler's overturn is only the final link in the chain of counter-revolutionary shifts.

A petty bourgeois is hostile to the idea of development, for development goes immutably against him; progress has brought him nothing but irredeemable debts. National Socialism rejects not only Marxism but Darwinism. The Nazis curse materialism because the victories of technology over nature have signified the triumph of large capital over small. The leaders of the movement are liquidating 'intellectualism' not so much because they themselves possess second and third-rate intellects but primarily because their historic role does not permit them to draw a single thought to its conclusion. The petty bourgeois takes refuge, in the last resort, in a mythology which stands above matter and above history, and which is safeguarded from competition, inflation, crisis, and the auction block. To evolution, economic thought, and rationalism—of the twentieth, nineteenth, and eighteenth centuries—is counterposed in his mind national idealism, as the source of the heroic beginning.

Hitler's nation is the mythological shadow of the petty bourgeoisie itself, its pathetic delirium of a millennium on earth.

In order to raise it above history, the nation is given the support of the race. History is viewed as the emanation of the race. The qualities of the race are construed without relation to changing social conditions. Rejecting 'economic thought' as base, National Socialism descends a stage lower—from economic materialism it appeals to zoologic materialism.

The theory of race, specially created, it seems, for a pretentious self-educated individual who seeks for a universal key to all the secrets of life, appears particularly melancholy in the light of the history of ideas. In order to create the religion of the genuine German blood, Hitler was obliged to borrow at second hand the ideas of racism from a Frenchman, Count Gobineau, a diplomat and a literary dilettante. Hitler found the political methodology ready-made in Italy. Mussolini utilised widely the Marxist theory of the class struggle. Marxism itself is the fruit of union between German philosophy, French history, and English economics. To investigate retrospectively the genealogy of ideas, even those most reactionary and muddle-headed, is to leave not a trace of racism standing.

The immeasurable thinness of National Socialist philosophy did not, of course, hinder the academic sciences from entering Hitler's fairway, with all sails unfurled, once his victory was sufficiently established. For the majority of the professorial rabble the years of the Weimar regime were periods of riot and alarm. Historians, economists, jurists, and philosophers were lost in guesswork as to which of the contending camps would turn out in the end the master of the situation. The fascist dictatorship eliminates the doubts of the Fausts and the vacillations of the Hamlets of the university rostrums. Coming out of the twilight of parliamentary relativity, knowledge once again enters into the kingdom of the absolutes. Einstein has been obliged to pitch his tent outside the boundaries of Germany.

On the plane of politics, racialism is a vapid and bombastic variety of chauvinism in alliance with phrenology. As the ruined nobility sought solace in the gentility of its blood, so the pauperised petty bourgeoisie befuddles itself with fairy tales concerning the special superiorities of its race. Worthy of attention is the fact that the leaders of National Socialism are not native Germans but interlopers from Austria, like Hitler himself, from the former Baltic provinces of the Tsar's regime like Rosenberg, and from colonial countries like Hess, who is Hitler's present alternate for the party leadership. A school of barbaric national pothering along the cultural frontiers was required in order to instil into the 'leaders' those ideas which later found response in the hearts of the most barbarous classes in Germany.

Personality and class—liberalism and Marxism—are evil. The nation—is good. But at the threshold of private property this philosophy is turned inside out. Salvation lies only in personal private property. The idea of national property is the spawn of Bolshevism. Deifying the nation, the petty bourgeois does not want to give it anything. On the contrary, he expects the nation to endow him with property and to safeguard him from the worker and the bailiff. Unfortunately, the Third Reich will bestow nothing upon the petty bourgeois except new taxes.

In the sphere of modern economy, international in its ties and anonymous in its methods, the principle of race appears as an interloper from a medieval graveyard. The Nazis set out with concessions beforehand; the purity of race, which must be certified in the kingdom of the spirit by a passport, must be demonstrated in the sphere of economy chiefly by efficiency. Under contemporary conditions this means competitive capacity. Through the back door racialism returns to economic liberalism, freed from political liberties.

Nationalism in economy practically comes down to impotent though savage outbursts of anti-semitism. The Nazis abstract the usurious or banking capital from the modern economic system because it is of the spirit of evil, and, as is well known, it is precisely in this sphere that the Jewish bourgeoisie occupies an important position. Bowing down before capitalism as a whole, the petty bourgeois declares war against the evil spirit of gain in the guise of the Polish Jew in a long-skirted caftan and usually without a cent in his pocket. The pogrom becomes the supreme evidence of racial superiority.

The programme with which National Socialism came to power reminds one very much —alas—of a Jewish department store in an obscure province. What won't you find here—cheap in price and quality still lower! Recollections of the 'happy' days of free competition, and hazy traditions of the stability of class society; hopes for the regeneration of the colonial empire, and dreams of a shut-in economy; phrases about a reversion from Roman law to the Germanic, and pleas for an American moratorium; an envious hostility to inequality in the person of a proprietor in an automobile, and animal fear of equality in the person of a worker in a cap and without a collar; the frenzy of nationalism, and the fear of world creditors. All the refuse of international political thought has gone to fill up the spiritual treasury of the neo-Germanic Messianism.

Fascism has opened up the depths of society for politics. Today, not only in peasant homes but also in the city skyscrapers there lives alongside of the twentieth century the tenth or thirteenth. A hundred million people use electricity and still believe in the magic power of signs and exorcism. What inexhaustible reserves they possess of darkness, ignorance, and savagery! Despair has raised them to their feet, fascism has given them the banner. Everything that should have been eliminated from the national organism in the course of the unhindered development of society comes out today gushing from the throat; capitalist society is puking up the undigested barbarism. Such is the physiology of National Socialism.

German fascism, like the Italian, raised itself to power on the backs of the petty bourgeoisie, which it turned into a battering ram against the working class and the institutions of democracy. But fascism in power is least of all the rule of the petty bourgeoisie. On the contrary, it is a most ruthless dictatorship of monopolist capital. Mussolini is right: the intermediate classes are incapable of independent policies. During periods of great crisis they are called upon to reduce to absurdity the policies of one of the two basic classes. Fascism succeeded in placing them in the service of capital. Such slogans as state control of trusts and the elimination of illegitimate profits were thrown overboard immediately on the assumption of power. On the contrary, the particularism of the petty bourgeoisie, gave place to capitalist-police centralism. Every success of the internal and foreign policies of National Socialism inevitably means that small property is crushed by big capital.

The programme of petty-bourgeois illusions is not discarded; it is simply becoming divorced from reality, and dissolves into ritualistic acts. The unification of all classes reduces itself to the semi-symbolism of compulsory labour and to the confiscation of the labour holiday of May Day for the 'benefit of the people'. The preservation of the Gothic script as against the Latin is a symbolic revenge for the yoke of the world market. Dependence upon international bankers, including Jewish bankers, is not eased an iota, wherefore it is forbidden to slaughter animals according to the Talmudic ritual. If the road to hell is paved with good intentions, then the avenues of the Third Reich are paved with symbols.

Reducing the programme of petty-bourgeois illusions to bureaucratic masquerades, National Socialism raises itself over the nation as the ugliest form of imperialism. Absolutely false are hopes to the effect that Hitler's government will fall tomorrow, if not today, a victim of its internal incoherence. The Nazis required a programme in order to assume power; but power serves Hitler not at all for the purpose of fulfilling the programme. His tasks are assigned him by monopolist capital. The compulsory concentration of all national forces and resources in the interests of imperialism—the true historic mission of fascist dictatorship—means the preparation for war; and this brooks no internal resistance and leads to further mechanical concentration of power. Fascism cannot be reformed or dismissed. It can only be overthrown. The political orbit of the regime leads to the alternative, *war* or *revolution*.

The first anniversary of the Nazi dictatorship is approaching. All the tendencies of the regime have had time to take on a clear and distinctive character. The 'socialist' revolution imagined by the petty-bourgeois masses as a necessary supplement to the national revolution is officially condemned and liquidated. The brotherhood of all classes found its culmination in the fact that on a day especially appointed by the government the haves renounced their *hors d'oeuvre* and dessert in favour of the have- nots. The struggle against unemployment has resulted in the cutting of the semi-starvation doles by half. The rest is manipulated statistics. Planned autarchy is simply a new stage of economic disintegration.

The more the Nazi police regime is impotent in economics, the more it is forced to transfer its efforts to the field of foreign politics. This corresponds fully to the inner dynamics of German capitalism, aggressive through and through. The sudden turn of the Nazi leaders to peaceful declarations could deceive only utter simpletons. What other method remains at Hitler's disposal for throwing the responsibility for domestic disasters on external enemies and accumulating, under the press of the dictatorship, the explosive force of imperialism?

This part of the programme, outlined openly even prior to the Nazis' assumption of power, is now being fulfilled with iron logic before the eyes of the whole world. The date of the new European catastrophe will be determined by the time necessary for the arming of Germany. It is not a question of months, but neither is it a question of decades. It will be but a few years before Europe is again plunged into war, unless Hitler is forestalled in time by the inner forces of Germany.

Notes

Introduction

1. Membership of the Catholic unions was 690,000 in 1931 according to figures cited in Hilda Greber, **The History of the German Labour Movement** (Woolf, London 1969) page 195.
2. Figures cited in Franz Neumann, **Behemoth: The structure and practice of National Socialism** (Harper and Row, New York 1966) page 412.
3. Figure is for the end of 1928. Cited in Ben Foulkes, **Communism in Germany under the Weimar Republic** (Macmillan, London 1984).
4. For an account of this period see Chris Harman, **The Lost Revolution: Germany 1918-23** (Bookmarks, London 1982).
5. It should however be borne in mind that the crash deepened but did not cause the slump. German production was already declining when it occurred. See Chris Harman, **Explaining the Crisis** (Bookmarks, London 1984) pages 61-2.
6. Neumann, pages 412-3.
7. Industrial production in Germany in 1932 was 61 per cent of the 1929 level: at the height of the depression 30.1 per cent were unemployed (Harold James, **The German Slump: politics and economics 1924-36** (Clarendon Press, Oxford 1986) page 6). James' book is a treasure trove of statistical material (see especially chapter six), despite the repellent politics of its author.
8. Quoted in David Beetham, **Marxists in face of Fascism** (Manchester University Press 1983) page 261.
9. Quoted in Beetham, page 263.
10. Leon Trotsky, 'What Next?', see above page 173.
11. **The rise of Italian Fascism** (London 1938) by Angelo Tasca, a leading Italian Communist of the 1920s writing under the pseudonym of A Rossi, is still the most informative account in English. Its political standpoint is similar to that of Eurocommunist A Davidson in **The Theory and Practice of Italian Communism** (London 1982). Both support 'united fronts' with social democracy; both think this means blurring essential differences with it.

12. Speech to Enlarged Executive of the Comintern, June 1923, quoted in Beetham, page 112.

13. Quoted in Trotsky, 'What Next?', see above page 90, and in Beetham (page 143), where the source is given as *L'Internationale*, 1928.

14. For a summary account of these events see the essay by Chris Harman in Binns, Cliff and Harman, **Russia: From workers' state to state capitalism** (Bookmarks, London 1987); for a more detailed treatment, see M Reiman, **The Birth Of Stalinism** (I B Tauris, London 1987).

15. The notion that Stalin 'foresaw' the depression was widespread in the 1930s among those who attributed to him magical powers. Today, new superstitions are fashionable in Euro-communist circles, but the old survived amongst devotees of Mao Tse-tung thought. Nicos Poulantzas wrote of the 'remarkable foresight' of the Comintern's Sixth Congress in this regard (see his **Fascism and Dictatorship** (NLB, London 1974) page 46). But as Ben Foulkes rightly remarks of Varga, the economist upon whom the Comintern relied: 'Every year, he prophesied a capitalist crisis; he had to be right sooner or later. For the year 1928 Stalin and Varga were wrong. Varga might have found this embarrassing; for Stalin it did not matter. The economic analysis was advanced to justify the elimination of the right and the sharp move to the left in international communist strategy.' (Foulkes, page 146).

16. The increase in German strike figures in 1928 did not signify any mass movement towards revolutionary politics. As Trotsky had explained in July 1928: 'The communist party is growing alongside of the social democracy, but not yet directly at the expense of the latter...up to now the flow towards the social democracy is the larger.' And again: 'Can one say that "the situation is becoming more and more revolutionary" if the social democracy, the main prop of the bourgeois regime, is growing?' (Trotsky, **The Third International after Lenin** (Pathfinder, New York 1974) pages 261 and 260). Indeed, although the KPD vote improved from 2.76 to 3.26 million votes between the Reichstag elections of December 1924 and those of May 1928, votes for the Social Democrats rose from 7.88 to 9.15 million. The result was encouraging in that it demonstrated a strengthening of both the working-class parties, but it hardly amounted to a revolutionary vote of no confidence in the Republic. KPD membership then actually declined from 130,000 at the end of 1928 to 112,000 at the end of 1929.

17. For the Third Period and the Comintern, see Duncan Hallas **The Comintern** (Bookmarks, London 1985) chapter 6.

18. Hallas, page 129.

19. Quoted in Foulkes, pages 148-9.

20. Thalheimer developed a theory of fascism, which, though superior to that of the Comintern, looked at it from the angle of the state machine rather than from that of workers' democracy, and was therefore prone to stress the continuities, rather than the crucial differences, between the Bonapartist pre-Hitler regimes and the 'finished article'.

21. Quoted in Foulkes, page 154.

22. **Rote Fahne**, quoted in Foulkes, page 158.

23. **Trotsky on the Trade Unions** (Pathfinder, New York 1969) pages 28-9.

24. 'The Trade Union movement and the united front'(France) in Trotsky, **The first five years of the Communist International** (New Park, London 1974) page 100.

25. Trotsky, 'The turn in the Communist International', see above page 54.

26. Letter to the Paris Convention, 13 September 1922 in **First five years of the Communist International**, page 172.

27. 'Theses On the United Front', in **First five years of the Communist International**, pages 94-5.

28. Letter to the Paris Convention, in **First five years of the Communist International**, page 168.

29. Thälmann, speaking at the twelfth plenum of the Comintern Executive in August-September 1932, quoted in E H Carr, **Twilight of the Comintern** (Random House, New York 1982) page 72. Stalinist politics today has had to learn more sophisticated arguments than Thälmann's. Euro-communists must of course condemn the 'Third Period' but invariably do so by counterposing it to the Popular Front, which is defended as a variant of the united front. It should be clear that the two are fundamentally different in purpose and effect. The United Front was an alliance against reaction which aimed to defeat it by mass struggle; it did not abandon the struggle against reformism but tried to demonstrate reformism's inferiority in practice. The Popular Front was also an alliance against reaction, but it aimed to conceal fundamental disagreements within the alliance by subordinating independent revolutionary politics to the politics of both reformist and openly bourgeois parties (such as the Radicals in France). The temporary *agreement for action* was converted into a *political bloc* for conserving the supremacy of bourgeois politics. Euro-communist critics of Trotsky's assault on the Third Period have to conceal the diametrically opposed nature of the two fronts, and must therefore misrepresent his views on *both of them.* See for example the essay by Monty Johnston in Jim Firth (editor) **Britain, Fascism and the Popular Front** (London 1985).

30. Carr, **Twilight of the Comintern**, page 12.

31. Carr, **Twilight of the Comintern**, page 24.

32. Hallas, page 137.

33. Martin Broszat, **Hitler and the Collapse of Weimar Germany** (Berg, New York 1987) page 72.

34. Broszat, page 65.

35. Broszat, page 15.

36. Thus Bracher in **The German Dictatorship** (Penguin, Harmondsworth 1971) page 201: 'What they wanted was not socialism but the protection of small property owners against the growing incursion of big capital. The middle classes, contrary to Marxist expectations, did not come over into the ideological realm of socialism. Generally, in times of crisis, the hopeless elements in the middle class tend to listen to fascist

slogans, while the working class, on the other hand, tends towards communism'. Generally, the hopeless elements amongst middle class historians tend to treat political struggle as reducible to vapid psychological nostrums; the possibility of their learning anything can be wholly excluded unless, in times of crisis, the working class takes history and its practitioners by the throat.

37. Figures cited in Alan Bullock, **Hitler, a study in tyranny** (Odhams, London 1952) page 153, and Broszat, page 118.

38. Bullock page 193. His use of this phrase, with its connotation of indiscriminacy and irrationality reflects Bullock's perception of Nazism and Communism as symmetrically anti-democratic manifestations of unreason. He regrets the triumph of the Nazis, though from the standpoint of British decency (which is a rational value if your country already controls one third of the land surface of the planet), and not from that of the German working-class movement, whose fate merits scarcely a mention in his book.

39. Figures in Neumann, page 423.

40. Broszat, page 19. Some instances of the class nature of justice in the Weimar republic are given in Neumann's book: 'After the downfall of the Bavarian Soviet Republic in 1919, the courts handed down the following sentences: 407 persons: fortress imprisonment; 1737 persons: prison; 65 persons: imprisoned at hard labour. Every adherent of the Soviet Republic who had the slightest connection with the unsuccessful coup was sentenced. The contrast with the judicial treatment of the 1920 right-wing Kapp Putsch could not possibly have been more complete. Fifteen months after the *putsch*, the Reich ministry of justice announced officially on 21 May 1921 that a total of 705 charges of high treason had been examined. Of them "412, in the opinion of the courts, came under the amnesty law of 4 August 1920, despite the fact that the statute specifically excluded the *putsch* leaders from its provisions. 108 had become obsolete because of death or other reasons; 174 were not pressed; 11 were unfinished." Not one person had been punished.' (Neumann, pages 21-2).

41. Quoted in Bullock, page 161.

42. Broszat, page 117.

43. Broszat, page 118.

44. Evelyn Anderson, **Hammer or Anvil** (Left Book Club edition, London 1945) page 145. This is an excellent short summary of the history of the German labour movement, in spite of its illusions in the possibilities of a rejuvenated social democracy. Reprinted in the 1970s, it may be available in one edition or another in some libraries.

45. Broszat, page 121.

46. Trotsky, 'What Next?', see above page 93.

47. Quoted in Foulkes, pages 161-2.

48. *Rote Fahne*, 2 December 1930, quoted in Foulkes, page 26.

49. *Rote Fahne*, 22 March 1931, quoted in Foulkes, page 163.

50. Remmele in the Reichstag, October 1931, quoted in Hallas, page 131.

51. *Internationale Presse-Korrespondenz*, page 1553 (14 June 1932), quoted in Carr, page 60.

52. Quoted in Carr, page 62.

53. Quoted in Foulkes, page 168.

54. Quoted in Anderson, page 153.

55. Anderson, page 152.

56. Quoted in Neumann, page 31.

57. Bullock, page 237.

58. L J Edinger, **German Exile Politics** (University of California Press 1956) page 10. The author also shows (page 21) that Hitler persuaded the SPD leaders to mute their criticisms of these and other repressive measures, hinting that good behaviour in this matter might be rewarded by the return of their newspapers.

59. Quoted in Joachim Fest, **Hitler** (Penguin, Harmondsworth 1977) page 593.

60. Quoted in Edinger, page 20, who dates it to 'April or early May'. It is more likely to be April: it is difficult to believe that even Kautsky could believe that in the light of the events of 2 May.

61. In *Gewerkschaftzeitung*, official organ of the ADGB; quoted in Anderson, page 155.

62. Heckert, in **Rundschau**, 7 July 1933, quoted in Anderson, page 157.

63. **Rundschau**, 17 November 1933, quoted in Anderson, page 159.

64. See Allan Merson, **Communist Resistance in Nazi Germany** (Lawrence and Wishart, London 1985) page 66.

65. See Jan Valtin, **Out of the Night** (Fortress Books 1988) pages 448-473.

66. Tim Mason's point, however, that the class struggle did not cease under the Nazis, but took highly indirect forms, is absolutely right. Not even their machine could suppress resistance altogether, though it could be prevented from taking shape politically. See his article in **History Workshop Journal** no 11.

67. Psychological theories of fascism are widespread, ranging from Shirer to Theodore Adorno. These usually hinge on 'Prussian' characteristics—in Shirer's account these were established by the time of Peace of Westphalia in 1648!—and/or Hitler's personality disorders. There is a useful survey in M Kitchen, **Fascism** (though the author's attachment to Popular Front politics leads him to misrepresent Trotsky's positions). For Beetham (page 58) the Frankfurt School's work on fascism helps explain 'the social-psychological aspects of its mass appeal'. He comments: 'The absence of this dimension is one of the most obvious inadequacies of the Marxist analyses considered here'. It is difficult to agree. Trotsky's own account continually stresses the importance of this 'dimension', but subordinates it to a class and historical framework. His work did not, and could not in the circumstances, dwell on the complex process of historical selection whereby the social base of Nazism, 'maddened' by its misfortunes, 'chose' this man and his once insignificant sect to express its rage and frustration, how the heterogeneity of these

layers, bound together only in the myth of the *volk,* demanded the establishment of the leadership principle rather than the 'comrades in arms' bonhomie (typified by Rohm) of its Freikorps past, if the party was ever seriously to contend for state power, and so on. The personalities of leading figures, which so mesmerise bourgeois commentators, would of course enter into such a study, which appears in outline in 'What is National Socialism?'. But Hitler's impotence or monomania, Bruning's arrogance, Papen's lightmindedness, Schleicher's Machiavellianism, Hindenburg's 'senility' (why was he not replaced?), the industrialists' 'shortsightedness', and so on, would be understood, not as primary causes, but as symptoms of the political crisis. Such an approach contrasts sharply with the pessimistic generalisations of the Frankfurt School, which led its theorists—such as Horkheimer and Adorno—away from working- class politics.

1930: Background

1. Theses of the Tenth Plenum of the Executive Committee of the Comintern, published by the Communist Party of Great Britain, quoted in C L R James, **World Revolution** (London 1937).
2. Theses of the Tenth Plenum, quoted in James.
3. Quoted in Braunthal, **History of the International**, volume 2 (London 1967) page 366.
4. **Rote Fahne**, 15 September 1930, quoted in James.
5. **Rote Fahne**, 16 September 1930, quoted in James.

The Turn in the Communist International

1. The Ninth Plenum—full meeting—of the Executive Committee of the Comintern was held in February 1928, its Sixth World Congress in July the same year, and the Tenth Plenum in July 1929.
2. *Chvostism* means, literally, 'tailism', that is, the theory or practice of following behind the tail of events.
3. 'Young's noose' is a reference to Germany's war reparations programme, drawn up and administered by Owen Young, an American lawyer. See also Glossary.
4. Notes on individuals mentioned in the text will be found in the Glossary.
5. 'The epigone leadership', sometimes just 'the epigones', is Trotsky's way of referring derogatively to the Stalinist leadership in Russia and in the Comintern. The word 'epigone' means 'later and less distinguished'.

1931: Background

1. **Communist International**, 15 December 1931, quoted in James.
2. Quoted in Braunthal, page 366.
3. Quoted in Braunthal, page 378.

Germany: The key to the international situation

1. On 4 August 1914, at the outbreak of the First World War, the SPD

leaders in the Reichstag voted in favour of the war credits which were to finance the German war effort, thereby supporting the war and leading millions of workers to the slaughter of the trenches. At pre-war congresses, the party had committed itself to oppose any imperialist war, pledging itself to the cause of the international working class through the Second International.

2. Clemenceau and Millerand of France, Lloyd George of Britain, and Woodrow Wilson of the USA were the Western leaders whose covert support enabled the counter-revolutionary generals Kolchak, Wrangel and Denikin to wage the civil war after the Russian revolution of 1917.

What next?

1. Trotsky was writing from the Turkish island of Prinkipo, where he was in exile from Russia.
2. *Die Internationale*, January 1932.
3. Lenin, **Left-wing Communism: An infantile disorder**.
4. House of Ullstein and Mosse Verlag were two large publishing companies, producing both books and newspapers.
5. Trotsky, **First Five Years of the Communist International** (New York and London 1953) pages 91-6 and 127-8.
6. *Die Rote Fahne*, 22 December 1931.
7. The International Federation of Trade Unions, whose headquarters was in Amsterdam; it was dominated by the Social Democrats.
8. Minutes of the Seventh Plenum of the Executive Committee of the Communist International.
9. *Arbeiterpolitik*, 10 January 1932.
10. *Arbeiterpolitik*, 10 January 1932.
11. *Die Rote Fahne*, 2 February 1932.

1932: Background

1. Peter and Irma Petroff, **The Secret of Hitler's Victory** (London 1934).
2. Braunthal, page 388.
3. Braunthal, page 377.
4. Braunthal, page 377.

The Only Road

1. 'Manchesterism' is a reference to the British reform movement of the 1840s, which called for free trade and opposed the Corn Laws which imposed duty on grain imports. It was based in Manchester.
2. Papen had given two billion marks to German capitalists in the form of tax certificates.

1933: Background

1. Braunthal, page 380
2. Quoted in Braunthal, page 394
3. Quoted in Braunthal, page 383

Glossary

a

Adler, Max (1873-1937): Leading theoretician of the Austrian Social Democracy.

Austro-Marxism: Name given to the tendency that dominated Austrian Social Democracy. Resisted the revisionism of Bernstein in theory, but in practice behaved no differently. Opposed violent revolution; believed force should be used by socialists only defensively.

b

Balabanoff, Angelica (1878-1965): Russian-Italian leader of the Italian Socialist Party before First World War, who became secretary of the Comintern under Zinoviev; resigned after the Kronstadt uprising and returned to the PSI.

Bauer, Otto (1881-1938): Leader of the Austrian Social Democracy after the Frist World War; theoretician of Austro-Marxism.

Bebel, August: Founder (with Wilhelm Liebknecht) and leading member of German Social Democracy before the First World War.

Bernstein, Eduard (1850-1932): Theoretician of German Social Democracy who held that Marxism had to be 'revised'—hence 'revisionism'—and that socialism would now come through the gradual democratisation of capitalism.

Bethman-Hollweg, Theobald von: German Chancellor and Prussian prime minister 1909-17.

Blum, Leon (1872-1950): French Socialist Party leader; later to be prime minister of French Popular Front government 1936-1937.

Bogdanov, A A (1873-1938): The most wholehearted of Lenin's supporters at the time of the split with the Mensheviks in 1903. In 1909 became leader of the Vperyod group in the Bolshevik Party, together with Lunacharsky and

Gorky, which later broke with Lenin's faction. Denounced Lenin's attitude to participation in the Duma, the Tsarist parliament, as opportunist.

Bolshevik-Leninists: Supporters of the Left Opposition.

Bonapartism: A transitional form between the regimes of parliamentary democracy and fascism; a strong government which appears to stand 'above parties' and 'above classes' due to relative equilibrium between the working class and the bourgeoisie.

Bordiga, Amadeo (1889-1970): Leader of the opposition to the centrist policies of the Italian Socialist Party during and immediately after the First World War, and the major influence in the Italian Communist Party from its foundation in 1921 until 1924. Later expelled from the party.

Brandler, Heinrich (1881-1967): A building worker from Chemnitz, disciple of Rosa Luxemburg from 1916 onwards and a veteran Spartakist. Founder member of the German Communist Party, of which, together with August Thalheimer, he was the leader until the abortive Hamburg uprising of 1923. At the crucial period of 1923 he was a minister in the Communist-Social Democratic government of Saxony. Later made the scapegoat for failure of 1923 risings, and removed from leadership of party at Frankfurt Conference of 1924. Brandler then led a right-wing faction in the party until 1929, when expelled. With Thalheimer, he then led an independent group, the KPO. This was strongly critical of the policy of the German Communists, but refused to analyse the policy's origins or to criticise the role of Stalinism in Russia.

Braun, Otto: Social Democrat prime minister of Prussia, removed from office by Papen on 20 July 1932.

Breitscheid, Rudolf (1874-1944): Minister of interior in German republic 1918-19, then a leading Social Democrat deputy. Died at hands of Nazis.

Brüning, Heinrich (1885-1970): Leader of German Catholic Centre Party and Chancellor at head of a minority government, ruling through emergency decrees and only half-tolerated by Reichstag, from March 1930 until May 1932. Dismissed from office by Hindenberg, whose re-election as president he had masterminded—on the advice of Schleicher, head of the army. Left Germany in May 1933.

Bukharin, Nikolai (1888-1938): Youngest of the Bolshevik 'old guard'. Member of Bolshevik Party in Moscow until escaping abroad in 1911. During First World War, after being arrested in Sweden for anti-militarist activities, participated with Trotsky in editing Russian paper *Novy Mir* in USA. Returned to Russia after February revolution 1917. Member of Bolshevik Central Committee from July 1917, and later editor of *Pravda*. During the revolution and civil war was a 'Left Communist'. As such, opposed the peace of Brest-Litovsk and issued a factional paper, **Communist**. However from 1923 on increasingly adopted right-wing policies. In Russia he argued for slow building of 'socialism in one country' through policy of accommodation to the peasants; internationally this tended to mean surrendering the independence of Communist parties to bourgeois nationalists and left Social Democrat and trade union leaders. Between 1923 and 1927 Bukharin worked hand-in-glove with Stalin against the Left Opposition. In 1928 Stalin broke this alliance. By end of 1929 Bukharin had been removed from all positions of importance in the party and Comintern. After capitulating completely to Stalin, was made editor of *Izvestia* in 1933, only to be framed and executed in the last of the Moscow Trials in 1938.

c

Centrism: Political position which oscillates between reformism, which is the policy of the labour bureaucracy, and Marxism, which expresses the revolutionary interests of the working class.

Chiang Kai-shek: Military leader of the Chinese bourgeois nationalist Kuomintang during the Chinese revolution of 1925-27. On policy of Stalin and Bukharin, the Chinese Communist Party gave uncritical support to Kuomintang and Chiang Kai-shek was hailed as a great revolutionary; once his power was secure he turned on the Communists, massacring party members and trade unionists in Shanghai in 1927.

Cook, Arthur (1885-1931): Left-wing leader of the British Miners Federation before and during the General Strike of 1926.

Curtius, Julius: Minister for foreign affairs in German Müller and Brüning governments 1929-30.

d

Dawes Plan: One of series of measures that brought German crisis of 1923 to an end, reducing burden of reparations to be paid by Germany to a level the economy could bear in period 1924-28; accompanied by international supervision of German economy and by large flow of US credit to Germany.

e

Ebert, Friedrich (1871-1925): Right-wing leader of German Social Democrats during First World War. Abhorred revolution and favoured constitutional monarchy, yet became head of first government of German Republic in November 1918, later its first president; one of those responsible for agreement between Social Democrats and army high command which led to crushing of Spartakists and murder of Luxemburg and Liebknecht.

Ercoli (pseudonym of P Togliatti): Member of group of Italian socialists in Turin led by Gramsci; joined Italian Communist Party at its foundation in 1921. Became leader of party after Bordiga's removal and Gramsci's imprisonment. Rapidly became pliant tool of Stalin. Played crucial role in allowing reconsolidation of discredited capitalism in Italy after 1945.

f

Fischer, Ruth (1895-1961): Founder of Austrian Communist Party, later leader (with Maslow) of 'leftist' faction in German Communist Party, then leader of party itself 1924-25. Her book on the party in the 1920s, **Stalin and German Communism**, is interesting but factually unreliable.

Frick, Wilhelm (1877-1945): Leading Nazi, became minister for interior in 1933.

Frölich, Paul (1884-1953): Founder-member of German Communist Party who left to join Brandler's KPO, then the SAP; he fled Germany in 1933. Biographer of Rosa Luxemburg.

g

Gramsci, Antonio (1891-1937): Founder-member of Italian Communist Party; imprisonned by the fascists in 1926, he is know for prison notebooks and letters which made important contributions to Marxist theory—though his criticism of the party was suppressed by its leadership. Died in prison.

Gröner, Wilhelm (1867-1939): Leading general, instrumental in abdication of Kaiser in 1919. Minister of defence in Müller and Brüning governments 1928-32. Forced to resign when Reichswehr objected to his attempts to outlaw Nazi SA and SS.

Grzesinsky, Albert: Social Democrat police chief in Prussia under Braun and Severing.

h

Haase, Hugo (1863-1919): Social Democrat deputy who led centrist minority during Frist World War and was founder of USPD in 1917; assassinated in 1919.

Hilferding, Rudolf (1877-1944): Leading German Social Democrat theorist and economist, finance minister in Müller government 1928-30. Author of important books on imperialism and finance capital. Arrested by French Vichy regime in 1940 as he attempted to escape from France, and handed to Nazis.

Hirsch, Werner: Stalinist theoretician.

Hindenberg (1847-1934): Head of German army in First World War. Elected president of Germany in 1925 by right-wing bloc, and re-elected in 1932 by bloc containing both Social Democrats and big business interests. At first resented Hitler as an upstart, but made him Chancellor in 1933 under influence of big landowners, industrialists and army.

Hoover Moratorium: One-year moratorium of war debts and reparations declared in July 1931 on initiative of US president Herbert Hoover.

i

die Internationale: Official theoretical journal of German Communist Party.

Iron Front: Alliance for defence of the German Republic established by various organisations under Social Democratic influence, such as the Social Democratic Party, the Free Trade Unions, the Reichsbanner and Social Democratic sports clubs.

j

Jouhaux, Leon (1879-1954): General secretary of French CGT union federation; supported First World War.

k

Kautsky, Karl: Chief theoretician of Second International and of German Social Democratic Party before First World War. Between wars, chief apologist for Social Democratic policies—though he still employed Marxist language.

Kun, Bela (1886-1939): Comintern representative in Germany during the disastrously ultra-left March Action of 1921; member of CPSU throughout 1930s; shot in Russia in 1939.

Kuusinen, Otto: Communist leader in Finland; fled to Russia after failure of Finnish revolution in 1919. Directed German affairs for Comintern from 1924 on.

l

LaFollette, Robert: Wisconsin Republican who ran for US presidency on Progressive Party ticket in 1924.

Lassalle, Ferdinand (1825-64): One of founders of German working- class movement. Marx denounced his characterisation of all other classes in German society as 'one reactionary mass'—as leading him to support absolutist Prussian regime against its half-hearted bourgeois opponents. His followers and those of Marx later merged to form German Social Democratic Party.

Ledebour, Georg (1850-1947): Long-standing Social Democrat who became founder-member of USPD and member of Berlin workers' council in 1918; opposed proposal that USPD join Comintern in 1920; later joined SAP.

Leipart, Theodor: One of leaders of Free (Social Democratic) Trade Unions—later the ADGB. Attempted to cooperate with Hitler government, for instance in celebration of 'National Day of Labour' on 1 May 1933. Arrested on 2 May 1933.

Leninbund: Organisation founded by Fischer, Maslow and Urbahns after their expulsion from KPD in 1927; close to Left Opposition until 1930, when Opposition supporters were expelled.

Levi, Paul (1883-1930): Spartacist and founder-member of KPD; opposed March Action, then resigned.

Lozovsky, Salomon (1878-1952): Former Menshevik, secretary of Red International of Labour Unions from foundation in 1921, later deputy commissar for Russian foreign affairs and head of Soviet Information Office. Shot in 1952.

m

MacDonald, James Ramsey (1866-1937): Prime minister of first British Labour government 1924; betrayed party during second term 1928-31 to form National Government in alliance with Tories.

Manuilsky, D: Early Bolshevik, split from party as member of Bogdanov's Vperyod group in 1909, rejoined it with Trotsky and the Mezhrayontsy in summer 1917. Later loyal Stalinist and general secretary of Comintern during 'Third Period'. After Second World War was on central committee of CPSU and Ukrainian delegate to United Nations.

March Action: Period in March 1921 when newly-formed German Communist Party attempted to spread a violent miners' strike in central Germany, hoping for a general uprising. Mass of workers remained passive. In many places a minority, often unemployed, attempted to use force to drive majority out of factories. Action weakened influence of party among mass of workers.

Maslow, Arkadi: With Ruth Fischer, leader of left group which gained leadership of German Communist Party after removal of Brandler in 1924 by Zinoviev. In turn replaced when Stalin broke with Zinoviev in 1926. Expelled from party after supporting united opposition of supporters of Zinoviev and Trotsky.

Molotov, Viatoslav: Editor of Pravda before 1917; elected to Central Committee of Russian Communist Party in 1920 and aligned with Stalin; president of Council of Peoples Commissars throughout 1930s; in party leadership until 1957.

Münzenburg, Willi (1889-1940): Secretary of International Socialist Youth League 1914-21, then of Young Communist International. Leading figure in German Communist Party and behind-the-scenes organiser of many 'front' movements. Broke with party in 1937 after Moscow Trials. Found hanged in France after escaping from internment camp in 1940; his death ascribed variously to Gestapo and NKVD (Stalin's secret police).

n

National Communism: Name given to attempt by German Communist Party to win support of extreme nationalists by using slogans such as 'People's revolution', 'National Liberation' and 'Down with the Treaty of Versailles'—similar to Nazi slogans. First used by Radek in 1923, taken up in effort to outbid Nazis in 'Third Period'.

Neumann, Heinz: Leading German Communist, confidant and drinking companion of Stalin. Organised Canton Commune of 1927 in China. In 1931 began privately to oppose official Communist Party line in Germany, was removed from positions as Thälmann's secretary and member of party politburo. Sent to Spain, then Switzerland, then recalled to Moscow; arrested in 1937 and disappeared. His wife (Margarete Büber-Neumann) was sent to Russian prison camp, then handed to Gestapo after Hitler-Stalin Pact; she survived Nazi concentration camp to write her memoirs.

Noske, Gustav (1868-1946): Right-wing Social Democrat leader who supported First World War, became minister for war in second Ebert government of 1919. Responsible for suppression of Kiel Mutiny and Spartakist Rising, killing an estimated 15,000 in nine months. Forced to resign after Kapp Putsch 1920. Lived on in Germany under Nazis, being arrested twice after 1944.

P

Paragraph 48: Section of Weimar Constitution that permitted emergency rule by presidential decree without parliamentary approval.

von Papen: German politician and diplomat, made Chancellor in May 1932 by Hindenburg, under influence of Schleicher, political head of Reichswehr; lifted ban on Nazi SA and SS; forced out at end of 1932 by Schleicher; with General von Blomberg and Nationalist Party leader von Hugenburg, prevailed on Hindenburg to make Hitler Chancellor.

Die Permanente Revolution: Paper of the German Left Opposition.

Pilsudski, Joseph (1867-1935): Polish dictator. Founder of Polish Socialist Party in 1893, in opposition to Rosa Luxemburg's internationalist Social Democratic Party. Organised Polish troops to fight for Austrian side in First World War; minister for war in first Polish government of 1916; imprisoned by Germans 1917-18. Virtual dictator of Poland 1918-23, then again after coup of 1926. Suppressed both Communist and Socialist parties after 1930.

Purcell, Alfred: British trade union leader associated with Anglo-Russian Trade Union Unity Committee of 1925-26, a joint committee of General Councils of British Trades Union Congress and Soviet trade unions which played important role in 'Second Period' policy of Zinoviev and Stalin. British Communist Party discouraged from criticising 'left' members of committee, who played a role indistinguishable from the right during the British General Strike of 1926. Purcell was chairman of Strike Organisation Committee which tried to prevent leftists influencing local strike committees. (See Tony Cliff and Donny Gluckstein, **Marxism and Trade Union Struggle**, Bookmarks, London 1986).

Radek, Karl: Active on extreme left in Germany and Poland before Russian revolution, when he became one of inner circle of Bolshevik leaders. Escaped assassination when Luxemburg and Liebknecht were murdered in Berlin in 1919. Later blamed for failure of German revolution in 1923. A leader of Left Opposition until capitulated to Stalin in 1929 after latter broke with Bukharin. Wrote propaganda for Stalin until Moscow Trials, when he was sentenced to ten years' imprisonment and disappeared.

Radich, Stefan: Croatian independence leader who took part in 1924 Peasant International in Moscow.

Rakovsky, Christian (1873-1942): Leading Bolshevik and chairman of Ukhraine Soviet 1919-23; expelled from party with Left Opposition 1927 and exiled to Barnaul in Siberia; recanted in 1934 but was sentenced to 20 years imprisonment in Moscow show trials.

Red Referendum: Attempt by Nazis and nationalists to remove Social Democrat government of Prussia in 1931; supported after initial hesitation by German Communist Party.

Reichswehr: Army of German Weimar Republic. Under Treaty of Versailles, supposed to be limited to 100,000 men, but in fact supplemented by secret contingents—the Black Reichswehr. Exclusion of Communists ensured its political reliability for the right.

Reichsbanner: Parliamentary organisation of German Social Democrats, with 300,000 members pledged to defend German Republic against any coup. Unarmed, but expected to receive weapons from Prussian police should they be needed.

Remmele, Herman: Central committee member of German Communist Party, fled to Russia in 1933. Refusal to accept theory of 'orderly retreat' led to removal from leadership. Killed by GPU in 1937.

RGO (Revolutionary Trade Union Opposition): Communist-led German trade union organisation set up in opposition to Social Democratic union federation; as a tactic it was an appalling failure, since it separated Communist militants from the mass of trade unionists.

Rosenfeld, Kurt: Left Social Democrat deputy associated with opposition within the SDP and the split to form the SAP.

Die Rote Fahne: Daily paper of German Communist Party.

Roy, M N (1893-1953): Leading Indian Communist who proposed cooperation with bourgeois nationalists in struggle for independence; supporter of Bukharin and the Right Opposition; imprisoned by British government of India.

S

SAP: German Socialist Workers Party, a centrist party formed by leftists who broke with Social Democrats in 1931 but would not join Communist Party. In some ways similar to the British Independent Labour Party in the 1930s.

Scheidemann, Philip (1865-1937): Leading right-wing German Social Democrat who supported First World War. Proclaimed Republic during 1918 revolution in order to prevent Spartakists doing so. In exile after 1933.

Schleicher, Kurt von: General in charge of making political contacts for Reichswehr. Became power behind throne, selecting first ministers for defence, then chancellors. Attempted to use Nazis to build his own position. Became Chancellor in December 1932, only to be replaced by Hitler two months later. Murdered on Hitler's orders, along with Röhm, in 1934.

Semard, Pierre (1887-1942): French Communist Party leader.

Severing, C W (1875-1952): Social Democrat deputy from 1907, Prussian minister for interior 1919-26 and 1930-32. Arrested briefly when von Papen overthrew Prussian government in 1932, lived unmolested under Nazis until arrested after anti-Hitler 'Generals' Plot' of 1944. Again SDP deputy after 1945.

Seydewitz, Max: Leader of leftist opposition in German Social Democratic Party which split to form SAP in 1931.

Spartakists: Spartakusbund, or Spartacist League, led by Rosa Luxemburg and Karl Liebknecht; group within SPD which opposed First World War and, after it, formed nucleus of German Communist Party.

Stahlhelm: Paramilitary organisation of German right-wing veterans, merged with SA after election of 1933.

Ströbel, Heinrich (1869-1943): Left-wing Social Democrat who joined first USPD, then briefly SAP.

Sturm-Abteilung (SA): 'Stormtroopers', paramilitary organisation of the Nazi Party.

t

Tarnow, Fritz (1880-1954): Social Democrat deputy also active in trade unions. Left Social Democrats for SAP in 1931. In exile during period of Nazi rule, active in unions till his death.

Thälmann, Ernst (1866-1944): Leader of German Communist Party after Stalinisation, arrested by Nazis in 1933 and murdered in concentration camp at end of Second World War.

Thalheimer, August: With Brandler, leader of German Communist Party 1921-24, with a similar subsequent history.

Thorez, Maurice (1900-64): Stalinist leader of French Communist Party from 1930 until his death.

Turati, Filippo (1857-1932): Founder-member of Italian Socialist Party.

Two-and-a-half International: Centrist International founded in 1921 by Karl Kautsky and Otto Bauer; merged with reformist Second International in 1923.

U

Urbahns, Hugo: German Communist associated with Maslow and Fischer in leadership of party 1924-26 and in opposition after this. In exile in Sweden from 1933 to his death in 1947.

V

Victor Emmanuel III (1869-1947): King of Italy from 1900, through First World War and fascist rule of Mussolini; abdicated in 1946.

Vorwärts: Daily paper of German Social Democratic Party.

W

Walcher, Jacob: Spartakist and founder-member of German Communist Party; went with Brandler to KPO; led split in 1931 to join SAP.

Wang Chin Wei: Kuomintang leader in China. During 1926-27 policy of Stalin and Bukharin was to give uncritical support to leaders of Chinese national bourgeois revolution, at first Chiang Kai-shek, who was made honorary member of Comintern executive. Chinese Communists worked to build Kuomintang without criticising its leaders, even though Chiang had made strikes illegal and was disbanding unions and peasant leagues. Workers who had captured Shanghai from the warlords and imperialists in March 1927 were told to receive Chiang as a revolutionary leader; he then proceeded to murder Communists and trade unionists. Despite this, Stalin and Bukharin tried to continue the same policy, transferring support to the group of Kuomintang leaders around Wang Chin Wei in Wuhan—which Stalin characterised as the 'revolutionary centre'. Almost as Stalin spoke, the Wuhan leaders came to terms with Chiang Kai-shek and started murdering worker-militants.

Warski, Adolf (1868-1938): Leading Polish Social Democrat before First World War, associated with Rosa Luxemburg. Founder-member of Polish Communist Party, removed from leadership 1924-26 for protesting at anti-Trotsky campaign. Returned to leadership, taking 'Second Period' policy so seriously as to support dictatorship of Pilsudski—which Moscow opposed. Quickly recognised mistake and organised resistance to Pilsudski. Removed from leadership at start of 'Third Period', but remained in party in exile and docilely supported Stalin. When Polish Communist Party liquidated by Stalin in 1938, Warski was killed as 'a traitor, a spy and a Pilsudski agent'.

Wels, Otto (1879-1939): Right-wing German Social Democrat, military commander of Berlin who crushed Spartakist rising in December 1918 on orders from Noske. Led opposition to Hitler in Reichstag in 1933, calling for 'lawful non-violent opposition'. Exiled in Paris after 1933.

y

Yaroslavsky, E (1878-1943): Author of Stalinist histories falsifying events; fell from favour with Stalin 1930-31.

Young Plan: Named after an American banker and accepted by German government in 1929; set annual reparation payments at lower level than under existing Dawes Plan—but said they were to continue for another 59 years. Violent opposition to this from extreme nationalists, Stahlhelm and industrialists. By supporting this, the Nazis began to obtain substantial sums from big business.

z

Zinoviev, Grigory: Old Bolshevik, Lenin's closest collaborator during First World War. In hiding with Lenin in summer 1917, but with Kamenev opposed October insurrection. First president of Comintern and responsible for major policy errors in Germany, Bulgaria and other places. Nominal leader 1923-25 of bloc with Kamenev and Stalin, and most virulent opponent of 'Trotskyism'. Stalin broke with him in 1925 and deprived him of post in Comintern and control of Leningrad party apparatus. Formed joint opposition with Trotsky 1926-27, expelled from party with Trotsky in 1927 but immediately recanted. Expelled again and deported to Siberia 1932, but again recanted and re-admitted to party. Imprisoned after Kirov assassination in 1935, he was 'star victim' in Moscow Trials a year later. Executed after yet again recanting to Stalin, this time admitting to being a 'traitor'—and a 'fascist'.

Zorgiebel, Karl: Social Democratic commissioner of Berlin police force; defended police action in attacking Communist May Day demonstration in 1929 killing 25 people.

Other Bookmarks Revolutionary Classics

The Mass Strike / *Rosa Luxemburg*
The first book to show the revolutionary implications of the mass general strike, by examining those that led to just such a climax in Russia in 1905. 96 pages. £1.95 / $4.50

Labour in Irish History / *James Connolly*
A challenge to the Irish nationalists in whose company Connolly was to fight and die in the Easter Rising of 1916, based on a historical analysis of Ireland's struggle for freedom. 160 pages. £2.95 / $4.95

Lenin's Moscow / *Alfred Rosmer*
An account of the 'centre of world revolution', when Moscow was capital city of the first workers' revolution and headquarters of the Communist Internationalof which Rosmer was a leading member. 288 pages. £4.95 / $9.95.

The Lessons of October / *Leon Trotsky*
The first serious political analysis of the tactics of the Russian Bolsheviks in the months that led up to the 1917 revolution—by one of its leaders. 96 pages. £1.95 / $3.95

State Capitalism in Russia / *Tony Cliff*
An analysis of Russia under Stalin, when a new state capitalist ruling class rose to power on the ashes of the revolution, now with a postscript covering the years between Stalin and Gorbachev. 377 pages. £5.95 / $9.00

Reform or Revolution / *Rosa Luxemburg*
The first work to recognise reformism as a distinct political movement—and whose major tenets it countered with an intellectual power rarely surpassed since. 96 pages. £2.50 / $4.75

All available from good bookshops, or by post from Bookmarks (add 10 per cent to cover postage—minimum 35p or $1).

BOOKMARKS

265 Seven Sisters Road, London N4 2DE, England.
PO Box 16085, Chicago, IL 60616, USA.
GPO Box 1473N, Melbourne 3001, Australia.